THE PARADOX
OF AMERICAN UNIONISM

THE PARADOX
OF AMERICAN UNIONISM

WHY AMERICANS LIKE UNIONS MORE THAN
CANADIANS DO BUT JOIN MUCH LESS

Seymour Martin Lipset and Noah M. Meltz

with Rafael Gomez and Ivan Katchanovski

FOREWORD BY THOMAS A. KOCHAN

ILR PRESS

AN IMPRINT OF

CORNELL UNIVERSITY PRESS
ITHACA AND LONDON

In memory of Noah Meltz, our friend and colleague
SML, RG, IK

To Sydnee
SML

Copyright © 2004 by Cornell University

All rights reserved. Except for brief quotations in a review, this book, or parts thereof, must not be reproduced in any form without permission in writing from the publisher. For information, address Cornell University Press, Sage House, 512 East State Street, Ithaca, New York 14850.

First published 2004 by Cornell University Press

Printed in the United States of America

Library of Congress Cataloging-in-Publication Data

Lipset, Seymour Martin.
  The paradox of American unionism : why Americans like unions more than Canadians do but join much less / Seymour Martin Lipset and Noah M. Meltz, with Rafael Gomez and Ivan Katchanovski ; foreword by Thomas A. Kochan.
      p. cm.
Includes bibliographical references and index.
    ISBN 0-8014-4200-1 (cloth : alk. paper)
    1. Labor union members—United States. 2. Labor unions—United States. 3. Labor union members—Canada. 4. Labor unions—Canada. I. Meltz, Noah M. II. Title.
    HD6508.L53   2004
      331.88′0973—dc22

                                                          2003024992

Cloth printing   10 9 8 7 6 5 4 3 2 1

CONTENTS

FOREWORD

The paradoxical patterns observed in union membership in Canada and the United States pose challenging questions to industrial relations researchers and provide a convenient laboratory to explore some of the most important theoretical and public policy questions facing our field. Why has union membership historically been higher in Canada than in the United States even though unions are rated more favorably in the United States? Why, after moving in parallel for nearly sixty years, did membership grow in Canada and decline in the United States between 1965 and 1985? And, finally, why has union membership declined in both countries in the past two decades, even though an increasing number of workers indicate an interest in becoming union members? This welcome book provides us with the historical and contemporary data and analysis we need to address these questions.

The Paradox of American Unionism is especially welcome because it is the product of two of the most knowledgeable and renowned students of Canadian and U.S. unions and related political and social institutions of our time. Seymour Martin Lipset is perhaps best known to students of political science and sociology for his classic book *Political Man* (Lipset 1960/1981). However, most students of industrial relations were first introduced to him in his seminal case study of union democracy in the International Typographers Union (Lipset, Trow, and Coleman 1956). Since then, Lipset and his colleagues have explored the sources of U.S. "exceptionalism," that is, why socialism and radicalism have been relatively unsuccessful in the United States, and he has been a pioneer in using survey data to examine the roles that attitudes and values play in shaping social and political institutions, unions, and professional associations. Throughout his career he has shown a special interest in comparing political developments in Canada and the United States for what they might tell us about how deep-seated values and culture shape political institutions and outcomes.

For the past thirty years Noah Meltz contributed intellectual and organizational leadership to the task of building the field of industrial relations in Canada. At the University of Toronto he guided the Center for Industrial Relations to become one of the preeminent locations for teaching, research, and policy analysis in our field. He helped create and chair the study group devoted to industrial theory for the International Industrial Relations Association and kept it focused on what he saw as the twin responsibilities of scholarship in our field, namely to promote efficiency and equity at work (Meltz 1989a). As early as 1982, Noah began to note and study one sign of the paradox examined in this book. He used labor force data to show that, although union membership trends in the two countries had moved generally in parallel for most of the twentieth century, beginning in 1965 they began to diverge. Moreover, he showed that this divergence could not be explained, as many thought at the time, by differential rates of industry or occupational growth experienced in our two countries (Meltz 1985). Consistent with his inquisitive mind and dedication to empirical analysis, Noah pursued answers to this puzzle throughout the remaining years of his life.

I was therefore delighted when Noah told me in early 1996 that he and Marty Lipset were planning a survey of Canadian and U.S. workers to see if they could help solve this puzzle. This book is the capstone publication from this project.

The authors offer four interrelated hypotheses to explain why U.S. workers express a higher degree of support for unions but join them less than Canadians do: (1) the push to the left prompted by the Great Depression was more of an anomaly in the United States than in Canada—as prosperity returned, U.S. individualism reemerged as the dominant political value and culture while the deeper-seated communitarian traditions in Canada helped strong social democratic movements to take hold and provide continued support for unions; (2) approval of unions tends to be negatively related to union power—the weaker unions become, the more the public in both countries voices support for unions as institutions; (3) U.S. labor law and its administration make it more difficult for workers to join a union in the United States than in Canada; and (4) differences between the two countries in the values and political culture make it more difficult for the United States to change its labor laws.

Although each of these hypotheses appears to play a role, Lipset and Meltz give greatest weight to the effects of political culture and values. They accept as a fact that unions in the United States do experience less support from their government and suffer under a labor law that makes organizing more difficult than in most of Canada's provinces and in the federal sector. But they push the question to the next level and ask why this is the case. Their answer lies in what they see as the strong individualistic, limited government political values and culture the U.S. forefathers favored and built into our form of government and the resulting political institutions these values perpetuate.

Some readers might quarrel with this explanation. Critics might ask: If deep differences in values and political culture are the root causes of the mean differences observed in union membership in these two countries, why did membership patterns depart so dramatically in the 1960s after nearly six decades in which the differences were relatively small in magnitude and moved in parallel? That is, what explains the variations from the long-term trend at different points in time? Lipset and Meltz offer an answer to this question. They suggest that the real anomaly in the data is found in the 1935–60 time period in the United States, when the effects of the New Deal labor and social legislation played out and union membership grew more in the United States than in Canada. It took a depression and major social crisis to overcome the resistance to enacting and supporting labor legislation that might be construed as favoring collectivist, communitarian values over individualism. As the effects of this legislation wore off, labor was not able to build sufficient political support to reform labor law in ways that might overcome its weaknesses. In Canada, in contrast, unions used their coalition with social democratic parties to gain stronger federal labor legislation covering government employees and provincial labor laws protecting or promoting unionization for private-sector workers.

I will leave it to readers of this volume to decide where they might come out in this debate. Indeed, work on these issues needs to continue. Unions in both countries once again face a deep crisis because their memberships have been decreasing in parallel for nearly two decades. An accurate diagnosis of the root causes of this decline is essential to any effort to predict or propose alternative strategies for union renewal. And, as both of these authors have taught us, a vibrant and growing labor movement is essential to a democratic society that aspires to achieve both efficiency and equity at work.

Once again, Seymour Martin Lipset and Noah Meltz have done our field a great service in providing the data, historical material, and contending arguments needed to encourage continued examination of these issues.

Putting these materials together in this careful fashion and placing them in the context of the major theoretical and policy debates in our field is just what we have come to expect from these two intellectual giants. Noah Meltz lost his battle with cancer in January 2002. This volume is a fitting tribute to him and his work. We may miss having Meltz and Lipset to join future debate and examination of these issues in person, but their presence will be felt for many years to come.

THOMAS A. KOCHAN
George M. Bunker Professor of Work and Employment Relations
MIT Sloan School of Management

ACKNOWLEDGMENTS

This book would not have been possible without assistance from many people. We appreciate help and advice from Shmuel Eisenstadt, Don Kash, Bruce Kaufman, Tom Kochan, Phillipe Schmitter, John Stephens, and Jelle Visser. Seymour Martin Lipset expresses his intellectual debt to his teachers, colleagues, and friends, in particular to Robert K. Merton, Reinhard Bendix, Daniel Bell, S. D. Clark, Lewis Coser, Larry Diamond, Nathan Glazer, Alex Inkeles, Gary Marks, Daniel Patrick Moynihan, Earl Raab, David Riesman, and Philip Selznick. Research assistance was provided by Gabriel Lenz, Marcella Ridlen Ray, and Scott Talkington.

Noah Meltz passed away January 29, 2002, before he could complete this book. His family thanks Rafael Gomez, who took over when Noah could no longer continue. They also thank colleagues and staff at the Centre for Industrial Relations and Woodsworth College, University of Toronto, for the help and kindness they showed throughout Noah's illness, in particular William Bateman, Deborah Campbell, Morley Gunderson, Eva Hollander, Doug Hyatt, John Kervin, Frank Reid, Jeff Reitz, Anil Verma, the library staff—Monica Hypher, Elizabeth Perry, Vicki Skelton, and Hilary Shelton—and the regular staff.

The authors are indebted to the Donner Canadian Foundation, the Russell Sage Foundation, the Academic Office of the Canadian Embassy in Washington, D.C., and the Friedrich Ebert Foundation for financial support. The School of Public Policy of George Mason University, the Woodrow Wilson Center for Scholars, the Hoover Institution, and the Progressive Policy Institute have given us intellectual and physical venues. We thank Angus Reid (Ipsos-Reid) and in particular Mag Burns, who conducted our survey in both the United States and Canada. We are grateful as well to Barry Hirsch, whose provision of proprietary data files allowed us to calculate unionization rates by detailed occupational and professional categories. We are greatly indebted to our editor at Cornell University Press, Fran Benson. Last but not least, we owe more than we can possibly acknowledge to Sydnee Lipset, Rochelle Meltz, and Sophia Katchanovski.

1　Paradoxes, Anomalies, and Hypotheses

Paradoxes

This book deals with unions and labor relations in Canada and the United States. The rationale for the book can be found in the two diagrams that follow: one showing the dramatic divergence that has developed in the percentage of employees belonging to unions in the United States and Canada and the other showing the percentage of people who approve of unions in both countries. Figure 1.1 shows how over the past four decades a huge gap in the extent of union representation has emerged between the two countries. In 1963, 29 percent of employees in each country were union members (Kumar 1993). By 2001, however, only 14 percent of employees belonged to unions in the United States compared to 30 percent in Canada. Figure 1.2 displays the results of cross-national surveys for the past fifty years showing that Americans approve of unions far more than Canadians do. Although a majority of people have approved of unions in both countries (except for 1982 and the Anti-Inflation Board[1] years of 1976 and 1978 in Canada), U.S. approval has exceeded Canadian approval in most years from 1941 to 2001, in some cases by as much as 18 percentage points. The few exceptions are close to the margin of error.

How can we explain this paradox? Why do Americans approve of unions more than Canadians, yet since the mid-1960s have joined unions to a much lesser extent? Indeed, how do we explain that even in Canada twice as many people approve of unions as join them, and in the United States approval of unions exceeds membership by more than fourfold?

Although these questions seem daunting enough to be the subject of a book unto themselves, there is also a second paradox to be explored. A

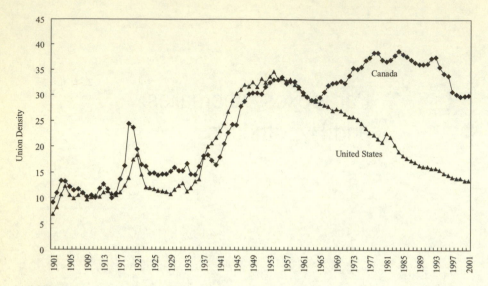

FIGURE 1.1
Union density in Canada and the United States, 1901–2001. (For data sources and methodology see app. A.)

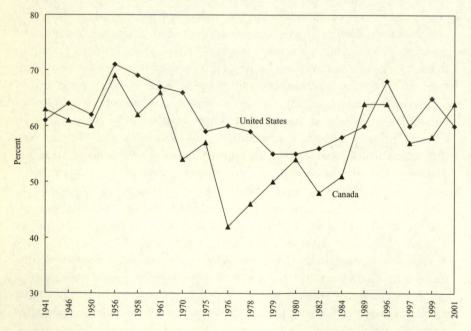

FIGURE 1.2
Union approval in Canada and the United States, 1941–2001 (*Source*: Gallup Poll, http://www.gallup.com.)

survey conducted for the authors suggests that U.S. managers are less resistant to union organizing than Canadian managers (see app. B for a description of the survey). This, like the general survey data already discussed, seems counterintuitive. One of the major explanations that has been offered for lower union membership in the United States is that management is much more aggressive in opposing unions than is management in Canada (e.g., Kochan, Katz and McKersie, 1994; Gomez, Lipset, and Meltz 2001). In the United States there is even a highly visible industry providing advice to companies on how to avoid being unionized. Should we conclude that the results of the surveys are not to be trusted? We do not think so. Instead we believe that there are answers to these paradoxes, but in order to resolve them we have to probe more deeply into the factors that distinguish Americans from Canadians.

The Not-So Invisible Border

Americans and Canadians often refer to the world's longest undefended border that separates them as an invisible border. At a superficial level, there is some truth to this statement because there are few obvious differences between the two countries. In fact, Canada's largest city, Toronto, is the third largest location for filming movies in North America, after Los Angeles and New York, and, along with Vancouver and Montreal, often substitutes for almost any U.S. city. Until recently, Vancouver was even the location for the popular U.S. television program *The X-Files*. However, as Lipset (1990) has shown previously, there are significant differences lying below the surface in many of the attitudes and values of Americans and Canadians. In this book, we plumb these differences to see whether they contribute to the union representation gap between the two countries and, if so, how.

This is not the first book to offer an explanation for divergent unionization trends in Canada and the United States. Since 1983 many studies have suggested various reasons for the large gap that has emerged in the extent of union membership between the two countries. A full list of these factors is discussed later, but among those that are considered to have the greatest impact are labor laws and the nature and extent of the enforcement of those laws by labor relations boards. What is not considered as important are the differing attitudes and values of Americans and Canadians that in large measure underpin these same laws and legal institutions. To quote an expert analyst of the differences, "There is no empirical support for the hypothesis that the Canada-U.S. gap in union coverage is due to differences between the two countries in the underlying social attitudes toward unions" (Riddell 1993, 143). We hope to convince our readers that there is indeed a relation between attitudes and the extent of unionism, and that to locate it we must look beyond simple attitudinal responses and instead examine the value systems of both countries.

Anomalies

Consider figure 1.1, which tells us about trade union membership in Canada and the United States in the twentieth century. The figure shows that both countries followed similar paths for the first half of the century. Canada was somewhat ahead of the United States in union membership rates during the first three decades of this century, and then the United States led Canada from the late 1930s to the late 1950s. But apart from these broadly congruent patterns, there are also some noticeable differences.

Both countries experienced a surge in membership during World War I, but after that war ended, the U.S. membership rate dropped back to prewar levels, whereas the decline in Canada was relatively less dramatic, leaving the Canadian unionization rate at a much higher plateau than in the prewar period. Figure 1.1 also indicates that for the entire twentieth century, with the exception of only one or two years, the only period in which the United States had a higher union density rate (that is, proportion of employed who are members) was during the period 1938–55, years that included the end of the Great Depression of the 1930s, World War II, and the early postwar period—the heyday of the New Deal.

Could it be that the exception proves the rule—that it took the extraordinary conjunction of the Depression, government encouragement by the New Deal administration of Franklin Delano Roosevelt, and the greatest war in history to boost unions in the United States? This interpretation suggests that the dramatic growth of unions in the 1930s through the early postwar period may have been an anomaly. This is no way negates the fact that even today pockets of union strength exist in the United States. The success of unions such as the Auto Workers, the American Federation of Teachers and the National Education Association, the Service Employees Union, and the Teamsters brings the labor movement to more than 16 million workers. But, in relation to the work force as a whole, the union sector has been continually eroding since the mid-1950s and especially after the late 1970s when the actual number of union members stopped growing and began to decline. Private-sector union membership in 2001 was 9.0 percent, lower than the rate preceding World War I. In Canada the comparable statistic in the first half of 2001 was twice as high at 18.1 percent.

If the dramatic growth of unions in the United States for almost two decades, beginning in the Depression, is an anomaly, why did it occur? Does this mean that in the United States, but not in Canada, the share of the workforce in unions increases only during wartime or peaceful periods when there is strong government support? And are the workers who join unions in Canada the same kind who belong to unions in the United States or are there major differences? These questions are the subject matter of this book.

Four Hypotheses

Central to our argument are four hypotheses about the U.S. labor movement that arise from sharp contrasts with Canada, which (even aside from geographical proximity) resembles the United States economically and socially more closely than any other country.

1. Although the experience of the Great Depression pushed both the United States and Canada toward the political left, Canada's strong social democratic movement took root in a preexisting statist, communitarian tradition. In the United States, the statist and communitarian values that emerged during the Depression and lasted into the postwar years declined under the impact of postwar prosperity. The country soon returned to an individualistic state tradition that was not supportive of collectivist approaches. The first hypothesis, therefore, is that the surge in union membership relative to labor force growth in the United States from 1938 to 1958 was an anomaly in the overall U.S. experience with unionism, as was the increase in union membership during World War I.

2. If these gains were indeed an anomaly, how do we explain the apparently high levels of public approval of unions? Union approval is high across all fifty states, but a big majority express little confidence in unions, less than for business (see Lipset and Schneider 1983). There is historical and comparative evidence that approval of unions tends to be negatively related to the perceived power of unions; that is, the weaker unions are, or at least appear to be, the more they are endorsed as an institution that is speaking for the interests of working people. This phenomenon has been noted in the United Kingdom and Australia as well as in North America. Public approval of unions has increased as their numerical strength has fallen. The second hypothesis is that, ironically, the greater historical approval of unions in the United States is a result of the union movement's relative weakness. We suggest that if unions were relatively stronger, as in Canada, public support would be lower.

3. Evidence suggests that for the past several decades it has been more difficult to join a union in the United States than in Canada because the underlying government institutions in the U.S. labor field—both the labor legislation and enforcement of the legislation—have not been as supportive of unionization as they generally have been in its northern neighbor. Our third hypothesis is that a major component of the paradox in unionism is the greater difficulty that Americans have in joining unions compared with Canadians. In other words, even though Americans express a greater desire or willingness to join unions, they cannot join as easily as Canadians, thereby perpetuating the weakness of the union movement and leading to an ingrained rooting-for-the-underdog syndrome.

4. One final perplexing question still remains: If U.S. citizens really are more desirous of unions and are prevented by state policies, why do U.S. governments not change their behavior? The difference in culture and values between the United States and Canada, we argue, is what contributes significantly to limitations in political and legal support for unions in the United States. Our fourth hypothesis is that in the choice between freedom for the individual and collective rights for the group, more weight is given to the individual than to the collective in the United States, except in extreme circumstances. Our fourth hypothesis also states that in Canada, compared to the United States, more emphasis is placed on the common good than on individual freedom. It is no accident, we argue, that the U.S. Declaration of Independence speaks of an individual's ". . . right to life, liberty and the pursuit of happiness," whereas the Canadian Constitution speaks of "peace, order and good government."

The evidence presented in this book clearly suggests that Americans do want to join unions. Impeding them from joining is the U.S. emphasis on individual freedom, combined with the peculiarities of Congressional government which make changes to labor law very difficult. This has led the United States to maintain institutional barriers against unions. These barriers have only broken down in extraordinary circumstances, such as those occasioned by wars and depressions.

In subsequent chapters we probe U.S. and Canadian views on a range of subjects related to work, social values, and political institutions to try to understand the apparent paradox that Americans approve of unions more than Canadians do but join them less. The results are based, in part, on an in-depth survey of over three thousand people, mostly employees, conducted exclusively for the authors in the two countries.

Structure of the Book

The book is organized into eleven chapters. Chapter 2 provides an international context for the analysis by examining trends in union membership in industrialized countries in western Europe, Australia, New Zealand, and Japan, along with the United States and Canada. The data in some cases go back to 1900. The main finding that emerges from this cross-country evidence is that support for unions is associated with social democratic strength.

Chapter 3 presents a historical overview of the evolution of trade unions in the United States and Canada from 1901 to 2001. Six subperiods are discussed: 1901–16, 1916–36, 1936–56, 1956–81, and 1981–2001. The focus is on the patterns of change in union membership in the two countries measured against the background of changes in the structure of the labor movements, in labor legislation, and in the political context in which these developments took place.

Three main observations emerge from this analysis. First, union density has traditionally been higher in Canada, except for the period of the New Deal (from the late 1930s to the late 1950s). Second, the turning points in union membership in both countries are associated with significant political, social, and economic events—including wars, depressions, and changed social attitudes—that caused a shift toward the rights of workers being represented collectively in bargaining. In terms of Canadian-U.S. patterns, the major finding in this context is the much greater freedom that public-sector workers were given in Canada after the mid-1960s to bargain and even strike. A final factor that affected private-sector workers and the extent of union organizing and management opposition to unions was the difference in labor legislation and its enforcement, which in Canada was more union friendly.

Chapter 4 continues the discussion of the social, political, and economic factors that underlie the more robust legislative protection and the much greater strength of unions in Canada than in the United States. It begins with the examination of the results of our survey. The focus is on measures of political culture in the two countries and how they differ, specifically after the mid-1960s when trade union membership in the two countries parted ways. As a summary statement, it can be said that the ethos in the United States is one of individualism and an appeal to exit, as opposed to voice, as a means of protecting workers. In Canada, the underlying dominant view is still largely a social democratic one.

Chapter 5 explores our two paradoxes. The first is the central paradox of this book, that Americans approve of unions more than Canadians, but are less likely to join. The second paradox is both counterintuitive and counter to what most researchers in industrial relations believe: U.S. managers are less hostile to unions than are Canadian managers. Our analysis is based not only on what workers and managers in the two countries say about unions, but on the broader societal attitudes and values that our survey reveals. The findings of this chapter corroborate the extent of frustrated demand for unions that is examined later in chapter 6. But this chapter also qualifies the extent of demand for unionization and differences in managers' attitudes toward unions.

Chapter 6 uses the results of our survey to measure the extent to which there is a frustrated demand for union membership in the United States. Using all the ways in which demand by workers to join unions could be determined, one finding is absolutely clear: far more Americans want to join unions than actually belong. More Canadians also want to join unions than are members, but it is on the U.S. side that the extent of frustrated demand easily outstrips observed membership rates.

Chapter 7 considers Canadian-U.S. union differences not from an aggregate perspective but rather from differences in union density within each country. What is most surprising is that differences *within* each country, particularly within the United States, are far greater than are the differences in the extent of union membership *between* the two countries. A worker in New York state, for example, is seven times more likely to belong to a union than a worker in North Carolina. That same worker in New York is about five times more likely to belong to a union than the average worker in Texas. Almost the same union density differences apply in other high-density states such as Washington, Oregon, Alaska, and Hawaii. One possible reason for these large interstate differences emerges when we look at a map. As we see in chapter 7, the map reveals that the closer a state is to the Canadian border, the higher the probability that its workers will be unionized. Is this a coincidence or is there some shared set of values between border provinces and states?

Chapters 8 and 9 examine the attitudes and behaviors of white-collar workers and professionals toward unions in the United States and Canada. These populations are extremely important not only as occupations that have been recent sources of strength for unions in both countries, but also because their size and the changes that are taking place in the knowledge economy provide measures that are harbingers for the future development of unions on both sides of the border. This is part of the shift to a post-industrial society and the decline in industrial work. The key for unions is seen to be the combination of desire for representation and special needs for professional development.

Chapter 10 looks at the location and extent of nonunion employee representation. The issue we raise is whether nonunion forms of employee representation are substitutes for, or complements to, formal union representation. We find that a surprisingly high proportion of workers have nonunion representation. In fact in the United States the proportion of workers with such representation, 11 percent, is almost as great as the 14 percent who belong to a union (if we add the additional 2 percent of workers who are covered by a collective agreement). The proportion of employees covered in Canada by nonunion organizations is similar to the United States (10 percent), but of course this is only one-third of the total union representation. The differences that do exist between the two countries are explored, setting the stage for a discussion of what this means for employee representation in the future.

Chapter 11 sums up the explanations for the paradoxes that have been observed in union representation in the United States and Canada. It asks whether, on the basis of this study, the future holds a turnabout in union representation in the United States or whether, instead, Canada is destined to decline to U.S.-style levels of union membership.

2   Union Density in a Cross-National Context

This book deals primarily with the sources and consequences of the sizable variation in union density and coverage between U.S. and Canadian unions. In this chapter we provide an international context in which to analyze the variation in union density between the two countries. After first comparing differences in union density and collective agreement coverage across twenty-four industrialized countries, we then examine the factors affecting cross-national variation in union density.

Patterns of Union Density in Advanced Western Countries

Union density varies greatly among the different cultural and geographic groupings of advanced Western countries. The range, using international data from the mid-1990s, is from 88 percent in Sweden to 10–14 percent in France and the United States. French unionism is actually much stronger than this estimate of low membership suggests.[1] For collective bargaining coverage, that is, the proportion of employees represented by unions, France is close to the top, 95 percent, while the United States is at the bottom, 16.7 percent. Canada is much more unionized, with 37 percent density and 40 percent coverage, clearly much more than its southern neighbor but less than much of Europe (tables 2.1 and 2.2).

TABLE 2.1
Union Density and Collective Bargaining Coverage in the Mid-1990s (%)

Country	Union Density, Dependent Labor Force, 1995	Collective Bargaining Coverage, 1990s[a]
Northern European countries	*76.6*	*78.8*
Sweden	87.5	85.0 (1995)
Iceland	83.3	n.a.
Finland	79.6	95.0 (1995)
Denmark	77.0	69.0 (1994)
Norway	55.4	66.0 (1996)
Low countries	*40.2*	*85.0*
Belgium	52.9	90.0 (1994)
Luxembourg	43.4	n.a.
Netherlands	24.3	80.0 (1996)
German-speaking countries	*31.1*	*79.3*
Austria	40.7	98.0 (1994)
Germany	29.1	90.0 (1996)
Switzerland	23.6	50.0 (1993)
English-speaking countries	*33.2*	*47.0*
Ireland	52.3	90.0 (1994)
Canada	37.0[b]	40.0 (1994)
United Kingdom	36.4	47.0 (1994)
Australia	35.2	65.0 (1995)
New Zealand	24.3	23.1 (1995)
United States	14.2	16.7 (1995)
Southern European countries	*23.4*	*84.2*
Italy	38.5	83.0 (1993)
Portugal	25.6	71.0 (1993)
Greece	24.3	90.0 (1994)
Spain	18.2	82.0 (1996)
France	10.3	95.0 (1995)
Outliers	*23.5*	*n.a.*
Japan	24.0	25.0 (1994)
Israel	23.0	n.a.

Source: Daily Labor Report (Jan. 29, 1997); Ebbinghaus and Visser (2000); International Labour Organisation ([ILO] 1997, 248); Organization for Economic Development and Cooperation ([OECD] 1997); Traxler (1996, 274).

Note: The density data for Japan, Australia, and New Zealand (ILO 1997) are not adjusted. The 1994 density data for Canada (OECD 1997) have a coverage rate somewhat higher than the density data for Sweden, Denmark, and New Zealand. This discrepancy can be attributed to the fact that the estimates are obtained from different sources and refer to different years (see OECD 1997, 72, 84).

[a] n.a., not available.   [b] For 1994.

Cultural and Geographic Groupings

The proportion of workers organized is highest in the northern European countries. Union density in these nations exceeded 75 percent in 1995. It

TABLE 2.2
Union Density in Developed Countries, 1950–1995, Ranked by 1995 Estimates

Country	1950[a]	1960	1970	1980	1990	1995
Sweden	67.3	70.7	66.6	78.2	82.4	87.5
Finland	29.9	29.3	51.4	70.0	72.5	78.8
Denmark	53.2	60.2	62.1	77.5	74.5	78.1
Belgium	40.2	40.7	42.3	56.6	56.7	59.8
Norway	n.a.	51.6	50.0	54.1	53.1	52.5
Ireland	38.9	45.8	54.2	57.4	48.2	44.4
Austria	57.9	57.8	55.4	50.8	45.2	38.9
Canada	n.a.	28.3	29.8	36.0	36.0	37.0[b]
Australia	n.a.	49.1	44.4	48.0	41.0	35.2
Italy	40.3	22.4	34.0	44.4	33.6	32.4
United Kingdom	44.1	44.3	48.6	52.8	40.1	32.2
Germany	33.9	34.2	31.8	33.6	29.9	26.5
New Zealand	n.a.	54.0	46.1	56.0	45.0	24.3
Japan	n.a.	32.2	34.5	31.0	25.0	24.0
Netherlands	42.0	41.0	36.0	32.4	22.3	22.9
Switzerland	n.a.	n.a.	29.9	30.7	26.3	22.7
United States	n.a.	28.9	25.9	22.0	16.0	14.2
France	30.2	19.2	21.0	17.1	9.2	8.6

Source: Ebbinghaus and Visser (2000); OECD (1997); ILO (1997); Visser (1994, 1993).
Note: Percentage of employed wage and salary earners. The 1980 and 1990 data for the United States, Canada (including 1994), Japan, Australia, and New Zealand (OECD 1997) and the 1995 data for these countries (ILO 1997) are not adjusted.
[a] n.a., not available.
[b] For 1994.

is 88 percent in Sweden, 83 percent in Iceland, 79–80 percent in Finland, and 77–78 percent in Denmark.[2] A smaller proportion, but still more than one-half of wage and salary workers or the dependent labor force (53–55 percent), is unionized in Norway (see tables 2.1 and 2.2). With the exception of Finland, the northern countries form a culturally uniform group.

Union density in the nations with populations of European origin and that have been part of the British Commonwealth is much lower than in northern countries. Ireland is the most unionized of this group, with about one-half of the dependent labor force (52 percent), or 44 percent of the gainfully employed, unionized compared to 32–36 percent in the United Kingdom. The membership rates in Australia and Canada are similar to that of Britain—in Australia it is more than one-third (35 percent), and it is about the same in Canada—while the rate in New Zealand is lower at one-fourth (24 percent). The United States is the lowest, with only one-seventh (14 percent) of its wage and salary earners as union members. Collective bargaining coverage, the other measure of union strength, is low in English-speaking countries compared with the other regional culture groups. With the exception of Ireland and Australia, the rate in the English-speaking world is less than one-half, while in all other countries for which data are available, except Japan, it ranges from 50 to 95 percent (table 2.1).

Union densities in the Low Countries, German-speaking nations, and southern European nations, plus the outliers, Japan and Israel, are also lower than in northern European countries. However, there is significant variation among them. More than one-half of the dependent labor force or gainfully employed workers (53–60 percent) are union members in Belgium. In contrast, union density in Luxembourg is 43 percent and in the Netherlands the rate is less than one-quarter (23–24 percent) (see tables 2.1 and 2.2).

Austria leads the German-speaking nations with about two-fifths of the dependent labor force (41 percent), or of the gainfully employed (39 percent), as union members as of 1995. In Germany, the density figures are slightly over one-quarter (27–29 percent). In Switzerland, which is over two-thirds German-speaking, fewer than one in four workers (23–24 percent) belong to unions.

The southern European countries are culturally Latin and Catholic, with the exception of Greece. In Italy, about one-third of gainfully employed workers (32 percent), or the dependent labor force (39 percent), belongs to labor unions. In contrast, the union membership rate in France is much lower, 9–10 percent. One in four (26 percent) wage and salary workers in Portugal is a union member, while in Spain union density is lower—depending on the definition, 14 percent of gainfully employed workers or 18 percent of the dependent labor force belong to unions in Spain. The union membership rate in Greece is 24 percent.

Two quite different outlier industrialized countries, Japan and Israel, report similar rates, 24 and 23 percent in 1995. In the past, the rate for the Israeli Histadrut was much higher, but it was more than a union, including many nonworkers because it provided a variety of social welfare functions, such as medical coverage and pensions. Its membership also included many pensioners. As a result, Israeli union density was estimated at 80 percent in 1979 (Wallerstein 1989, 482). But by the mid-1990s, after it gave up these functions, the unionization rate declined to 23 percent (table 2.1).

Although culture (predominantly political culture) seems to be linked to these considerable differences in union density, it has proven very difficult to order and estimate cultural variables in a fashion that permits statistical analysis. We have, for example, no good measures of the degree of class awareness or class consciousness in various countries, unless we rely on left party voting. But, such parties themselves are too varied in ideology to be of use. In general, the cross-national analysis of union density is complicated because of the large number of independent variables and the relatively small number of countries.[3] Many factors associated with cross-national variation are difficult to quantify. The unreliability of the international data also complicates statistical analysis. Measures of density and collective bargaining coverage are not always consistent and compatible because of differences in methodology and data collection. National definitions of union members and labor force measures vary. For instance, Ebbinghaus and Visser (2000) and Visser (1994) calculate union density as the ratio of union members to the dependent labor force and to the gainfully employed. The first measure includes the unemployed, but the second does not. Also the unionization estimates in some countries (e.g., the United Kingdom and Ireland) include economically inactive union members, and the comparative data on collective bargaining coverage are derived from different sources (see tables 2.1 and 2.2).

Factors Affecting Cross-National Variation in Union Density

A number of studies have looked at union density in industrialized Western countries and analyzed the factors behind cross-national and temporal variations (e.g., Ebbinghaus and Visser 1999, 2000; Golden, Wallerstein, and Lange 1999; Western 1997; Visser 1993, 1994; Ebbinghaus 1993; Blanchflower and Freeman 1992; Neumann, Pedersen, and Westergard-Nielsen 1991; Stephens 1991; Freeman 1990; Wallerstein 1989). Most of the studies focus on cross-national variations in union density at a given time. The historical data required for a longitudinal cross-national analysis are not always available or reliable. Nevertheless, we can report that the rank order of countries according to unionization level has remained relatively stable over the postwar period (Visser 1994, 165). The intertemporal association is also quite strong. The correlation between 1995 and 1970 of union densities among eighteen Organization for Economic Cooperation and Development (OECD) countries is 0.81 (calculated from Visser's data reported in table 2.2).

We have analyzed the determinants of union membership rates in 1995 among the employed wage and salary earners in advanced OECD countries. The independent variables reflect various political, structural, economic, and religious cleavages as formulated in Lipset and Rokkan's (1967) analysis of cross-national political variation. Variables identified in other studies of unionization are also included in the analysis.

The following indexes, which provide a quantitative assessment of various factors that appear to affect union density, have been used: left cumulative power (how long left parties have held national office); Catholic cumulative power (how long Catholic parties have held national office); corporatism; legal regulation of labor relations; and religious, political, and economic divisions in union systems. Our independent variables also include the Ghent system, labor force size, the proportion employed in government and private industry, the state's share of GDP revenue, the extent of ethnolinguistic diversity, and the religious composition of the population (table 2.3).[4]

The Relationship between Left Parties and Union Strength

Unions and left parties have been seen as different parts of same movement. Comparative analyses of labor organizations points to their varied relationships with left parties, for example, social democratic, labor, socialist, and communist. In some countries, left parties were basically an offspring of the trade union movement; in others, the labor organizations were created by the political movements or developed in parallel with them. Unions played a significant role in the founding of left parties in Great Britain and other English-speaking countries, as well as in Scandinavia. United States is the exception (Marks 1989; Western 1997, 67–69). The variations in the historical patterns of union formation and party-union relationships have been related to differences in cleavage structure (see Lipset and Rokkan 1967; Lipset 1983; Ebbinghaus 1993, 1996; Western 1997, 67–69).

Class-consciousness has traditionally been strong in the Scandinavian countries. Unions founded social democratic parties in Sweden and Denmark and the Labor party in Norway by the end of the nineteenth century. In Iceland, then a dependent territory of Denmark, the Icelandic Federation of Labor acted also as the Social Democratic Party from the time of its founding by unions in 1916 (Ebbinghaus 1996; Kjartansson 1992).

Similarly, unions were involved in the formation of labor parties in Great Britain, Ireland, Australia, and New Zealand (Western 1997, 67–69). Labor activists took part in the formation of the first electorally viable social democratic party in Canada, the Cooperative Commonwealth Federation

TABLE 2.3
Political, Structural, and Economic Characteristics of Eighteen OECD Countries

Country	Left Cumulative Power, 1946–94	Catholic Cumulative Power, 1946–94	Corporatism Index	Ethnolinguistic Fractionalization	Proportion of Catholic Population (%)	Employed and Unemployed (millions)	Government Revenue, 1995 (% of GDP)	Government Employment, 1995 (% total employment)	Industry Employment, 1995 (% total employment)	Legal Regulation Index	Occupational Split	Religious Split	Political Split
Sweden	38.86	0	1.70	0.065	1.4	4.27	57.4	32.0	25.0	16	40	0	0
Denmark	26.91	0	1.60	0.028	0.6	2.73	59.1	30.5	26.8	16	21	0	0
Finland	19.29	0	1.80	0.105	0.1	2.47	53.2	25.1	26.8	16	34	0	0
Norway	36.88	0	1.80	0.070	0.3	2.12	50.5	30.6	23.4	16	18	0	0
Belgium	15.87	26.06	1.30	0.364	90.0	4.20	50.8	19.4	27.7	15	0	0	53
New Zealand	16.25	0	0.95	0.148	18.7	1.70	n.a.	22.1	24.9	14	0	0	0
Australia	18.77	0	1.10	0.113	29.6	8.78	34.2	16.6	23.5	14	24	0	0
Austria	30.54	18.05	1.80	0.033	88.8	3.88	47.3	22.4	33.2	14	0	0	0
Ireland	4.86	0	1.15	0.090	95.3	1.42	38.9	13.4	27.6	15	0	0	0
United Kingdom	16.16	0	0.95	0.106	13.1	28.32	37.3	14.4	27.7	11	0	0	0
Italy	5.57	38.65	0.75	0.039	83.2	22.72	44.5	16.1	32.1	13	0	34	63
Germany	12.31	0	1.40	0.044	35.0	39.22	45.9	15.9	37.6	12	13	3	0
Canada	0	0	0.80	0.376	46.6	14.83	46.7	19.6	22.6	10	0	3	0
Switzerland	12.50	13.83	1.40	0.308	52.8	3.91	37.4	14.0	28.8	14	17	13	0
Japan	0.81	0	0.40	0.010	0.6	66.45	32.2	6.0	34.0	10	0	0	51
Netherlands	11.11	14.02	1.40	0.063	42.6	7.12	51.6	12.7	23.0	15	13	20	0
United States	0	0	0.85	0.209	30.0	131.06	31.7	14.0	24.0	9	15	0	0
France	12.59	3.97	0.60	0.146	76.4	24.87	46.8	24.8	26.7	12	22	4	55

Source: Huber, Ragin, and Stephens (1997); La Porta et al. (1998); "OECD in Figures" (1997); Redding and Viterna (1999); Wessels (1996).

(CCF), and played a significant role in the organization of the New Democratic Party (NDP), the CCF's successor (Horowitz 1968; Lipset 1996, 96; Meltz 1985, 326). But in contrast to other English-speaking countries, unions in the United States never created or supported their own labor or social democratic party (Lipset and Marks 2000, 85–112; Marks 1989).

Unions in Germany were formed under the influence of socialist and labor parties that later formed the Social Democratic Party (Marks 1989; Verberckmoes 1996a). Labor organizations in Austria and Finland developed in parallel with social democratic and socialist parties. In Switzerland, Belgium, and Netherlands, the ties of emerging union movements with left parties were weakened by the church-state cleavage, which led to the formation of Christian unions (see Broeck 1992; Ebbinghaus 1993, 1996; Gruner 1992; Pasture 1996; Schonhoven 1992; Soikkanen 1992; Voorden 1992). Reformist-revolutionary ideological differences fragmented organized labor in France, Italy, and Spain, countries in which the church-state cleavage was also strong. Unions in these Latin countries initially developed under the influence of syndicalists and anarchists; hence, they formed separately from socialist parties. In these nations, the power of the ideologically revolutionary anarchosyndicalists facilitated strong communist parties, with strength among unions (see Bianchi 1996; Ebbinghaus 1993, 1996; Esenwein 1992; Verberckmoes 1996b). The strength of revolutionary parties and unions in the Latin societies is related to the late development of a full-grown industrial system and state repression of working-class political and economic rights (Lipset 1983).

The differences in historical origins and links of left parties and unions affect their present relationships. Left parties that were originally formed by unions continue to have much closer organizational and political ties with organized labor (Western 1997, 67–69). Scandinavian countries represent an example of this relationship (Galenson 1998). In contrast, links between left parties and unions are weaker where they emerged independently of one another.

Previous cross-national studies have reported a strong and significant relationship between the strength of left parties in government and unionization levels (see Stephens 1991; Visser 1994; Wallerstein 1989; Western 1997). Our statistical analysis indicates that the index of left cumulative power strongly correlates with union density in eighteen OECD countries. The left cumulative power index, developed by Huber, Ragin, and Stephens (1997) and based on the percentage of parliamentary seats held by left parties in government from 1946 to 1994, correlates positively with

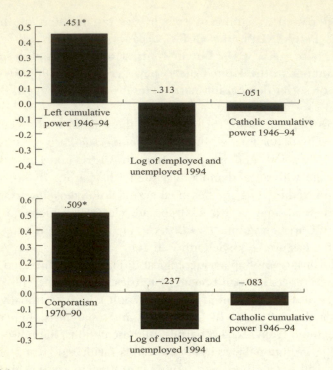

FIGURE 2.1

Determinants of union density in eighteen OECD countries, 1995 (standardized coefficients). *$p < 0.10$. (For data sources see tables 2.2 and 2.3.)

union density (0.63). The association holds when tested in multivariate regressions and is statistically significant at $p < 0.10$ (figure 2.1).[5]

Left parties have never been represented in the national governments of the United States and Canada (table 2.3). Social democratic parties, however, have had considerable strength at the provincial level in Canada, much more than in the U.S. states. This is particularly important because provincial governments are responsible for labor legislation that covers approximately 90 percent of the Canadian work force. Since the 1970s, social democratic parties have on various occasions governed in five of the ten provinces and the territory of the Yukon. In the early 1990s, three NDP governments (Ontario, British Columbia, and Saskatchewan) covered more than one-half the Canadian population, while the Parti Quebecois was the governing party of Quebec. The Parti Quebecois tried to affiliate with the Socialist International but was prevented from doing so by the NDP, which had the right to prevent another Canadian party from joining.

Social democratic parties and labor unions clearly have been much stronger north of the border.

Beyond reflecting working-class values, social democratic strength affects the legal environment in which unions operate, a factor obviously related to union bargaining power. An index of legal regulation of labor relations is very strongly associated with the left cumulative power index (0.81).[6] Left governments are more likely to provide state support for unions during conflicts, as well as union-friendly legislation. The latter, as expected, is positively correlated with union density in the eighteen OECD countries (0.62).

The Ghent System

The Ghent system, in which unions are involved in administration of unemployment insurance schemes, is very favorable for unionization. This system originated in Belgium when the local governments started to subsidize unemployment funds run by unions, but its development has varied in different periods and countries. The Ghent system now exists in Belgium, Sweden, Denmark, and Finland, all of which have very high unionization rates. The other advanced Western countries have public unemployment insurance schemes (see Galenson 1998; Western 1997).

Because trade unions run unemployment insurance funds and pay unemployment benefits, many workers in these countries remain union members even when they lose their jobs. The Ghent system is also favorable to unionism because it gives unions control over labor market competition (Western 1997, 55–56). The Ghent system dummy variable is highly correlated with union density (0.87). However, it is also associated with the cultural and geographic cluster of northern European countries to which all these nations, except Belgium, belong.

A comparison of otherwise similar countries within the same cluster with and without the Ghent system allows us to better evaluate its effect on the unionization rate. Among the Low Countries, Belgium has a much higher union density than the Netherlands. Similarly, the unionization rate in Sweden exceeds the rate in Norway, which lacks the Ghent system (see table 2.1; Western 1997, 57).

Corporatism

Some cross-national studies seek to evaluate the effect of corporatism on union density. Corporatism generally refers to systems in which business, unions, and government negotiate regularly with one another on economic issues. The literature focuses on varying aspects of corporatism and employs somewhat different indicators. Nevertheless, the various indexes of corporatism tend to be positively intercorrelated (see Pennings and Vergunst 2000). Our index reflects the organizational unity of labor and scope of collective bargaining in 1970–90.[7] The corporatism and left power indexes are highly correlated (0.78), a finding reported by Wilensky (1981) and Western (1994). Corporatism clearly has a social democratic character.

Other researchers report that corporatism has significant positive effects on union density in advanced Western countries (Ebbinghaus and Visser 1999; Freeman 1990).[8] Our corporatism index is correlated with union density (0.67); the finding is statistically significant in a regression analysis (figure 2.1). Government involvement in collective bargaining is one of the core elements of corporatism (Lange, Wallerstein, and Golden 1995, 87). Government and parliamentary participation in bargaining is positively associated with union density in sixteen OECD countries (Golden and Londregan 1998, 7).[9] Correlations between these two variables and the union membership rate in 1995 are 0.36 and 0.63 respectively.

Occupational, Ethnic, and Linguistic Cleavages

Ebbinghaus and Visser (2000) report that the differences in levels of union organization among countries are similar to a large degree to the analysis of party systems and structural cleavages of Lipset and Rokkan (1967). They also report that the strength of union movements cross-nationally are linked to the depth of the labor-capital cleavage and the extent of the status gap between nonmanual white-collar and professional employees and manual workers.

The high unionization rate in the Scandinavian countries has been attributed to the organization of white-collar and professional employees (Galenson 1998, 133). As of 1985, white-collar union density was 79 percent in Denmark, 71 percent in Sweden, and 62 percent in Norway, compared to 51 percent in Austria, 45 percent in Britain, 34 percent in Switzerland, 28 percent in Germany, and 25 percent in the Netherlands.[10] There is a significant correlation between the overall national union membership rates and intraclass variations in union strength, 0.46.[11] The measure of the latter indicates the relative strength of white-collar, professional, and other occupationally based unions (see Wessels 1996; table 2.3).

The examination of the effects of ethnic diversity produces ambiguous results. Visser (1994) and Stephens (1991), as well as our own analysis, find limited support for the hypothesis that ethnic heterogeneity hampers union organizing. There is even less significant evidence of support for the linguistic diversity hypothesis. Using the ethnic diversity index employed by Stephens (1991) we find a negative, but not statistically significant, relationship with union density. Similarly, our use of an ethnolinguistic fractionalization index, derived from La Porta and colleagues (1998), does not yield significant regression results.

Catholic Parties Power and Religion

Christian Democratic party strength is associated with unionization (Misra and Hicks 1994, 304). Wilensky (1981) notes that Catholic party power is as important a source of welfare state development as left party power. Catholic-based parties favor unionization, albeit by Christian union confederations, which exist in several western European countries, but a religious confederation represents the majority of union members in only one nation, Belgium (see Ebbinghaus and Visser 2000, 46; Western 1997, 80–83).

Our analysis indicates that a Catholic cumulative power index, which measures Catholic parties seats as a percentage of seats held by all government parties in 1946–94, does not significantly correlate with union density in multivariate regressions (Huber, Ragin, and Stephens 1997). The proportion of Catholics in the population is negatively related to union strength in our statistical analysis (see also Misra and Hicks 1994). Conversely, our Protestant variable is positively associated with density, that is, unions are stronger in Protestant than Catholic countries.[12]

Economic Factors

Our statistical analysis indicates that the size of the labor market, defined as the log of the 1994 employed and unemployed population, is negatively associated with union density in the eighteen industrialized Western countries (figure 2.1). The correlation coefficient is −0.57. Country size is of obvious importance. It may be noted that the majority of small countries have strong labor movements: Austria, Belgium, Denmark, Finland, Iceland, Ireland, Luxembourg, Norway, and Sweden. Union density, however, is low in Greece, the Netherlands, New Zealand, Portugal, and Switzerland compared with larger countries inside their cultural areas.

Such large countries as the United States, Japan, and Germany, have low density. Wallerstein (1989) seeks to explain the relationship by noting that in countries with larger labor markets, unions face higher costs of organizing additional union members. He points out (1989, 487) that union organizing is especially expensive in the United States, which has the biggest labor market in the industrialized world.

This finding that union membership rates are higher in smaller countries, however, may be a spurious one. Stephens (1991) points out that labor-force size is highly correlated with economic concentration, a variable that may be used as a proxy for industrial structure.[13] Such a high correlation (−0.90) in a small sample results in a multicollinearity problem. Statistical analyses are not able to distinguish the relative effect of these factors because of the very strong link between the two independent variables.

Union membership rates vary greatly among different industries and sectors of employment. In most advanced countries, it is higher in manufacturing and the public-sector than elsewhere in the economy (Ebbinghaus 1993, 186; Western 1997, 125). Curiously, measures of industrial and occupational structures, such as the proportion of wage and salary earners employed in industry (manufacturing, mining, utilities, and construction), public-sector, or blue-collar occupations, have no significant effects on union density when tested cross-nationally (Visser 1994, 177; Wallerstein 1989). Our computations also show that the proportion in industrial employment does not significantly affect the union membership rate. Estimates of trade dependence, such as the proportion of the merchandise exports in the GDP, produce similar results (Visser 1994).

The extent of government employment as of 1995 is positively correlated with union density, but our analysis indicates that this relationship is not significant when controlled for size of labor force and the left power index. The proportion of government revenues in the GDP is similarly associated with union density. These variables, of course, correlate highly with the left-party index, which leads again to a multicollinearity problem. Causation may also run in the opposite direction (Ebbinghaus and Visser 1999, 148).

As can be seen from the results reported earlier, cross-national statistical analysis of union density in advanced Western countries has its limits. The number of countries is small and comparable data are not always available. Moreover, there are many independent structural, economic, and political variables that can logically be posited to affect union density. Correlations are often difficult to interpret, and as our treatment of the left power, legal regulation of labor relations, and corporatism indices illustrates, union-linked variables are often interrelated. Multivariate regressions are problematic, given the interaction between independent variables or interconnected effects.

Cultural Clusters

To reiterate, union density and collective bargaining rates vary greatly within the English-speaking and European clusters, that is among northern European, southern European, German-speaking, and the Low countries. Statistical analysis cannot account for the differences among these cultural groupings (see Ebbinghaus and Visser 1999, 150). In contrast to the other culture regions, union densities in the highly unionized northern European countries have remained stable or even increased since 1980. Social democratic, class, and corporatist traditions and the Ghent system are especially strong in these states, all of which are small and Protestant (table 2.3). Norway is somewhat of an exception because its density and collective agreement coverage rates are significantly below the other northern European countries and it does not follow the Ghent system. There are greater absolute differences in these rates between Norway and Sweden (19 percentage points on coverage and 32 points on density) than there are between the United States and Canada (23 points on coverage and 23 points on density). In relative terms, however, the U.S.-Canadian gap is greater.

Union density differs greatly among the Low Countries. Belgium, which has the Ghent system, is the most highly organized country in the group, whereas the Netherlands has a much lower unionization rate. These two occupy the middle ground on the index of corporatism in 1970–90 (table 2.3). Belgium has the strongest Christian unions among advanced Western countries.

Membership rates also vary considerably among the southern European countries; the range between the highest, Italy, and the lowest, France, is quite large. However, collective bargaining coverage among them and the Low Countries is uniformly high (table 2.1). These two groups of countries are Catholic, with the exception of Greece, which is Orthodox, and the Netherlands, which has about equal proportions of Catholics and

Protestants. Among the German-speaking countries, Germany and Switzerland stand in the middle of the range on density. However, Austria, the smallest country, has the highest levels of union density, coverage, and corporatism in this group (table 2.1).

Both union density and collective bargaining rates differ significantly among English-speaking countries. Union density is highest in Ireland, the smallest country in the group. Ireland has almost one and one-half times higher the unionization rate and two times the bargaining coverage of Great Britain. The same pattern of variation applies to Australia and New Zealand. Union density in Australia is almost one and one-half times higher than New Zealand, and the coverage rate is almost three times higher.

As we have stressed, the United States and Canada, two neighboring, predominantly English-speaking societies with similar economic structures, have shown considerable divergence in union density and political culture (Lipset 1996, 77–109; 1986; 1990; Meltz 1985; 1989b; 1990; Western 1997, 18). Union density in Canada in the mid-1990s (37 percent) was more then two times higher than in the United States (14 percent). The collective bargaining coverage rate in Canada (40 percent) also exceeds that in the United States (17 percent) by more than two times. Corporatism does not differentiate, given that in the English-speaking countries, including the United States and Canada, it is generally very weak.

As noted, Canada is much more social democratic in its values and social policies than the United States; the majority of its provinces and population have been governed by social democratic parties, whereas few states in the United States have. The exceptional weakness of labor unions in the United States would appear to be linked to the same factors as those related to the absence of a visible socialist or labor party (Lipset and Marks 2000). A systematic comparison of the two nations, made possible by the 1996 Lipset-Meltz survey data and qualitative and historical materials, allows us to overcome some of the methodological problems posed by the too-few-countries, too-many-variables problem that undermines statistical research. Clearly, the comparative study of variation in trade union support would benefit much by case study analyses of the variations within small national clusters (e.g., the Low and southern European countries).

The picture is somewhat different when looking at the extent of collective bargaining coverage in the advanced Western countries. The overwhelming majority of employed people in two low-density Latin countries,

France and Spain, are covered by collective bargaining, 95 percent in the first and 82 percent in the second. A similar pattern exists in Greece and Italy. The coverage rate in Greece was 90 percent in 1994, and in Italy it was 83 percent in 1993.

Collective bargaining coverage is much weaker in English-speaking nations (Adams 1995). In Ireland, which is an exception to this generalization, 90 percent of workers are covered by collective bargaining. Collective bargaining coverage and union density, defined in terms of the dependent labor force, are closely related with one another in the United States (17 and 14 percent), Canada, (40 and 37 percent), New Zealand (24 and 23 percent), and Japan (25 and 24 percent). In Great Britain and Australia, the coverage rates (47 and 65 percent) are notably higher than densities (36 and 35 percent) (see table 2.1).

The Gap between Collective Agreement Coverage and Union Density

What causes collective agreement coverage to differ from the union membership rate? In the United States and Canada, a contract negotiated by a union certified to represent employees in a bargaining unit covers all employees in the unit, whether or not they belong to a union. Because not all employees in the bargaining unit join the union, there will be a gap between collective agreement coverage and the union membership rate. Similar factors are at play in the narrow gaps in Japan and New Zealand. Since 1980, the relative decline in the union membership rate was largest in New Zealand (table 2.2).[14] Union density in New Zealand in 1995 was less than one-half the rate in 1980. This drop has been attributed to the deregulation of the labor market (Harbridge and Honeybone 1996). In many countries, industry sector agreements negotiated between an employers' association and union(s) are extended to cover all employees in the industry. In addition, some governments make provision for wage-rate extensions. Deregulation is usually accompanied by the elimination of these industry extension provisions.

Why should any employee want to join a union and pay union dues if the industry or the government determines their terms and conditions of employment? Why not be a free rider? Although there is no statistically significant inverse relationship, if the northern European countries are excluded along with the United States, Canada, Japan, and New Zealand, there is a huge gap between coverage and density rates in a large number of countries (France, Greece, Spain, Germany, Austria, the Netherlands,

Portugal, and Italy). The widest gap occurs in France, 95 versus 10 percent, but even the narrowest gap, in Italy, is more than double the union density rate, 83 versus 38.5 percent. Ireland and Belgium have narrower but still substantial gaps of over 37 percentage points each. In Ireland, it appears that industry-level bargaining is responsible for the high level of coverage (Western 1997, 162).

These data suggest that regulations and government legislation not only affect the extent to which employees are covered by collective agreements, but they may also have a negative effect on the rate of union density. Much more analysis is needed to determine specifically what impact these regulations and legislation have on a country's union density.

Patterns in Union Density across Time

The trends in international union density in developed countries by percentage of employed wage and salary earners from 1950 to 1995 are presented in table 2.2, ranked by the 1995 estimates. Until 1960, the European pattern in terms of the direction of change is roughly similar to the patterns in both the United States and Canada. That is, union density grew in each decade up to 1920, decreased in 1930, and grew thereafter until 1960. European union density in 1910 (9.7 percent) was similar to that in the United States (9.1 percent) and Canada (10.6 percent).[15] Although the direction of change was similar, the magnitude of the change in Europe was much greater than in the two North American countries. By 1960, the European average (43.0) was 50 percent higher than the rates for both the Unites States (28.9 percent) and Canada (28.3 percent).

The most significant changes took place after 1960 (see table 2.2). In Europe, the average union density rate continued to rise, peaking in 1980, and then declined somewhat after that, but it was still above the 1960 rate. The pattern in Canada was very much like that in northern Europe, with growth continuing until 1980, and then some easing, but remaining above the 1960 level. The pattern in the United States, however, was far different from either Canada or northern Europe, but similar to Japan—a continuing decline after 1960 to a 1995 U.S. rate below that of 1920. Private-sector union density in 1999 at 9.4 percent was also below the 1910 rate of 10.1 percent. Density in Japan fell from 32 percent in 1960 to 24 percent in 1995. These figures provide some useful benchmarks for the remaining chapters of this book.

The Cross-Country Evidence: Implications for the United States and Canada

From the mid-1960s, Canadian union density diverged from the U.S. pattern and has been similar to that in the northern European countries. It should, however, be noted that between 1900 and the mid-1930s, union density was consistently slightly higher in Canada, the less industrialized and urbanized country.

Based on international studies, the primary source of Canadian-U.S. union density differences in the post-1960 period appears to be the differences in political parties that have held power. There has been much greater representation by the left in governments in Canada, provincially more so than federally. This in turn leads to the further question of why the political parties and the orientation of Canadian governments were so different in the United States and Canada. This question, beyond the scope of past labor research, is central to our study. Why did Canada and the United States have such divergent political patterns after the 1960s, with social democratic and socialist parties holding power in Canada but not in the United States? (In fact, the first major divergence was in 1944 by the socialist government, which enacted pro-union legislation in the province of Saskatchewan, giving workers in the public sector the right to bargain and strike; Lipset 1950/1968.) This difference in the strength of political forces is especially important when considering that a large left cross-partisan bloc held office in the Unites States between 1934 and 1938, was strong in the U.S. Congress in reaction to the Great Depression, and gave the primary push to legislation favorable to unions, whereas the equivalent groups in Canada had less legislative impact because they sat on opposition benches.

These questions go to the core of the hypotheses of our book: for much of recent history, with the exception of the Depression-era New Deal policies of Roosevelt, social democratic values, which have been more conducive to support for the collective rights of workers everywhere, gradually became stronger in Canada than in the United States. One manifestation of the greater strength was legislation more supportive of unions in Canada and more vigorous enforcement of the legislation by labor relations boards. This theme is examined in subsequent chapters. Some analysts have even argued that a social democratic orientation permeated Canada's two major bourgeois parties. Western (1997) includes the Liberal Party, at times referred to as "socialists in a hurry," in the group of social democratic or working-class parties, using data from Wallerstein (1989), whereas

others speak of the Progressive Conservatives as "Red Tories." Both parties
supported a wide range of legislation that was very union-supportive. What
is most significant about Canada is the broad support that almost all this
country's political parties have given in the post–World War II period to
labor and welfare state legislation. This has led some, such as novelist
Robertson Davies, to describe the country as a "socialist monarchy."

The international data and North American findings presented in the
following chapters indicate a continuing strong link between trade unionism and the strength of left parties and movements, which in turn is related
to the degree of class awareness. Union density is positively associated with
left party power in government. In the context of the United States and
Canada, this means that a country that has a strong social democratic orientation in politics should also have strong unions.

3   The Evolution of Trade Unions in the United States and Canada

The Emergence of the Gap in Union Density

A fundamental observation about the evolution of unions in Canada and the United States in the twentieth century is that, with the exception of the two-decade period 1938–58, a greater percentage of Canadian than U.S. workers belonged to trade unions. This prompts three questions. Why has the trade union membership rate been consistently higher in Canada? What happened between 1938 and 1958 that led to a greater union membership share in the United States? And finally, why after 1964 were the differences in union membership between the two countries magnified as never before? We start with the early history of trade unions and follow these developments over time.

Early History

Trade unions are voluntary associations of workers formed to ensure the fair treatment of workers by employers and to protect and improve wages and working conditions. The major mechanism for attaining these goals is collective bargaining with employers over the terms and conditions of employment, with the additional pressure of strikes on occasion to move toward union goals. In Canada and the United States, unions experimented with different structures to attain some permanence as a vehicle to represent workers. The first strike of wage earners in a single trade seems to have been that of the journeymen printers in Philadelphia in 1786. In 1799, the journeymen shoemakers' union in Philadelphia struck for nine weeks against a wage cut and hired one of their members to picket outside the employers' shops (Lester 1964).

One of the first national labor organizations in the United States was the Knights of Labor, established in 1869. Its members included farmers and merchants as well as workers from many trades. By the late 1800s, a stable form of unionism had emerged, which came to be known as business unionism. It became dominant in North America with the formation (in 1886) and growth of the American Federation of Labor (AFL), which concentrated on trades or skilled workers.

Initially, there was competition between the AFL and industrially based organizations, such as the Industrial Workers of the World (IWW, also known as Wobblies). However, by the beginning of World War I it was generally clear that business unionism was the only form able to withstand the frequent recessions and depressions that devastated union membership. The AFL had affiliates in Canada as well as in the United States (Marks 1989; Hattam 1993).

Background and Overview

In 1901 total union membership is estimated at 7 percent of employees in the United States and 9 percent in Canada (see fig. 1.1). One hundred years later the figures for the two countries are 13.5 and 30.0 percent respectively. To begin, we present an overview of the evolution of the trade union movements in the twentieth century in both countries, focussing on the relevant behavior of workers, business, and government, as well as the key determinants of the changes in union membership. There is such a broad and deep wealth of writing on the history of the labor movements that we can only scratch the surface. Our main contribution is in analyzing the ways in which the three main actors (unions, government, and employers) both responded to and shaped their structural environments up to the start of the twenty-first century. We also combine an analysis of the results of the survey we have conducted of workers in the United States and Canada with the major themes of the long-term patterns in the evolution of trade unions in the two countries. We begin with a quantitative examination of changes in union strength, using the changing statistic of the percentages of employees who were unions members, as set out in figure 1.1. The technical term for this statistic is *union density*. It provides a rough estimate of the proportion of workers eligible to join unions who actually belong. This measure usually excludes people who are self-employed or

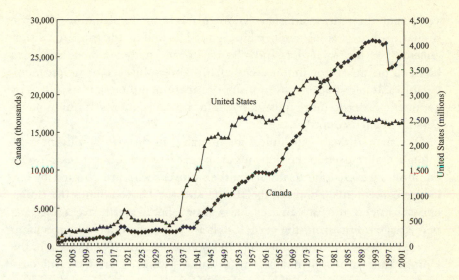

FIGURE 3.1

Total union membership in Canada and the United States, 1901–2001 (in thousands). The scale for the U.S. is approximately ten times that for Canada to reflect the fact that the population of the United States is roughly ten times that of Canada; in 1998 the populations were 270 million and 30 million, respectively. (For data sources, see app. A.)

work for their families because they normally cannot or do not join unions. Of course, nothing is straightforward. Some self-employed workers in specialized areas may belong to associations that are unions, such as fishermen who belong to associations that bargain with the owners of ships and of fish-processing plants or physicians who form unions to deal with HMOs (health maintenance organizations). The statistics in figure 1.1 include new estimates of the early period (1901–1936) prepared by the authors, as described in appendix A.

The years from 1901 to 2001 are divided here into six periods reflecting the most fundamental changes in the shares of union membership in the employed workforces of the two countries. The six periods are 1901–16, 1916–36, 1936–56, 1956–64, 1964–81, and 1981–2001. These are somewhat arbitrary divisions, intended to capture the broad developments that occurred in the two countries during these periods. Figure 3.1 shows the actual growth in the number of union members in the two countries.

As discussed in chapter 1, there are small variations in the evolution of the share of union membership in the two countries up to 1964, but after that there appear to be large differences; that is, the proportion of employees who belonged to unions followed roughly the same patterns up to

1964, but then diverged sharply. We offer some explanations for the similar early trends in membership density, as well as for the later differences. In trying to understand these patterns in detail, we distinguish between private-sector union membership and public-sector union membership and later patterns by industry occupation and by state as well as by gender, in order to more fully understand the components of union membership in each country.

Our analysis deals with union membership in the two countries, even though, as discussed in the previous chapter, there are differences between employees who belong to unions and employees who are covered by collective agreements. However, in Canada and the United States the differences between the two figures have always been small, averaging 2–4 percentage points from the earliest data we have on collective agreement coverage versus union membership. In 1998, 2 percent of employees in the United States who did not belong to unions were covered by collective agreements, compared with 3 percent in Canada.

The figures for Europe are far different, with collective agreement coverage running between 70 and 80 percent for most countries, while membership averaged 45 percent. The reasons for the trans-Atlantic differences go to the heart of differences in history as well as economic and social legislation. Although in this respect Canada is close to the United States, our discussion of union membership shows how and why Canada is much closer to Europe.

1901–1916

The period from 1901 to 1916 is one of relative stability in the share of union membership, averaging 10.3 percent in the United States and a slightly higher 11.3 percent in Canada. Because the United States was a more industrialized, urbanized country during this period, the raw union density figures may even understate the extent of unionization in Canada. The evolution of unions as institutions took a major step forward as a result of the *Commonwealth v. Hunt* decision in the United States (1842) and the Trade Union Act (1872) in Canada—trade unions were no longer considered conspiracies in restraint of trade. However, governments did little to protect a worker's right to join a union. In Canada, the Industrial Disputes Investigation Act (IDIA) of 1907 provided for a cooling-off period if there was a strike or the threat of a strike. A tripartite conciliation board (union representative, employer representative, and jointly chosen chair or government representative) was to be appointed in the event that a concilia-tion officer failed to settle the dispute. If the dispute could still not be settled, then the board would issue a nonbinding report on the terms that it thought were reasonable to settle the strike. This moral suasion was intended to put pressure on the parties to settle. In the end, it was a test of strength between labor and management, but it did at least formally rec-ognize that unions had a role to play in the collective bargaining process.

Under this approach of survival of the fittest, or laissez-faire, the form of unionism that evolved had to be one that could resist the determined efforts of employers to avoid unions. Such unions, as Samuel Gompers foresaw in establishing the AFL in 1886, were based on skilled workers who could pay union dues and whose threat of a withdrawal of their labor serv-ices had some economic impact on the companies targeted.

The five largest unions in 1916 are shown in figures 3.2 and 3.3 for each country. Three points deserve mentioning. First, many of the large unions in the United States were international unions, meaning that they had branches or affiliates in Canada, such as the United Mine Workers, United Brotherhood of Carpenters, International Union of Bricklayers, and the International Association of Machinists.[1] Second, the unions were entirely in the private sector; there were no government or other public-sector unions (the government-owned Canadian National Railways was created in 1923 when five private railways went bankrupt). Third, organizations con-nected with the railways dominated union membership in Canada, whereas in the United States a broader range of skills made up the leading groups. This clearly reflects the importance of transportation and communication and the lesser role of industry in the Canadian economy. For the purposes of our later discussion, it is important to note that the Canadian govern-ment, in establishing a sovereign country north of the forty-ninth parallel, directly fostered the growth of the transportation sector.

Both countries also had a number of independent radical unions, of which the IWW was the most important. By 1916, however, these unions had been weakened considerably in both the United States and Canada; the IWW had strength only in a few mining communities in the west.

The higher union density in Canada in the first period reflects some-what greater union strength than is initially apparent because there was a proportionately smaller industrial and urban base in Canada, as indicated in table 3.1. For example, between 1921 and 1941 employment in manu-facturing in the United States averaged about 30 percent, compared with just under 20 percent in Canada. Agriculture was about 10 percentage points less in the United States than in Canada. Because manufacturing

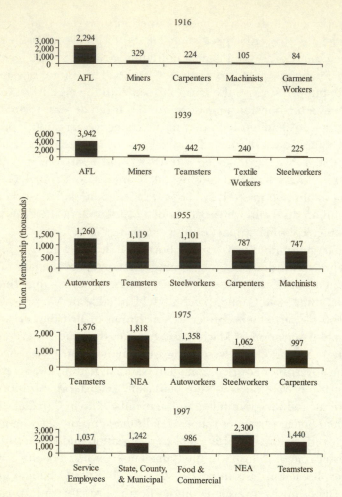

FIGURE 3.2

Membership in five largest union organizations, United States 1916–1997 (in thousands). AFL, American Federation of Labor; Autoworkers, United Automobile Workers of America; Carpenters, United Brotherhood of Carpenters and Joiners of America; Food & Commercial, Food and Commercial Workers; Garment Workers, United Garment Workers of America; Machinists, International Association of Machinists; Miners, United Mine Workers of America; NEA, National Education Association; State, County & Municipal, State, County, & Municipal Employees; Teamsters, International Brotherhood of Teamsters; Textile, Clothing & Textile Workers of America. (*Source*: Gifford 1998; Troy and Scheflin 1985; *Directory of Labour Organizations in Canada* for selected years, http://labour.hrdc-drhc.gc.ca/ millieudetravail_workplace/ot_lo/index.cfm/doc/english.)

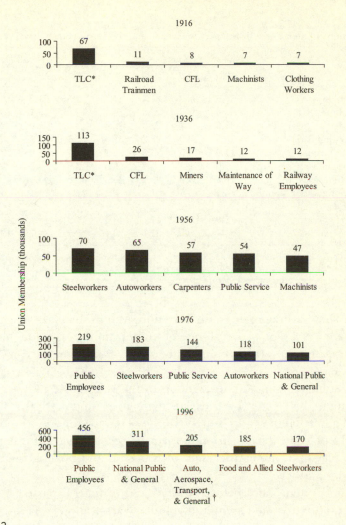

FIGURE 3.3

Membership in five largest union organizations, Canada 1911–1996 (in thousands). Auto, Aerospace, Transport & General, National Automobile, Aerospace, Transportation and General Workers Union of Canada; Autoworkers, United Automobile Workers of America; CFL, Canadian Federation of Labor; Carpenters, United Brotherhood of Carpenters; Clothing Workers, Clothing Workers of America; Food and Allied, United Food and Allied Workers; Machinists, International Association of Machinists; Maintenance of Way, International Brotherhood of Maintenance of Way Employees; Miners, United Mine Workers of America; National Public & General, National Union of Public and General Employees; Public Employees, Canadian Union of Public Employees; Public Service, Public Service Alliance of Canada; Railway Employees, Canadian Brotherhood of Railway Employees; Railroad Trainmen, Brotherhood of Railroad Trainmen; TLC, Trades and Labour Congress of Canada. *Refers to Canadian organizations. †In 1984 the Canadian Auto Workers (CAW) separated from the United Automobile Workers of America (UAW). The CAW is also known as the National Automobile, Aerospace, Transportation and General Workers of Canada. (*Source: Directory of Labour Organizations in Canada,* http://labour.hrdc-drhc.gc.ca/millieudetravail_workplace/ot_lo/index.cfm/doc/english; 1956 data from Eaton and Ashagrie 1970).

TABLE 3.1
Distribution of Labor Force by Industry in Canada and the United States, 1921–1951 (%)

Industry	Canada				United States			
	1921	*1931*	*1941*	*1951*	*1921*	*1931*	*1941*	*1951*
Primary industries	36.6	33.0	31.4	21.1	22.5	21.6	18.2	11.3
Agriculture[a]	35.0	31.2	29.2	19.1	19.6	19.7	15.5	9.2
Mining	1.6	1.8	2.2	2.0	3.9	2.9	2.7	2.1
Secondary industries	26.5	24.9	28.2	32.3	32.5	32.2	36.7	40.6
Manufacturing	17.5	18.5	23.0	25.7	29.7	28.0	32.9	35.5
Construction	9.0	6.4	5.2	6.6	3.6	4.2	3.8	5.1
Tertiary industries	36.9	37.9	39.2	45.3	41.6	44.9	43.8	46.6
Transportation and public utilities	8.4	7.7	7.0	8.8	12.4	11.1	9.1	9.1
Trade	11.8	9.9	11.1	13.4	16.5	18.1	19.2	21.1
Other services	—	20.3	21.1	23.1	12.7	15.7	15.5	16.4

Source: Canadian data from Denton and Ostry (1967); U.S. agriculture data from Bancroft (1958); all other U.S. data from *Handbook of Labor Statistics* (1921–1951).
   [a] Including fishing, trapping, and forestry operations.

had an above average rate of unionization even in the early years, the fact that there was a higher overall rate of unionization in Canada may reflect a higher base rate in that country and even greater union activism from the earliest days.

A possible explanation, in addition to the role of the railways and the stimulation this sector by the Canadian government, is the Canadian federal government's more supportive views toward unions, as reflected in the IDIA of 1907. That legislation formally recognized that unions had a role to play in a public discussion of issues in, and possible solutions to, industrial conflict.

In the United States before World War I, Congress passed a series of laws providing for mediation and voluntary arbitration of labor disputes. However, these were limited to the railroad industry—the Railway Act of 1888, the Erdman Act of 1898, and the Newlands Act of 1913 all provided for mediation and arrangements for arbitration for railroad-operating employees.

A second early distinguishing factor between the countries was the role of the province of Quebec and its labor movement. The British had conquered the French colony of Quebec in 1759, but the French were granted use of their own language, their own legal system, and the maintenance of their own religion, Roman Catholicism. These freedoms and distinctiveness were incorporated in the British North America Act of 1867, which created the Dominion of Canada through a confederation of several of the

British provinces. The French in Quebec also had a different approach to trade unions, supporting the concept of unions and employers working together for the larger common good. The United States was also multi-ethnic to a greater extent than English Canada, which was largely made up of immigrants from the British Isles. These workers of British origin were in turn more sympathetic to a labor party and socialism than were Americans.

In this early period, U.S. and Canadian unionists were therefore taking a different approach to politics and political parties. In the United States, Gompers's dictum was nonaffiliation: "reward your friends and punish your enemies." In Canada, the Trades and Labour Congress (TLC), the affiliate of the AFL, did not formally support a political party and did not favor socialism, but its association with the Liberal Party was much stronger than comparable political links in the United States (Babcock 1974). Whereas the AFL formally rejected socialism, the TLC did not oppose it. The differences in the political systems in the two countries, a congressional system versus the Canadian parliamentary system, were especially important for the later differences in political affiliations.

Before World War I, socialists in the United States were organizationally stronger than in Canada. Socialist mayors and legislators were elected there. At that time in Canada, there was no effective federal socialist or labor party, but local socialist and labor parties elected members of the provincial legislatures in British Columbia and in Winnipeg. There was also a small group of independent labor progressives under the leadership of James Shaver (J. S.) Woodsworth.

In summary, by the onset of the U.S. entry into World War I there was a core of unionists in both countries in areas where they held sizable economic power, but proportionately somewhat more in Canada than in the United States.

1916–1936

The entry of Canada and the United States into World War I ushered in dramatic increases in trade union membership and participation in the economy, but as the data in figure 1.1 show, the changes were short-lived, especially in the United States. In Canada there were longer-term effects that lifted the extent of union membership strength significantly above that in the United States. Canadian union density rose to 24.4 percent in 1919 versus a peak of 18.3 percent in the United States in 1921. For the entire 1916–1936 period, union density averaged less than 13 percent south of the border and just over 16 to the north. Why did union membership rise so much more during the war in Canada than in the United States? Why did Canada's union density, although falling precipitously, remain at a higher level?

Canada entered the war earlier (1914) than the United States (1917) and committed a higher proportion of its economic resources. As a British dominion, Canada came quickly to Britain's assistance. In order to send both troops and war materiel it was necessary to guarantee continuous production. The Canadian government moved quickly to head off possible worker unrest by supporting the recognition of unions in war industries. As a result, union membership increased sharply among trades in factory and other war-related production and transportation. The United States joined in the war later, but a similar pattern of union recognition was followed in the interests of war production. The fact that the United States was in the war for a shorter period may be responsible for the smaller increase in the percentage of U.S. workers who were union members.

In the aftermath of the war, the union share of employment dropped by almost the same extent in both countries. Two factors seem mainly responsible. First, the government removed its support for unionization with the end of the need for war production. The increase in the number of people looking for work, as a result of the return of millions of servicemen wanting to go back to their jobs and the drop in employment (especially in more unionized industries) because the end of war production, took pressure off the labor market. People who went on strike or who threatened to strike could be easily replaced. In Canada, events culminated in the Winnipeg General Strike of 1919. The Winnipeg General Strike was an outgrowth of a march from western Canada by unemployed ex-soldiers who were intending to go to Ottawa, the country's capital, to demand jobs. In Winnipeg, they were supported by a socialist union alliance known as the One Big Union. The demonstrators demanded jobs, unemployment insurance, and health care. Troops were called in and the organizers of the strike were jailed (see Morton 1990, 119). Union leaders were branded communist sympathizers and opponents of capitalism, further eroding support for unionism.

A second negative factor for unions was the increased anti-union militancy of employers. The experience of worker interest in unionization during World War I may have been a factor in the introduction of a Canadian-designed approach that became known, ironically enough, as the American Plan. A Canadian industrial relations expert, William Lyon

Mackenzie King, who was the first deputy minister of Labour of Canada in 1901 and later was prime minister for 22 years between 1921 and 1948, developed it. The plan was for the formation of nonunion employee representation groups. King had developed this approach for the Rockefellers following the bloody strikes in 1914 in their Colorado coal mines. King's philosophy on labor relations was set out in his 1918 book *Industry and Humanity*.[2] Although the Progressive Party did have some success on both sides of the border, this was a period of strength for conservatives in both countries.

Even though the 1920s was a very prosperous time, trade union membership in both countries remained at the low levels to which it had fallen by the early 1920s. The only difference is that the level in Canada was at a much higher plateau than in the United States. There is evidence that within the AFL some leaders were unhappy that unions did not represent industrial workers in the new mass-production areas of automobiles, steel, rubber, and electrical products. Although there was some representation among coal miners, a number of bloody battles had been fought over union representation. Many companies had introduced employee representation plans and some had unions in skilled trades who were members of the AFL, but the vast majority of workers in industry did not have a formal voice (Marks 1989).

There was growing interest in socialism in this period on both sides of the border. Ontario and Alberta had farmer-dominated third-party governments, which were linked to labor. The United States had farmer-labor political organizations that controlled state governments in North Dakota and Minnesota.

Passions were stirring among industrial workers, led in particular by mine workers. The most famous name was the president of the United Mine Workers of America, John L. Lewis. He was later to spearhead a committee within the AFL to attempt to organize industrial workers. Initially called the Committee for Industrial Organization (CIO), it began vigorously promoting unionization among workers in mass-production industries in the 1930s. The efforts of the CIO in the United States spread to Canada, both as branch operations and by invitation from Canadian workers. However, as figure 1.1 shows, there was little impact on total union density until after 1937.

On the political scene in the United States, there was a return of government support for unionization not seen since World War I. The Great Depression that began in 1929 was proving intractable. The Republicans were defeated in 1932 and Franklin Delano Roosevelt was elected on a platform promising to get the economy moving. The decision by the Supreme Court that the National Industrial Recovery Act (NRA) of 1933 was not constitutional focused attention on the role of the labor movement in assisting the economy out of the depression.

The National Labor Relations (Wagner) Act of 1935, often called the Magna Carta of organized labor, for the first time recognized the right of employees to join unions without interference from employers and required employers to bargain collectively with unions. The act also established the National Labor Relations Board to enforce the provisions of the act and designated certain unfair labor practices from which management was to refrain. It has been said that the Depression introduced a "social-democratic tinge" in the United States (Hofstadter 1972, 208).

In spite of this act and the evident government encouragement for unions—CIO organizers told workers that "the president wants you to join the union" (Kochan and Katz 1989, 25)—there were only small gains in the share of unions before 1937 (see fig. 1.1). Although it has been the standard view of labor historians that the Wagner Act was responsible for the explosive growth of union membership from the late 1930s to the mid-1950s, the data show that the sharp growth really began two years after Congress passed the Wagner Act. The standard view has been criticized in particular by Roy Adams, who has said, "by most objective standards the Wagner Act must be judged a long term failure" (1994, 2). The implication is that union strength was growing on its own and that the Wagner Act approach may actually have reduced the extent of unionization by requiring a formal process for the certification of unions as opposed to a demonstration of union strength.

One possible explanation for the delayed impact of the Wagner Act is that the act did not take effect until 1937 when the Supreme Court, in the *Jones and Laughlin* decision, held that the Wagner Act was constitutional. This came at about the time of the Little Steel Strike, the bloody battle by the United Steelworkers of America for recognition as the bargaining agent of employees at Republic Steel. Security agents hired by Republic Steel killed some of the strikers. The Supreme Court decision also coincided with General Motors's capitulation to the CIO United Auto Workers, following a two-month sit-down strike. The Wagner Act was intended to do away with recognition strikes because the act required employers to bargain with a union certified as the exclusive representative of the employees in a designated bargaining unit. (This concept of exclusive representation did not exist in Europe.) Whatever the merits of the arguments concerning the impact of the Wagner Act, it is clear that union membership growth only spurted ahead in 1937 after the act was declared constitutional.

On the political front in Canada, no Wagner Act was in the offing. However, events were to take place in this period that later transformed the politics of Canada and the role of trade unions. In 1933, in the western provinces, a new political party was formed, the socialist Cooperative Commonwealth Federation (CCF). In June 1933 this party issued the Regina Manifesto calling for, among other demands, government ownership, support for trade unions, and government-sponsored health care. Specifically, the manifesto advocated fourteen public-policy proposals ranging over such issues as planning, the socialization of finance, socialized health services, social justice, and an emergency program to alleviate the effects of the Great Depression. The CCF ran candidates in both provincial and federal elections and formed the first socialist government in North America in the province of Saskatchewan in 1944.

1936–1956

The period 1936–56 has been termed labor's golden age in the United States, and figure 1.1 confirms this. The union membership share in the United States leaped forward from 13.7 percent in 1936 to the high-water mark of 34.7 percent in 1954, and then eased somewhat to 33.4 percent in 1956. Canadian membership followed with a lag, but caught up to the U.S. figure in 1955. Organized labor had arrived in the United States; it had become part of the political mainstream. The general view, at least among academics and perhaps government officials, was that unions had become an accepted part of the industrial fabric of the country. Books such as Richard Lester's *As Unions Mature* (1958) describe what appeared to be the natural place for unions in the fabric of society.

An indication of this new role could perhaps be seen in the merging of the two giant labor federations in the two countries. The Committee for Industrial Organization, founded in 1935, had split from the AFL to become an archrival known as the Congress of Industrial Organizations (still called the CIO). The rivalry between the two former allies was regarded as divisive within the house of labor, but the competition surely spurred membership growth (Meltz 1985). In 1955, the AFL and the CIO merged to form the AFL-CIO. In 1956 the Trades and Labour Congress (TLC), which was the Canadian branch of the AFL, merged with the Canadian Congress of Labour (CCL), the Canadian branch of the CIO, to form the Canadian Labour Congress (CLC). Whether by coincidence or not, the mergers in each country were followed by declines in the union share of employment.

While the U.S. government was giving tacit and formal support for union organizing, the events connected with World War II provided a major impetus, as had been the case in World War I. Again there was the production imperative and the need to avoid strikes that would damage the war effort. The labor movement in both countries, in relation to the workforce, was twice the size it had been at the outset of World War I, although the movement in Canada was much larger relative to the workforce. The combination of size and government recognition gave a huge boost to organized labor in both countries.

It was said in the United States that if Roosevelt had a problem with production he would say "clear it with Sidney"—Sidney Hillman of the Clothing Workers was head of the political action committee of the Democratic national convention (Galenson 1960, 292). Roosevelt was a Democrat and the unions were openly supporting the Democratic Party. The Gompers notion of reward your friends and punish your enemies had been replaced by labor, especially the CIO, as a strong backer of the Democratic Party, the party that had brought in the Wagner Act. But there were clouds on the political horizon.

Concern over the issue of communists in some trade union leadership positions, particularly within the CIO, as well as their association with the Democratic Party led to a backlash against organized labor. In 1948 and 1949 communist leaders and unions were expelled from the CIO following the earlier lead of its Canadian affiliate, the CCL. The CCL acted after the revelations of the Guzenko Affair, which showed communist penetration of the Canadian and U.S. labor movements, as well as political activities by unionists.

Organized labor also suffered a big reverse when the Republican Congress in 1947 passed the Taft-Hartley Act. This act, which was dubbed "the slave labor law," curbed some trade union freedoms, such as closed shops (the requirement that only union members could be hired), and identified unfair practices by unions. The act also permitted states to enact more restrictive labor legislation. Specifically, Section 14(b) of the act allowed states to adopt right-to-work laws; these are laws that prevent a union from negotiating a union shop agreement, that is, the requirement that all employees in the bargaining unit join the union and pay union dues. The act also prohibited the use of the secondary boycotts, sympathy strikes, and jurisdictional strikes.

The Taft-Hartley Act was introduced during a period of postwar strikes following the end of wage and price controls. The great strike wave, along with shortages of goods, aroused public ill will and produced a public backlash against organized labor. This also occurred at a time when the Republican Party controlled Congress (in 1946 it won majorities in both houses of Congress for the first time since 1928). Public support for unions—although still above 60 percent and consistently higher in the United States than in Canada—also fell somewhat in the 1940s (see fig. 1.2). This development seems to have foreshadowed the reemergence of antistate laissez-faire values that accompanied the postwar prosperity. The act and the somewhat reduced public support for unions at that time also prefigured the disappearance in the United States of Richard Hofstadter's "social-democratic tinge." Simply put, politics had become more conservative in the United States.

Political events, however, were moving in a different direction in Canada. Canada advanced industrially very rapidly during the war, bringing with it tremendous prosperity. But in the postwar period, Canada did not become more conservative because, we suggest, these were not core Canadian values. Instead, in 1944 the socialist CCF party was elected to form the government of the province of Saskatchewan. The government immediately introduced legislation not only giving industrial workers the right to join unions and strike, but also giving public-sector employees (government workers, health-care workers, and teachers) the same rights.

In other provinces, in particular Ontario, and in the federal Parliament, the CCF became a party to be reckoned with. Opinion polls in 1944 showed the CCF was close to the Liberal Party, which was the governing party nationally. Prime Minister MacKenzie King, fearing a CCF victory in the upcoming 1944 elections, introduced labor legislation similar to the Wagner Act, incorporating the tripartite committee provisions of the 1907 Industrial Relations Democracy In Industry Act (IRDIA). Privy Council Order (PC) 1003 covered not only the federal jurisdiction but also the provinces under the wartime regulations. In 1948, when the act was changed to apply only to the federal jurisdiction, it was given the name the Industrial Relations and Disputes Investigation Act. Canadian union membership had been growing rapidly even before PC 1003, spurred by the necessity for a wartime accommodation between labor and management and by the active industrial organizing by the CCL and the TLC.

Labor organizations in Canada were divided in their approach to politics. The CCL (the branch of the CIO) actively supported the CCF. The

TLC (the branch of the AFL) was at times supportive of the Liberal Party. For example, in the 1945 federal election the TLC urged its members to reelect the Liberal government of Mackenzie King (Morton 1990). When the two union federations united in 1956, the newly created CLC was clearly leaning toward a more politically activist approach. Interaction between labor and politics grew in Canada while its effectiveness decreased in the United States.

One final important development in Canada during this period should be noted. In 1946 a Supreme Court justice made a decision in the case of a strike at the Ford Motor Company of Canada that was the opposite of right-to-work laws in the United States. Justice Ivan Rand—in what is now known in Canada as the Rand Formula—decided that employees who were represented by a union had to pay dues to the union, or the equivalent to a charity, even if they did not choose to belong to the union. The reasoning was that if a union was negotiating wages and working conditions on behalf of all employees it was therefore entitled to the financial support of all employees. In effect, Justice Rand was saying that there should be no free riders.

1956–1964

The short period 1956–64 witnessed virtually identical union membership declines in the two countries, from densities of 33 to 29 percent. We can speculate as to the reasons for this gradual decline in membership shares. As figure 3.1 indicates, membership was still growing, but it was not growing as fast as employment. One possible reason for the reduced membership growth is the lessening in competition within each country's labor movement as a result of the mergers of the two main federations.

Another possibility is that employer opposition to unions was slowly increasing in a period of weakening government support and the return to laissez-faire values (Kochan, Katz, and McKersie 1994). In the United States, revelations of union racketeering and corruption led to the passage of the Landrum-Griffin Act of 1959, further restricting union freedoms. The John F. Kennedy administration also identified the Teamsters Union as a target because of that union's corruption. At the same time, President Kennedy signed Executive Order 10988 in 1962, which provided limited collective bargaining rights for federal government employees (Western 1997, 72).

Economic factors also played a role in the decline of union density in both countries. With the reduction in the competition to organize new members following the federation mergers in both countries, the gradual changes that were taking place in the economies of both countries may have had an impact—the start of a trend away from employment in manufacturing toward service industries.

This development was the result of several factors. First, services that had been provided within manufacturing companies were beginning to be purchased from other suppliers, such as food services, building cleaning, and security. The main motivation was reduced costs from lower-wage nonunion suppliers. A second factor was the beginning of a move away from very large plants to smaller establishments. One reason was the ending of the war, which had put a premium on larger, standardized production units. Another reason was the move to more diversified units of production. The result was that larger units that had been easier to unionize were gradually giving way to medium-size units that were somewhat harder to unionize. These developments were just beginning in the period 1956–64 and were to have a much greater impact in the two subsequent periods.

An interesting might-have-been in labor history in the United States relates to developments in this period. In 1967 Walter Reuther, president of the United Auto Workers (UAW), broke with George Meany, head of the AFL-CIO, over the direction of the U.S. labor movement. Reuther, who had been the head of the AFL-CIO Economic Policy Committee from its founding in 1955, wanted a more activist approach for the labor movement both to social issues and to organizing. Meany, however, adopted a much more conservative approach. In 1968 the UAW withdrew from AFL-CIO and in 1969 Reuther created the American Labor Alliance (ALA) between the UAW and the Teamsters. This new federation was to be socially and politically activist. In fact, much of its platform had a similar direction to the newly formed CLC in Canada. However, the ALA was short-lived. When Reuther died in a plane crash in 1970, the ALA and the goal of a more socially activist labor movement died with him.

In Canada, on the other hand, the relations between unions and politics were taking a different direction, one that was to lay the foundation for the enhanced political support of labor. In 1961 the CLC and the CCF jointly founded the New Democratic Party (NDP). This party was directly in competition with the Liberal Party, which part of the labor movement had supported.[3] Whether the labor movement could deliver the votes was another issue, but the new party clearly was committed to representing union interests. The stage seemed to be set for major changes in the direction of a stronger union movement in Canada compared with the United States.

1964–1981

The period 1964–81 is perhaps the most significant in the entire twentieth century for understanding the differences as well as the similarities in the evolution of the trade union movements in the two countries. As figure 1.1 boldly displays, this was the first lengthy period when the union densities in the two countries dramatically diverged. Canada's average density of 34 percent was substantially above that of 25 percent in the United States.

In the case of the United States, union density continued the decline that had begun in 1956. Although there was a slight upward blip in 1981, the decline resumed after that. Two main factors account for the decline in the United States. First, membership in unions actually stopped growing and started to drop from the mid-1970s, as shown in figure 3.1. Initially, growth was still taking place, but at a slower rate than the growth of the labor force. Specifically, employment was not growing fast enough in the unionized, blue-collar sectors, such as manufacturing, mining, construction, and transportation, to offset growth in the predominantly nonunion sectors of trade, finance, restaurants, accommodation, and personal services. Although some union growth began in the rapidly increasing public (government) sector—20 percent between 1968 and 1978 (Kumar 1993)—this was not enough to compensate for the declines in union density in the private sector.

Data on membership in the five largest unions in the United States (fig. 3.2) show the decline in the industrial unions after 1975—the Steelworkers, United Auto Workers, and International Association of Machinists—and the rise of public-sector and service workers unions such as the National Educational Association (NEA), Service Employees, State and Municipal Employees (SCME), and Food and Commercial Workers (FCW). The Teamsters continued to increase beyond 1975, but by 1997 declined to less than 1.5 million members.

In Canada, there were similar patterns, as the membership figures by decade from 1956 to 1996 show (fig. 3.3). Although the declines were not nearly as steep as in the United States, many blue-collar unions experienced declines after 1976—the Steelworkers, United Brotherhood of

Carpenters, and International Association of Machinists. The exceptions included the Canadian Auto Workers—initially known as the UAW and then in 1985 as CAW after the split from the UAW (Kumar and Meltz 1992)—and the International Brotherhood of Electrical Workers (IBEW). Huge increases took place in public-sector unions the Canadian Union of Public Employees (CUPE), Public Service Alliance of Canada (PSAC), National Union of Public and General Employees (NUPGE)—and the public-sector unions in Quebec—the Quebec Teachers Corporation, and Social Affairs Federation, Inc.

On the U.S. political front, the AFL-CIO made a major effort to change labor legislation during the Democratic Carter Administration of 1976–80. The partnership between the union movement and the Democrats was aiming to make the National Labor Relations Act friendlier to labor. It had become apparent, not just to academics but to the labor movement as a whole, that the gradual erosion of union power could be slowed or reversed only by stronger enforcement of provisions against unfair practices by employers and by adopting the Canadian approach of certification based on the signing of membership cards. This was preferred over requiring a vote in each case of certification application because the election system often permitted employers to delay and mobilize employees against the unionization efforts.

Introduced into Congress in 1977, the bill known as the Labor Law Reform Act was stiffly opposed by employer groups. The act imposed harsher penalties on violators of labor laws, required stricter time limits on the election process, expanded the membership of the National Labor Relations Board by two members, and provided more effective remedies for victims of unfair labor practices (Kochan 1980). Although passed in the House, the bill died in 1978 when it was defeated in the Senate by a vote of 51 to 49. This failed effort was one of the last major political efforts of organized labor in the United States for almost two decades.

Right-to-work (RTW) laws, which prohibit unions and management from signing collective agreements that enforce universal membership or dues check off, were spreading rapidly in the United States during the 1970s. By 1998, twenty-one states had adopted such legislation. Studies have shown that the existence of RTW laws has a significant downward effect on union density (Meltz 1989b).

On the positive side for unions, by 1979 a majority of state governments (thirty-eight) had moved to give public-sector workers the right to organize and bargain collectively. It is not surprising that the earliest states to grant public employees the right to organize, such as New York, Oregon,

Washington, and Minnesota, were also those known for historically having
more left-of-center political leanings. On balance, increased union organizing in the public sector, to about 35 percent by 1981, was not sufficient
to offset the declines in the private sector—first relatively and then in
the mid-1970s absolutely—and the labor movement began losing total
membership.

Developments in Canada were very different in the period 1964–81. In
fact, this might be termed the high-water mark of unionism in Canada. The
changes in Canada were initiated by developments occurring in the
Province of Quebec, during what is termed the quiet revolution of the early
1960s. As a result of cultural and political changes, the province emerged
from domination by the Catholic Church, the Anglo-Canadian business
sector, conservative politicians, and a restrictive government. It modern-
ized and moved quickly toward the establishment of social democratic
institutions.

With the quiet revolution came greater militancy by trade unions and
the abandonment of the tradition of labor-management-government cooperation. Legislation was passed in 1964 that gave all Quebec public-sector
workers (government employees, as well as those employed in education
and health), the rights to be represented by a union, to bargain collectively,
and to strike.

This set the stage for a move in Canada toward more union-friendly
labor legislation, in both the public and private sectors. We have mentioned earlier that the socialist government in the province of
Saskatchewan introduced similar public-sector labor legislation two
decades earlier than Quebec. The same government was to be a pioneer
again in North America by introducing a comprehensive medical insurance scheme (universal health care) in 1961. In these and other cases,
Saskatchewan and Quebec seem to have served as a laboratory for Canada
to test new and often social democratic ideas. If viewed as successful at
the provincial level, these ideas were then adopted in other parts of
Canada.

The Quebec legislation of 1964 clearly heralded a transformation of
public-sector labor relations in Canada. The legislation went far beyond
President Kennedy's permitting union representation in the federal public
sector, but not necessarily permitting bargaining and not permitting the
right to strike. Indeed, with the exception of developments in the public
sector, U.S. labor legislation and its enforcement was becoming more
negative, whereas the reverse was occurring in Canada.

In 1967, the Canadian federal government followed the lead of Quebec
and introduced the right of federal government employees to bargain and

strike through the Public Service Staff Relations Act (PSSRA). This followed a period of turmoil in the federal public-sector industrial relations, with illegal strikes by postal workers and seaway workers in 1965–67. Bargaining-unit employees were given the option when they started a round of negotiations to opt either for arbitration of the terms of the agreement without being able to strike or to bargain with the option that if they did not reach an agreement they could strike. Employees designated as performing essential services were subject to binding arbitration, with no right to strike.

In Canada, unlike the United States, labor legislation is a provincial responsibility rather than a federal responsibility. Roughly 10 percent of employees in Canada are covered by federal legislation, compared with 90 percent in the United States. This means that each province decides its own labor legislation. After the Quebec and federal legislative initiatives, most provinces made major changes, giving their public-sector employees the right to bargain, although not always the right to strike. Where public-sector employees were denied the right to strike, as in the case of the largest province, Ontario, they were given compulsory arbitration of wages and other terms of employment (although the government retained much unilateral decision making in such areas as job classification).

What factors account for this fundamental divergence in labor legislation for public-sector employees in the two countries? We have already mentioned the transformation of the political situation in Quebec. At the federal level, there were minority governments throughout the 1960s that gave the newly created NDP more leverage on behalf of unionization. The labor scene had exploded in the mid-1960s with a series of wildcat strikes in the federal public sector by postal workers and by grain handlers. The federal government had made what were viewed as major wage concessions, which in turn fired the ambitions of other federal employees.

The changes in Quebec and at the federal level rippled across the country. In 1972 the third largest province, British Columbia, elected an NDP government. This election was followed by major changes in labor legislation (see Weiler 1980). In Ontario in 1974 and 1975 the teachers went on illegal strikes, which ended in the enactment of Bill 100, requiring every teacher to belong to a union and be allowed to bargain and strike. The right to strike was limited to the point at which the newly created Education Relations Commission determined that the students' academic year was threatened. Nurses in Ontario and other provinces also engaged in illegal strikes and again were given the right to bargain, but in many provinces (including Ontario) were not given the right to strike.

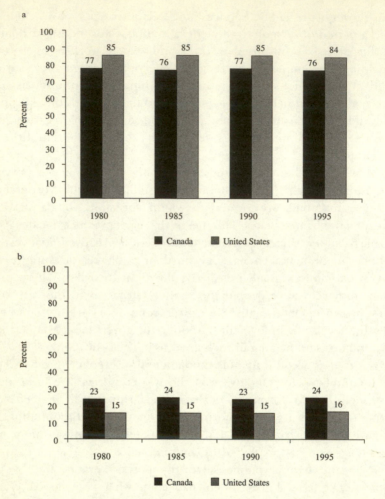

FIGURE 3.4

Canadian and U.S. shares of employment in the (a) public sector and (b) private sector (%).
U.S. data are for 1994. (*Source*: OECD Statistical Database, http://www.oecd.org/; proportion
of industrial public-private mix taken from Riddell 1993.)

Compulsory arbitration was provided instead. By the end of the 1970s, 56
percent of employees in the public sector were unionized.

It is also important to note that the public sector was (and still is) larger
in Canada than the United States, reflecting, we argue, basic differences in
values (see fig. 3.4).[4] There are several reasons for the larger public sector
in Canada. First, there is a great deal more state ownership in Canada than
in the United States. The state's role as owner occurs not just in utilities

such as electricity and water, in which there are presumed to be natural monopolies that require public protection, but also in transportation, communication, and even liquor sales. Crown corporations, companies whose shares are entirely owned by the federal or a provincial company, are the vehicles for governments to play a role in the economy. Also there were instances in which governments needed to provide universal service (a practice that private-sector companies would find unprofitable in a country as large and sparsely populated as Canada).

Second, state ownership arose because of private-sector bankruptcies following failed attempts to introduce competition, as in the formation of Canadian National Railways in the 1920s from five bankrupt private companies. Another reason was to provide economic stimulation and entrepreneurship, as in the creation of the Canadian Broadcast Corporation in the 1930s and the formation of Polymer Corporation during World War II. In the late 1980s, a move began in Canada to reduce the number of state companies through gradual privatization, such as the sale of the publicly owned Air Canada. Particularly relevant for the evolution of trade unions is that even after privatization state companies have tended to be very highly unionized. This also boosts the Canadian-U.S. trade union differences.

Major differences also emerged in the private sector that contributed significantly to the Canadian-U.S. gap that emerged in this period. While U.S. unions were losing ground in the private sector, such as in steel, chemicals, and mining, Canadian unions were holding their ground (Lipset and Katchanovski 2001). In fact, within manufacturing, the largest private sector in both countries, union density rose in Canada between 1966 and 1981, whereas union density fell in the United States (Meltz 1994). The rise in public sector unionization in Canada, together with the maintenance and even enhancement of private-sector unionization, contributed to the sharp upward move in union density.

By contrast, there was a proportionately smaller increase in public-sector density in the relatively smaller public sector in the United States and, at the same time, the relatively larger private sector experienced a decline in union density. These developments are depicted in figures 3.5 and 3.6, which compare patterns of change in union density in the two countries in the public sector (fig. 3.5) and in the private sector (fig. 3.6).

One final development in government policy during this period had implications for the evolution of unions: policies with respect to wage and price control. In 1970 Prime Minister Pierre Trudeau introduced voluntary wage and price guidelines (the Prices and Incomes Commission). In

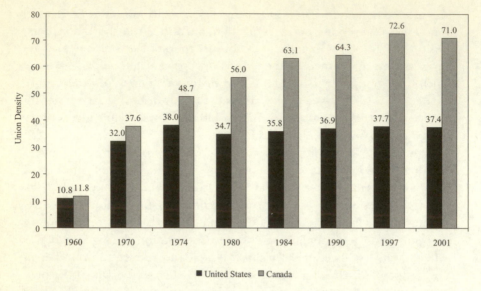

FIGURE 3.5
Public-sector union density in Canada and the United States, 1960–2001 (%). 2001 data for Canada are for the first half of the year. (For data sources see app. A.)

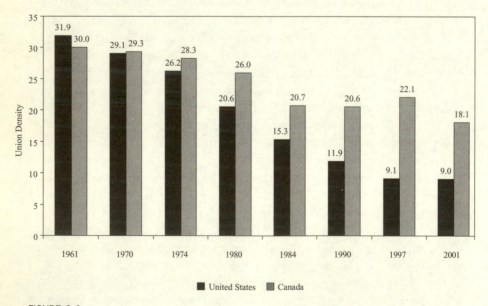

FIGURE 3.6
Private-sector union density in Canada and the United States, 1961–2001 (%). 2001 data for Canada are for the first half of the year. (For data sources see app. A.)

1971 President Richard Nixon introduced mandatory wage and price controls for a short period (three months). In Canada, the unions were little involved in the process, which had limited impact. In the United States, the AFL-CIO did not forcefully object. The recession in the United States in 1973–74 limited wage increases, but in Canada the government shielded the economy from recession by expansionary monetary and fiscal policy until 1975, when the establishment of the Anti-Inflation Board (AIB) for the period 1975–78 introduced mandatory wage and price guidelines. In 1976, on the first anniversary of the AIB, the trade union movement held a National Day of Protest. One million workers stayed off the job in what is said to have been the largest strike ever in Canada. In the end, there was no effect on the AIB process, although the government was defeated in the 1979 election that followed the end of the controls. The Liberal government under Pierre Trudeau had campaigned in the 1974 election on a platform of no controls. In spite of the controls, which were aimed particularly at the public sector in Canada, by 1981 labor was riding very high in Canada, while it was continuing to lose strength in the United States.

Significant changes in union density between men and women occurred in the 1960s and 1970s in both the United States and Canada. However, this gender gap narrowed in Canada to a greater extent than in the United States. In Canada, the union membership rate was almost two and one-half times lower among women (16 percent) than among men (38 percent) in 1966. It became 30 percent among women and 39 percent among men by 1985. In the United States, the union density among women (15 percent) was about one-half the density among men (31 percent) in 1956. In 1985, the figures became 13 and 22 percent (see Akyeampong 1998; Western 1997, 17).

1981–2001

The period 1981–2001 can be characterized by continuing decline in U.S. union density (the average density was 17 percent), and what may be the beginning of a decline in Canada from what for most of the period was a membership plateau of about 36 percent.

During this period, the gender gap continued to narrow in Canada faster than in the United States. In the first half of 2001, 29 percent of women and 31 of men were union members in Canada. In the United States, the union density in 2001 was 12 percent among women and 15 percent among men. The declining gender gap reflects in part, structural changes in the economy and the labor force. Employment in service and public sectors, which employ a high proportion of women, increased, whereas the male-dominated manufacturing sector, a traditional bastion of unionism, suffered a significant decline. As noted, the public sector in Canada is bigger, and this contributes to the gender-gap differences in unionization between the two countries.

In the United States there were small gains within the government sector, but as in the previous period, these were offset by losses in the private sector. The decline within the private sector was due less to the shift in employment away from unionized sectors than to the decline in the union share within sectors. Part of this decline came from the reduction in union organizing after the 1981–82 recession (Meltz and Verma 1996). This decline also coincided with the very high profile firing in early 1981 by President Ronald Reagan of the air traffic controllers who were on an illegal strike. The strike also won little favor with most Americans—a majority (59 percent) favored Reagan's handling of the strike, whereas 30 percent were opposed (Gallup Poll 1981, http://www.gallup.com).

Whether there is a connection between the reduction in organizing and the firing of the strikers has yet to be determined (Farber and Western 2002). What is clear is that the small upturn in union density that began in the early 1980s was reversed and the decline did not show any signs of recovery. If anything, Reagan's handling of the strike certainly sent a message that the U.S. government was not supportive of trade unions.[5]

The recession of 1990–91 a decade later further contributed to the decline in unionization, particularly affecting the areas of union strength. The Clinton administration in 1992, however, brought some prospects for support of reform in labor legislation with the establishment in 1993 of the Dunlop Commission. The commission reported two years later, just after the election of a Republican Congress eliminated the possibility of changes in labor legislation. In 1995 John Sweeney was elected president of the AFL-CIO on a platform of increased union activism and emphasis on organizing. There were also some union successes in 1997 and 1998 with the union victory in the United Parcel Service (UPS) strike and the successful organizing of 20,000 ticket clerks at United Airlines by the International Association of Machinists, the largest single gain in union members in twenty years. Nevertheless, union density was still declining at the end of the 1990s.

In Canada, the recession of 1981–82 was followed by public-sector wage controls at the federal level (known as "6 and 5," for the percentage wage increases permitted in 1982 and 1983). Several provinces followed the federal lead and introduced controls on wage increases in the public sector. In Ontario, the controls were 9 and 6 percent, respectively. Although these controls removed bargaining initiatives of the public-sector unions, they did not discourage union membership, which continued to grow during this period. By 1997, public-sector density reached 72.6 percent in Canada.

Union membership fell by 53,000 members in the aftermath of the 1981–82 recession, but growth resumed a year later when unions in Canada began vigorous organizing outside their traditional areas. For example, the steelworkers organized security guards and fast-food employees and the autoworkers brought in fishermen. The result was a recovery of union density for a while and then some erosion, followed by increases in the early 1990s. The gap between the United States and Canada was still huge, but it was no longer widening.

On the political front in Canada, support for unions was very mixed. In the early 1990s, there was a dramatic boost for unions when the unexpected victory of the NDP in Ontario in 1990 was followed by NDP victories in British Columbia and Saskatchewan. For several years, NDP governments represented provinces with over one-half the population of Canada. In 1993, the Ontario government passed Bill 40, the most liberal labor legislation in Canada, which included a ban on the use of replacement workers and increased opportunities for workers to join unions.

However, the political winds shifted markedly beginning in 1993 when defeat of the federal Conservatives brought not just a Liberal government, but an official opposition party, the Bloc Quebecois, dedicated to the separation of Quebec from Canada, and the Reform Party representing western Canada, dedicated to a very conservative, almost libertarian agenda. This was followed in 1995 by the victory in Ontario of the Progressive Conservative Party, whose tradition had been very moderate, but whose new leader Michael Harris and new neoconservative thrust represented a major break with the past. The first legislation passed in Ontario in 1995 by the new government was Bill 7, which took away all the pro-labor initiatives in Bill 40 and even did away with the long-standing practice of certifying unions on the basis of membership card checks.[6] In addition, the Harris government provoked confrontations with every public-sector union group: its own government employees, teachers, and even medical doctors. The basic thrust of the government was toward reducing the size of government and government-run organizations. All this clearly placed downward pressure on union membership in Canada's largest province, despite very active organizing in the private sector.

In both countries, there has been a restructuring of the labor move-ment. Although there have always been splits and mergers within and among unions, the late 1980s and 1990s witnessed major mergers, such as between the Communication Workers, the Energy and Chemical Workers, and the Paper Workers (Communication, Energy and Paper Workers Union of Canada; CEP). Whether or not unions are adapting to an eco-nomic world in which major corporations have gone through huge restruc-turing, some notable changes are taking place.

The largest change would have been the merger of the United Steel-workers of America (USWA), the United Auto Workers (UAW), and the International Association of Machinists (IAM) to create an international union of close to 2 million members. However, this merger did not mate-rialize. The proposed merger was to include both the U.S. and Canadian UAW branches; however, the UAW has only one small local in Canada because the bulk of its Canadian members split to form the Canadian Auto Workers (CAW) in 1985 over the Canadian branch's refusal to accept the concept of profit sharing (Kumar and Meltz 1992). As observed earlier, Canadian unions have had a tradition, at least since the merger in 1956 that created the CLC of much greater social activism and political parti-sanship than their counterparts to the south.

This development relates to another theme in the evolution of trade unions in Canada—nationalism—which may have provided further stimu-lus over the years for a higher level of union density. There have always been unions that were not affiliated with U.S.-based, international unions.[7] In fact, the percentage of international union membership in Canada has fluctuated considerably. In the early 1930s, the share had dropped to about 40 percent; then, following the CIO organizing drives and the growth of industrial unions, it grew to over 70 percent. In the late 1990s it was under 30 percent. Two factors were responsible for the later decline in the role of international unions in Canada. The largest factor was the huge growth in public-sector unions, almost all of them national unions. Second, there have been a number of separations of Canadian branches from the international unions, such as occurred within the pulp and paper unions, the Communication Workers, the Chemical Workers, and most dramati-cally with the creation of the CAW from the UAW. The growth of early unionism was based on unions following the market. Because this applied to private-sector employers and the market was becoming international, the unions followed the market and organized on both sides of the border. In the case of the public sector, there has been little international compe-tition in the provision of government, education, or health-care services.

This could, of course, change and lead to more organizing or at least more international cooperation among public-sector unions.

With respect to political involvement, Canadian unions are closer to their European counterparts than to their U.S. affiliates. As noted in chapter 2, trade union membership in Canada after the mid-1960s followed a pattern more similar to that in European countries than the United States. However, union densities have been under increasing pressure worldwide, so it is likely that density will decline in Canada, at least in the short term. On the other hand, as we discuss later in the book, surveys of employees show that there is support for unions and for a vehicle to represent employees in their dealings with their employers. In Europe, the decline in union density rates has not, or at least not yet, been matched by decreases in collective bargaining coverage rates. As a result, employees there have far more protection than U.S. employees do, and even more than do those in Canada. What form the desire for protection of employment takes on each side of the Canadian-U.S. border will be influenced by the factors that we explore in more detail in the chapters that follow.

Summary: 1901–2001

The central question in this overview of the evolution of trade unions in the United States and Canada is: Why are unions in Canada so much stronger than unions in the United States? The answer combines several factors. First, in looking back over one hundred years of statistics on the percentage of employees who belong to unions (union density), the most dramatic differences between the United States and Canada begin in the mid-1960s. Before that time the United States had a higher density from 1937 to 1956.

However, data from before and after the time when union density was higher south of the border (1937–56) suggest that this was the exception that proves the rule: Canada has always had a higher unionization base than the United States. Several factors seem crucial to the divergence in union density.

The role of government appears to have made a significant contribution to the maintenance of the union membership difference, not only through specific legislation but also through general recognition and support of unions. This was particularly true in wartime. The fact that Canada entered World War I earlier than the United States may explain the much greater union growth north of the border and its smaller proportional decrease after the war ended.

What we term the middle time period (1937–56; when the U.S. union density exceeded that in Canada) appears to be the result of a confluence of unusual events associated with the Great Depression and the Roosevelt Administration's encouragement of unionization. With the end of the Depression and the end of the wartime necessity for government involvement with unions to promote production, government support of trade unions drastically reduced and there was a return to the tradition of laissez-faire and at-will contracting in the U.S. labor market (Wright 1996 and Steinfeld 1991).

The long-term trends suggest that periods of lack of government support are associated with declining or, at most, stable trade union density. In Canada, government acceptance of unions seems to have been greater, at least from the beginning of the twentieth century. This support increased after World War II, when the political situation brought parties to power that had a strong identification with the labor movement. The CCF and the CLC joined together to found the NDP in 1961, and the Parti Quebecois was supported by the Quebec Federation of Labour and the teachers union in Quebec (Confedération d'Éducation Quebequois [CEQ]).

Although socialist parties existed in the United States as well as in Canada, the ethnic and cultural mix of the populations differed such that there was more acceptance of union affiliation with political parties in Canada. Whereas the American Federation of Labor adopted a policy of being independent of parties, its Canadian branch was not as opposed. In Quebec there was a syndicalist tradition, which endorsed associations between unions and political parties. On balance the union as an institution seems to have been more readily accepted in Canada (Lipset 1996; Lipset and Marks 2000).

The Parliamentary system in Canada—in which the party that wins the largest number of seats forms the government—favored the growth of parties supported by unions. Socialist and social democratic governments have held power in a number of provinces in Canada since 1944. When in power these parties tended to pass legislation favorable to trade unions, and they tended to support unions in other ways as well. But government involvement is always a double-edged sword. When there were economic difficulties, many of these same governments took action to control union bargaining activity. The imposition of wage cutbacks in the public sector in both Quebec and Ontario were major factors in the subsequent defeats of supposed labor-friendly parties at the polls.

A third factor is the greater social activism of Canadian unions associated with their political involvement. The split of the CAW from the UAW over the refusal to accept profit sharing and more aggressive Canadian organizing since the 1982 recession may have contributed to the growth of membership in some sectors and the retention of membership in others.

A fourth factor in the differences between the two countries is the larger size of the public sector in Canada. This is clearly related to the earlier point concerning the differences in values of the populations of the two countries. Whereas a laissez-faire role for government is regarded as the norm in the United States, Canadians have long accepted a leadership role for the government in the economic and social development of Canada. Harold A. Innis and William A. Mackintosh, two prominent Canadian economists writing in the early part of the twentieth century, even developed unique theories—the staples thesis and defensive expansionism—to account for the historically larger role played by the Canadian government in the economy (Norrie and Owran, 1991). This applies not just to the federal government, but also to the provincial governments, which under the Constitution are responsible for most labor and employment matters.

State-owned enterprises, which in Canada are termed *Crown corporations*, also have a long history north of the border. In the U.S. context, however, the Tennessee Valley Authority is viewed (accurately or not) as an exception. By way of contrast, governmental roles in social policy are still expected in Canada, although it remains to be seen whether the strong moves away from government involvement and against unions as witnessed in provinces such as Ontario with the Conservative (Mike Harris) government of Ontario elected in 1995 represent a trend in Canada or an aberration.

As many scholars have already suggested (Riddell 1993; Farber and Krueger 1993; and Fiorito, Stepina, and Bozeman 1996, to mention only a few), the greater extent of unionism in Canada, at least in the 1990s reflects less a difference in the demand for unionization by employees than a difference in the supply of unionization. The differences on the supply side are not simply due to the fact that employers are less opposed to unions in Canada.

Indeed, as we discuss in the next chapter, our data show that employers may be more opposed to unions north of the border. Moreover, it is also not the case that Canadians approve of unions more than Americans do;

Americans consistently report that they favor unions more than Canadians do. Rather, in contrast to the United States, Canadian society generally displays a greater receptiveness to the values conducive to union organizing and growth. These values exert their influence not just through the enactment of more favorable legislation and its enforcement, but also through the acceptance of the role of unions in the political, social, and economic structure of Canada.

4 Social Democratic Canada versus Free Market United States?

Why is trade unionism so much stronger in Canada than in the United States? Why do a larger proportion of employed workers belong to labor organizations north of the border than south of it? Why did Canadian density remain close to its 1950s high point, while the comparable figure for the United States dropped strikingly and continuously from the mid-1950s onward?

In chapter 3, we suggested that one of the most important factors is that the legislative and administrative agencies that govern labor relations are more union friendly in Canada than in the United States. Simply put, it is easier for unions to gain certification in a given company or jurisdiction in the north than in the south.

But granting that this is true, the question remains as to why Canada's political authorities and labor boards are more favorable to labor organizations. To address this question, we discuss briefly the ways in which the political culture of the two countries differs.

Canadian Political Culture

Canada has been described as a socialist or social democratic society, whereas there is general agreement that the United States is the leading example of a capitalist or libertarian society. In actuality, Canada obviously cannot be considered socialist using any description laid down by the Marxist fathers or even the revisionist school founded by Edward Bernstein. Its economy, like that of the United States, is primarily privately owned, to some degree by the same companies, although there is a relatively larger number of publicly owned companies in Canada. Neither country has a planned economy. There is no commitment in either to equality of income or status or to equality of opportunity. No socialist or social democratic party has ever governed Canada nationally. However, the U.S. founding fathers and the organizing principles, as laid down in the Declaration of Independence, tended toward libertarianism: That government governs best which governs least. Canada, the counterrevolutionary country, on the other hand, retained a more Tory or communitarian view of the polity. Both countries developed a welfare state, Canada much more so. As well, Canada has a commitment to regional income redistribution, from its three wealthiest provinces—Ontario, Alberta, and British Columbia—to its seven poorer provinces, that is absent in the United States.

Reflecting such differences, a U.S. *Dictionary of Modern English* contains the entry: "Canada, noun. A socialist protectorate full of nice people and clean streets" (Jackson 1988, 28). Robertson Davies, a great Canadian novelist and a political conservative, on a number of occasions described his country as a "socialist monarchy," noting also that "we are a people firmly set in the socialist pattern" (1977, 43). Kim Campbell, who served as a short-term prime minister in 1993 after holding various cabinet posts, told Lipset in a private discussion in 1995 that anyone who wants to play a role in Canadian politics must recognize that it has a "social democratic culture." Her predecessor as Tory prime minister for nine years, Brian Mulroney, during the 1988 election proclaimed the welfare state as Canada's "sacred heritage." On another occasion, he described it as a "sacred trust." Not surprisingly, perhaps, many of Canada's conservatives, who followed in the tradition of British noblesse oblige Toryism, once defined by Tory Prime Minister Harold Macmillan as "paternalistic socialism," have been referred to as Red Tories, an appellation they have accepted.

The Liberal Party, which governed Canada for most of the twentieth century, has generally been to the left of the Tories. Its leader for sixteen years in the 1970s and 1980s, Pierre Trudeau, was a socialist academic, who regarded the country's social democratic party, the NDP,[1] as too moderate and refused a parliamentary nomination from it in the early 1960s on ideological grounds. Shortly thereafter, however, Trudeau accepted a call from the Liberals, who desperately needed a politically appealing French-Canadian federalist, which Trudeau was, to counter the growing separatist movement in Quebec. Within three years, he became leader of the party and prime minister, a position he held for almost all of the next sixteen years. Seemingly his socialist history and concerns did not disturb the Liberals, who have a large left-wing caucus and a majority of the Canadian electorate who support this wing of the party.

The social democratic–Tory image of Canadian political culture may be challenged by the fact that no social democratic party has ever governed the country nationally and that in the 1990s the Progressive Conservative Party was overtaken on the right by a new, seemingly Reaganite, proponent of smaller and weaker government, the Reform Party (now known as the Canadian Alliance Party). Without detailing the complexities of Canada's party system, it may be noted that social democratic parties have governed provinces that contain a substantial majority of the population. This is also crucial for the trade union movement because almost 90 percent of Canadian employees are subject to provincial, not federal, labor legislation. This is the reverse of the situation in the United States, where state legislation deals with only 10 percent of employees while federal legislation covers about 90 percent of the country's employees.

The provinces that have had social democratic governments include the three largest and most industrialized ones, British Columbia, Ontario, and Quebec, as well as smaller provinces such as Manitoba, Saskatchewan, and the Yukon Territory. The English-speaking regions have been ruled by the CCF-NDP, while Quebec has been under the aegis of the Parti Quebecois (PQ), a separatist party with a social democratic program that applied for membership in the Socialist International (it was turned down because the largely Anglophone NDP vetoed the application, a right that the International's rules gave it as the representative of Canada).

The rise of the seemingly laissez-faire free market–oriented Reform Party in western Canada—it gained 19.4 percent of the national vote and won sixty seats in a five-party race in 1997, making it the Official Opposition in Parliament—does raise questions whether Canada, and particularly the country's conservatives, are departing from Brian Mulroney's "sacred trust" ("Official Voting Results" 1997).

There can be no question that in Canada, as in the United States, Britain, and elsewhere in the industrialized world, a new conservatism, which follows Hayek-Friedman Thatcher-Reagan laissez-faire or libertarian ideology, has developed. But in Canada, the traditional Tory party, the Progressive Conservative Party, which continues a more statist orientation, secures as many votes nationally as the Reform (Alliance) Party. It elected fewer members to Parliament in the 1990s because its strength was scattered across the country, not concentrated in a limited number of constituencies as Reform Party's was. The new leader of Progressive Conservative Party, Joe Clark, who was prime minister in 1979 between the

Liberal governments of Pierre Trudeau, rejected proposals from the Reform (Alliance) Party to merge the two parties and "unite the right." Joe Clark, it should be noted, is considered a Red Tory.

Most strikingly, however, as testimony that the rise of the Reform Party does not mean that Toryism is dead in Canada, is a statement made by Preston Manning, the leader of the Reform Party, during the 1993 election. He praised the effect on Canada of the policies of the country's socialists saying that "thanks largely to the NDP, the Canadian Parliament now has a social conscience that permeates every party. That's why medicare [Canada's single-payer government health plan], pensions and unemployment insurance are safe . . ." (in Bergman 1993, 15). In 1995, following the Republican victory in the U.S. congressional elections, Manning visited Washington to confer with his apparent ideological soulmates led by Newt Gingrich, then Speaker of House. On his return to Canada, Manning expressed some shock at the hard-heartedness of the congressional Republicans.

U.S. Political Culture: Is It All That Different?

The more libertarian country to the south moved left toward more statist welfare policies during the Great Depression of the 1930s and World War II. The Depression affected it more severely in terms of unemployment and bankruptcy rates than any other developed nation, with the possible exception of Germany, and Roosevelt's New Deal response introduced, as noted in chapter 3, a "social democratic tinge" for the first time in U.S. history (Hofstadter 1972, 308). Class divisions became more salient in differentiating political support than ever before (Lubell 1941). The Democratic Party took on a labor party cast in a number of northern and western states. The president and many congressional Democrats and state governors began to openly support trade union organization. The now-divided trade union movement began to grow rapidly, much faster than in Canada, to the point where the U.S. union density figure put the Canadian figure in the shade.[2]

But following World War II, the laissez-faire ideology of the United States gradually returned and refurbished itself, while Canada's ideology, which had also moved in a statist manner, did not move in a laissez-faire direction, in part, we argue, because its traditional values were statist Toryism, not Whiggish classical (libertarian) liberalism. Canada's social democratic and trade union forces gained in a relatively steady although uneven fashion, increasing from a majority in Saskatchewan in 1944 to control in three provinces containing a majority of the country's population in the early 1990s.

Nothing comparable occurred in the United States after 1950. Whereas Canadian socialists were gaining greatly in provincial and federal elections and in national opinion surveys, which on occasion reported them as the leading party, the American Socialist Party dissolved its minuscule organization in 1957. The Republicans won seven out of twelve presidential races. Both parties moved to their right, with the Democrats electing free market centrists or moderates in all but one of their four victories, Kennedy, Carter, and Clinton. The Republicans, following Barry Goldwater and Reagan, increasingly became a libertarian party almost totally in ideology and partially in practice.

Political Cultures Contrasted: The Postwar Period to the 1980s

The differences between the two countries are reflected in public policy, notably in labor legislation. Both countries have laws that provide for labor relations boards that can certify trade unions as the representatives of employees and require employers to negotiate with them. U.S. law, however, partly as a result of Republican postwar revisions to the 1935 Wagner Labor Relations Act (1947 Taft-Hartley and 1959 Landrum-Griffin), became less union friendly than Canadian law.

In most of the provinces, unions can be certified after submitting union representation cards signed by a majority of a company's employees. In three provincial jurisdictions, certification occurs after a representation election is held and won by the union and between five to ten days after cards signed by a majority are presented to the board.

In the United States, the showing of worker support for a union by signing cards does not enable the National Labor Relations Board to designate the union as the representatives of a company's employees but leads it to conduct a representation election, often held months after the union submission. Employers, however, are then free, in practice, to finance elaborate anti-union campaigns designed to produce a no vote, in which they posit various dire economic consequences for the company and individual employees if the union wins. The labor laws in both countries specify practices or actions that are forbidden to employers and unions. But the U.S. legislation, as amended in the Taft-Hartley Act (1947), allows employers much more leeway in fighting unions than does the Canadian law. Thus strikebreakers may retain their jobs after a dispute is settled in the United States, but not in Canada. In Canada striking employees are entitled to reclaim their jobs, depending on the jurisdiction, anywhere from six months to two years from the date the strike began.

Provincial legislation has been modified in an anti-union direction when business-oriented right-wing governments have held office, as in Alberta and Ontario and earlier in British Columbia (under the Social Credit Party). Such changes, however, have still left the labor laws more union friendly than in the United States. The Canadian political right and business seemingly have been less hostile to labor organizations than the American right.

State ownership of industry has been the hallmark of socialist programs and policy, although no governments, other than communist ones, have ever nationalized over 50 percent of the economy. Canada has had a variety of state-run industries, including railroads, airlines, bus lines, telephone and power companies, broadcasting networks and local outlets, and a variety of other activities, such as grain-marketing agencies, mines, oil, urban transit, and automobile insurance. This means that Canada has a higher percentage of government employees than the United States. As of 1995, almost one out of four working Canadians (23.7 percent) was employed by the government, compared with one out of six (16.1 percent) in the United States (National Accounts 1997).

Canadian analysts such as James T. Macleod have noted that in their country "the State has always dominated and shaped the economy"; that unlike "the United States, [Canada] has never experienced a period of pure unadulterated laissez-faire market capitalism" (1976, 6, 9). John Mercer and Michael Goldberg sum up the magnitude of government involvement in the Canadian economy as of 1982:

> Of 400 top industrial firms, 25 were controlled by the federal or provincial governments. Of the top 50 industrialists, all ranked by sales, 7 were either wholly owned or controlled by the federal or provincial governments. For financial institutions, 9 of the top 25 were federally or provincially owned or controlled. . . . Canadian governments at all levels exhibit little reticence about involvement in such diverse enterprises as railroads, airlines, aircraft manufacture, financial institutions, steel companies, oil companies, and selling and producing atomic reactors for energy generation. (1982, 27)[3]

Most European states are more directly involved in economic activities than is Canada, but the latter "does appear to represent a mid-point between the European and American patterns . . . both in the provisions of subsidies to the private sector and in the scope of public enterprise" (Mercer and Goldberg 1982, 27). Although below the norm for member nations of the OECD, Canadian subsidies to business and employment in public enterprise were each five times the level of those in the United States during the 1970s. "In Canada . . . the natural focus for collective activity has always been government." North of the border, private business is not "accorded the intrinsic value in and for itself that it receives in the United States . . . [where] even a badly functioning private marketplace often appears to be definitionally superior to a well-functioning public agency" (Evans 1988, 169).

These differences in the economic role of the state may be summed up quantitatively by the fact that as of the mid-1990s the proportion of the Canadian GDP in government hands was 47 percent, compared to 35 percent in the United States. Ten years earlier the ratio was 47 to 37 percent. Commenting in 1989 on the differences between conservative governments in North America, the *Wall Street Journal* noted that Brian Mulroney's policies were "the sort that Ronald Reagan and George Bush have refused to support" ("Canada" 1989, A14).

The Welfare State

The prototypical policy associated with social democracy in the Western world has been the development of the welfare state: the creation of a safety net that has upgraded the position of the less privileged, effectively transferring income from the upper strata to the lower economic groups. Heavy, progressive taxes have paid for these benefits.

A detailed comparative analysis of the development of the welfare state in North America in the 1960s and 1970s by Robert Kudrle and Theodore Marmor concludes that specific welfare policies have generally been adopted earlier in Canada and were "usually . . . more advanced in terms of program development, coverage and benefits," and "have exhibited a steadier development." They note further that it was "not just the typically earlier enactment of policy in Canada but also subsequent expansions and enhancements" (1981, 110–11). As detailed by a former Canadian official:

A remarkable collection of federally inspired programs was put in place that has had the effect of providing virtually cradle-to-grave basic protection and opportunity for every Canadian. Canadian federal and provincial governments put in place a *de facto* if not *de jure* guaranteed minimum income which embraced family allowances, a comprehensive social welfare program including widows and persons with disabilities, enriched unemployment insurance benefits, manpower training allowance, a greatly expanded post-secondary education program that covers about three-quarters of the real per student cost, old age pensions as a matter of right and an additional universal contributory pension program, subsidized housing, and a complete hospital-medical protection program. (Ostry 1985, 29)

The differences between the two countries are particularly striking with respect to the role of government in medical care. They have been well summed up in questions prepared for a Louis Harris cross-national opinion survey: "The American system is one in which the government pays most of the cost of health care for the elderly, the poor and the disabled. Most others either have health insurance paid for by their employers or have to buy it from an insurance company. Some have no insurance. Conversely, the Canadian system is one in which the government pays most of the cost of health care for everyone out of taxes, and the government sets all fees charged by doctors and hospitals" (Blendon 1989, 8–9). The Canadian system is much more liberal than government-financed medical care in most of Europe. Unlike in Britain and elsewhere, where the more well-to-do to are permitted to secure private medical caretakers, Canadian law forbids such policies.

Ironically, Canadian single-payer socialized medicine, although totally dependent financially on the governments, allows patients free choice of physicians, and doctors may send patients to any specialist or hospital they choose. The U.S. insurance plans, which are increasingly health maintenance organizations (HMOs), restrict patients to doctors and hospitals that are affiliated to specific HMOs. Physicians must secure approval from the HMO for specialist and hospital assignments.

Another irony is that the total cost of Canada's health care system as a proportion of the GDP is less (9.6 percent) than that in the United States (14 percent). Total expenditure per capita is U.S.$3,701 in the United States and U.S.$2,049 in Canada ("OECD in Figures" 1997). Canada's approach is widely supported throughout the country—poll data for 1988 show that an overwhelming 95 percent of Canadians preferred their system to the one in the United States. Several more recent polls consistently show that Canadians support public health care over a privately insured version. Even the idea of a Canada Health Allowance (in which the government would provide each Canadian with an individual health allowance that would always be sufficient to cover health services that are currently covered by provincial health plans, and the unused portion in one year could be used in future years for drugs, dental work, chiropractic work, and other currently uninsured services) has received only mixed reviews from Canadians.[4]

Most Americans (61 percent) also voiced a preference for the Canadian system over their own when interviewed in the Louis Harris cross-national opinion survey. There was much less satisfaction with "the health care services that you and your family have used in the last year" in the United States than in Canada; 35 percent of respondents were "very satisfied" in the south, compared to 67 percent in the north. Still, more than one-third of Americans, 37 percent, preferred the more pluralistic system in the United States; only 3 percent of Canadians did so (Blendon 1989).

In Canada, health care falls constitutionally under the purview of the provinces, though Ottawa funds about one-half of it through grants. It is both legislated and administered provincially (Glaser 1984, 319–22). Although there are important variations from province to province in amounts paid to physicians, cost controls, and care priorities, the Canadian programs are highly comparable.[5] This holds true for those sponsored by governments that are strongly oriented to free enterprise, such as the administration of British Columbia, when it was Social Credit (right wing), as well as for those introduced or operated by social democratic (NDP and PQ) and Liberal parties. Seemingly, all Canadian politicians, left and right, recognize that they cannot upset the commitment to public payment for all medical costs and to state control over the prices paid to physicians and hospitals. Obviously, there is no such consensus in the United States, where the medical profession and private insurance companies retain much more bargaining power, even in the publicly financed sectors.

Welfare policies have been under severe challenge since the mid-1980s and have been cut back in almost every country, usually with the agreement of the social democrats. But curtailment does not mean elimination. The welfare state remains much larger north of the border and in Europe, even if reduced in scope.

Public Opinion in the 1990s

Aggregate and institutional data have thus far sustained our argument that Canadian values are social democratic and more supportive of economic statism, of extensive welfare policies, and of income egalitarianism, whereas those of the United States are more individualistic, achievement oriented, competitive, and meritocratic. These values, we argue, have been instrumental in supporting legislation that has continued to be more union friendly north of the border. There are also abundant public opinion results that point to similar consistent and reliable differences between the two nations. A detailed account of relevant cross-national polls from the 1970s to the end of the 1980s is reported by Lipset in *Continental Divide* (1990, 97–100, 110–113, 121–123, 129, 131, 134, 140–142, 156–158, 166). These studies indicate that Americans are more libertarian and suspicious of the state, whereas Canadians are much more disposed to favor having the government deal with issues such as morality, health care, poverty, and economic inequality and opportunity. Canadians have been more committed to redistributive egalitarianism, whereas Americans place more emphasis on meritocratic competition. The northerners are more security and less achievement oriented, less disposed to be risk takers, and more supportive of seniority, as opposed to merit.

More recent cross-national surveys, including our own in 1996, document that these variations have continued into the late 1990s. Grouping the answers to a number of questions in our research into a social democratic index (running from most libertarian to most social democratic) yields clear evidence that Canadians are much more supportive of statist communitarian values than are Americans (fig. 4.1).

Specifying the items in the index points up the cross-national differences. Americans are much more likely than Canadians to strongly disagree that there "should be a maximum limit on income," by 55 to 41 percent. Not surprisingly, the populations react quite differently to the statement "It is the responsibility of the government to reduce the difference in income between people with high incomes and those with low incomes." Almost one-half of Canadians, 45 percent, agree, compared with 30 percent of their neighbors to the south. Canadians are more disposed to strongly favor an "obligation to ensure no child has to grow up in poverty," by 73 percent to 56 for Americans. The latter are less inclined to feel that the government "has an obligation to help people when they are in trouble," by 69 percent to 84.

Questions dealing with equality produce similar cross-national variations. Thus, when asked whether workers doing the same job but varying in efficiency or reliability should receive merit-related differences in pay, a majority of Americans, 57 percent, strongly supported paying the more able worker more, in contrast to 45 percent of Canadians. Respondents

Canada

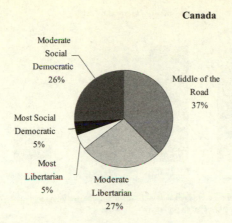

United States

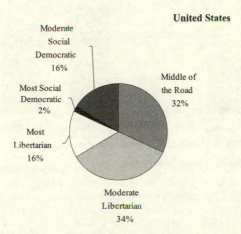

FIGURE 4.1
Cross-national ideological orientation (%). (*Source*: Lipset-Meltz survey.)

were asked which is more important: "Freedom, so that everyone can
live or develop without hindrance" or "Equality, so that nobody is underprivileged and social class differences are not so strong." Proportionately,
more Canadians, 43 percent, chose equality, in contrast to 36 percent of
Americans. Some of these results are summarized in figure 4.2.

The survey findings also indicate that workers living in the north are
more security oriented, whereas those in the south are more willing to take
risks. Close to two-fifths, 39 percent, of employed Canadians, compared

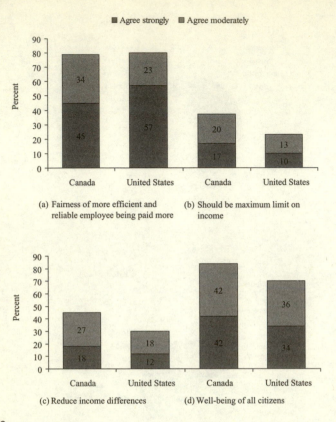

■ Agree strongly   ■ Agree moderately

(a) Fairness of more efficient and reliable employee being paid more

(b) Should be maximum limit on income

(c) Reduce income differences

(d) Well-being of all citizens

FIGURE 4.2

Cross-national attitudes on wage fairness, maximum income limit, income differences and responsibilities of the government (%). Survey questions (see app. B). (a) Imagine two workers of the same age, with the same years of service with their employer, doing nearly the same job. One earns (in Canada: 70 dollars; in the United States: 50 dollars) a week more than the other. The better paid worker, however, is quicker, more efficient, and more reliable at the job. In your opinion, how fair or unfair is it that one of these workers is paid more than the other—very fair, somewhat fair, somewhat unfair, or very unfair? (b) There should be a maximum limit on how much income people can make in salary and bonus. (c) It is the responsibility of the government to reduce the differences in income between people with high incomes and those with low incomes. (d) The government is responsible for the well-being of all its citizens and it has an obligation to help people when they are in trouble. (*Source*: Lipset-Meltz survey.)

with 31 percent of Americans, agree strongly that "job security is more important to me than opportunities for advancing my career." And Canadians are much more likely, by 46 to 19 percent, to feel that "when jobs are scarce, people should be required to retire early," the largest cross-national difference found in our survey.

Three Canadian scholars have sought to test the conclusions presented in *Continental Divide* concerning differences in the attitudes and values of Canadians and Americans by reference to surveys conducted by the National Opinion Research Center and the Canadian and American Gallup Polls in 1993–94. Jon P. Alston, Theresa M. Morris, and Arnold Vedlitz report that cross-national variations continued to hold up when they controlled the findings for nationality, age, religion, education, and income (1996, 301–14). They report anew that Americans are "more negative" toward government than Canadians. "There is a clear support for the continued collectivist orientation of Canadians" (309). A "less individualist orientation is also indicated . . ." among them. They conclude, "We find a great deal of support for Lipset's position in this new analysis. In general, Canadians are more supportive of civil and political institutions while Americans are more supportive of individual decision making. . . . With these 1993 and 1994 data, Lipset's thesis continues to be valid and the relationships he posits appear, for the most part, in the directions predicted. Canadians and Americans remain different under the same socioeconomic conditions. And we do not see any evidence of an 'Americanization' of Canadian positions" (313–14).

Clearly the results of sample surveys generally support the hypothesis that the institutional and policy difference existing across the border are linked to Canadians being more statist and social democratic in their basic values than Americans. But, because the two countries vary on several structural characteristics, as Alston, Morris, and Vedlitz (1996) note, it is possible that the variations in orientations are functions of such trait differences, a possibility that their analysis rejects. We have sought to test this possibility by a different, statistically more exacting method, multivariate regression, which tests for the independent effect of variables such as income, gender, and ethnic distribution. In the regression, the Canadian variable is strongly and positively associated with social democratic sentiments; the American variable is not. As noted, our social democratic scale includes questions on freedom and equality, fairness of pay, income limits, forced retirement, obligation that no children grow up in poverty, and the welfare role of government. The scale is continuous and takes values from 1 to 5. The average Canadian has stronger social democratic values by almost one-third of a scale unit than the average American does.

Standardized (beta) regression coefficients estimate the relative effect of independent variables on the dependent one, the social democratic scale. As might be expected, factors associated with deprivation or lower class position are positively associated with social democratic sentiments.

Personal and household income are very strongly and statistically significantly related to social democratic attitudes—the higher the income level, the less social democratic. The latter's beta coefficient (−0.29) is the largest in the regression. Less powerful or economically inferior ethnic and racial minorities, such as French Canadians, Blacks, and Hispanics, are strongly associated with holding social democratic attitudes. The beta coefficient for the ethnic minorities variable is 0.25. Males tend to be slightly less social democratic than females; the effect is relatively small but statistically significant. Religion is slightly correlated—Catholicism positively and Protestantism, particularly sectarianism, negatively. The differences between the national variables are expressions of the effects of factors other than income, religion, ethnicity/race, and gender, which are specific to Canada or the United States and not otherwise part of the regression.

The inclusion of structural variables such as employment sector, number of employees in the work location, and skill level in the regression turns the country variable into a proxy for the economy. The national variable has the largest effect on social democratic attitudes when the regression is limited to employed nonagricultural respondents. The effect of the country factor is stronger than income or ethnicity/race. Manual-skill level and government employment are positively associated with social democratic attitudes. Their effects are statistically significant, although smaller than the effects of country.

Essentially, structural variables do not explain away the cross-national differences. As illustrated in figure 4.3, with reference to the question "Which do you think is more important—freedom, so that everyone can live and develop without hindrance, or equality, so that nobody is underprivileged and social class differences are not so strong," the lower the class identification, the more disposed respondents are to opt for equality. Canadians, in keeping with the multivariate findings, are more likely to do so within each class identity, lower, working, middle, and upper. Hence, we may conclude from cross tabular as well as regression analysis that the statistical differences reported by survey data between the countries are real, that Canadians are personally more social democratic than Americans. It would, of course, be startling if otherwise.

Social Democratic Nation as Trade Union Nation: Not That Simple

The United States is obviously the more individualistic, laissez-faire nation of the two societies and has a weak trade union movement. It logically

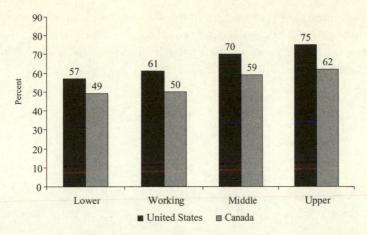

FIGURE 4.3
Cross-classification of preference for freedom over equality by nationality and social class (%). Survey question (see app. B): Which do you think is more important—freedom, so that everyone can live and develop without hindrance, or equality, so that nobody is underprivileged and social class differences are not so strong. (*Source*: Lipset-Meltz survey.)

follows that Canada, the more social democratic country, should, as it does, have the stronger labor movement. A comparison of the strength of unions in the developed world in chapter 2 shows a linkage between left party strength (Social Democratic, Socialist, Labor, and Communist) and union density or coverage. The Scandinavian countries are strongest in both, the United States is the weakest, and Canada falls in the middle, more difficult to locate politically because its statist values impact different parties.

It may be assumed therefore that cross-border differences in union density reflect the fact that a larger proportion of Canadian workers are social democrats than are Americans. The survey data do demonstrate, after all, a strong relationship between social democratic views and trade union membership. The answer to why Canada has a stronger labor movement, however, is not that simple. Although these differences account for a portion of the explanation, the relationship between unionism and political culture is more complex. As we document in the next chapter, the correlation between social democratic views and support for and membership in trade unions is much stronger within Canada than in the United States, but fear of the impact of union density on politics and on the economy is stronger north of the border. More important, the demand for trade union membership (the desire for or willingness to join a union) on the part of nonmembers is greater in the United States. In other words, on some questions, Americans appear more union friendly than Canadians. The reasons for this seeming discrepancy in the political culture hypothesis are discussed in chapter 5.

5   Attitudes and Values

An Inverted Relationship

We must reevaluate the cultural hypotheses with which this study begins given that Americans (as we show in this chapter), at almost every level and within all measurable subgroups in our research, consistently express more union-friendly attitudes than Canadians do. This cross-border pattern seemingly counters the different national values explanation for the variation in trade union strength in the two nations.

It is a major paradox that Americans, who are much less likely to belong to unions than their northern neighbors, should have more positive opinions about unions and, if nonmembers, be more disposed to want to join them (see chapter 6). This chapter aims to understand the reason(s) for this anomaly. Our principal contention is that Canada's social democratic tinge underpins, to a greater degree than in the United States, institutions that are more supportive of unionism and that this, in turn, generates greater levels of union power in Canada. The paradox of strong unionism and weak public support emerges because perceived union power is negatively correlated with union approval. In short, values (such as a preference for freedom over equality) and attitudes (the perceived power of unions and approval of trade unions) can often be in conflict because the latter are based on varying material conditions while the former are less susceptible to environmental changes. In this chapter, we outline the many attitudinal anomalies present in the data and discuss the role of perceived union power in explaining them.

The Anomaly in Detail

The cross-national linkage between social democratic values and trade union density seen in chapter 2 helps to explain the much greater strength of labor organizations in Canada. Ordinary least square and logistic regression analyses cohere with these findings.[1] The stronger effect that social democratic orientation has on individual behavior in Canada than in the United States affirms our linking of societal values to union strength. In the northern country, for example, such beliefs form a stronger predictor of union membership than any other variable measured.[2] South of the border, the social democratic effect is much weaker, with personal income and age having a stronger relationship. The weaker, although statistically significant, correlations of social democratic values with union membership in the United States as compared with Canada may reflect a lower commitment by social democratically–inclined Americans to such principles. Because context affects intensity, U.S. "social democrats" should be less strongly so than their northern neighbors, who live in a polity with two viable social democratic parties, the NDP in Anglo-Canada and the PQ, the governing separatist party of the French-speaking province of Quebec.[3] The NDP is the Canadian affiliate of the Socialist International, while the PQ applied for membership in the early 1970s.[4]

Canadians, therefore, clearly hold more statist and communitarian values, which are congruent with Tory–social democratic politics and collectivist or group-oriented (mosaic) orientations, while Americans exhibit more antistatist, individualistic and competitive (meritocratic) values, which imply laissez-faire politics. It would be natural to conclude, based on this and the fact that unions have higher membership rates north of the border, that Canadians should display a greater affinity for unions when directly queried about them. Unfortunately, such is not the case.

In spite of the cross-national variations in allegiance to social democratic values and in union density, when our sample employee population was asked, "If you had a choice, would you personally prefer to belong to a labor union or not," U.S. and Canadian employees were equally likely (39 percent) to answer that they would. And in line with this unexpected response, when nonmembers were asked how they would vote in an election to "decide whether your work place would be unionized or not" almost one-half of Americans (48.2 percent) would vote for a union, while only one-third of Canadians (33.3 percent) would do so.[5]

This anomaly is just as striking when we compare member and nonmember responses to other attitudinal questions (table 5.1). As might be

TABLE 5.1
Union Approval in the United States and Canada (% employed people)

Items	Canada		United States	
	Nonmembers	*Members*	*Nonmembers*	*Members*
Do you approve or disapprove of labor unions? approve	55	84	66	91
Most of my family and close friends don't like unions: agree	49	37	34	24
Unions are good/bad for Canada/the United States as a whole: good	42	66	52	80
Unions are good/bad for working people: good	55	75	60	83
Tend to side with the union in a labor dispute	41	73	57	88
N	384	540	952	199

Source: Lipset-Meltz survey.

expected, nonmembers voice less union approval than members in both countries, but in the United States 91 percent of unionists and 66 percent of nonmembers approve of labor unions, whereas in Canada 84 percent of members and 55 percent of nonmembers answer in this fashion. These cross-national differences in union approval apply also to the views of families and friends, as supplied by the survey respondents. One-quarter of union members (24 percent) and one-third of nonmembers (33 percent) in the United States report that most of their family and friends do not like unions. In contrast, 37 percent of Canadian union members and 49 percent of nonmembers report distaste for labor organizations by those close to them.

The same pattern is evident when we examine reactions to statements about the effects of unions. Substantial majorities, 83 percent of union members south of the border and 75 percent of those in the north, agree that unions are good for working people. Replying to the question of whether unions are good or bad for the country as a whole, more U.S. unionists than Canadian (80 vs. 66 percent) respond that unions are good. A majority, 52 percent, of nonmembers in the United States and 42 percent in Canada agree. Similarly, 57 percent of nonmembers in the United States, compared with 41 percent in Canada, report they usually side with the union rather than the company when they hear about a labor dispute.

When asked whether unions improve the wages and benefits of their members, U.S. unionists are again more positive than Canadian. Nine-tenths of U.S. members agree (a majority, 51 percent, strongly so) that unions increase wages. Fewer Canadian union members (76 percent) share this view (38 percent strongly). The same cross-national differential occurs within the population as a whole with respect to the statements that "Wage demands of unions don't reflect economic realities" (United States 56 percent to Canada 67 percent) and that unions "hurt the ability of companies to compete in international markets" (57 percent to 47 percent).

Americans not only express more favorable attitudes toward labor organizations, they also appear more willing to transform their words into deeds. Almost one-third of all employed Americans who do not belong to a union (31 percent) would join one if given a chance. Fewer of the smaller Canadian cohort of nonmembers (22 percent) express the same desire. U.S. unionists are also more willing to pay greater union dues to promote organization than are their Canadian counterparts. Three-fifths of members in the U.S. (61 percent) report they are "willing to pay a small increase in union dues to support efforts to organize more workers into unions." The proportion of Canadians, despite belonging to a much stronger labor movement, ready to do the same is a much lower 41 percent.

The responses to almost every question bearing on the roles of unions as defenders of employee interests or about the ways they affect national and economic interests clearly reveal more employees who are critical of organized labor in Canada than in the United States. More surprising still is that this pattern extends to unionists as well. Thus, 27 percent of Canadian unionists state that they side with the company when first hearing of a labor dispute, whereas only 12 percent of American members give the same response. When asked, "Who is more honest? Union leaders or corporate leaders?" almost one-quarter of Canadian members (24 percent) say corporate leaders, compared with 16 percent of U.S. members. When queried about confidence in unions and other institutions (quite a lot, a great deal, some, and very little) 43 percent of U.S. unionists answer "quite a lot" or "a great deal," responses given by only 27 percent of Canadian members. Perhaps more surprising is the extent to which union members, much more so in Canada, express agreement with the anti-union stereotype, "Unions enable workers to get away with being inefficient" (table 5.2).

Table 5.3 summarizes the details of the conundrum. On the one hand, as we have reiterated, Canadians are much more disposed than Americans

TABLE 5.2
Perceptions of Unions and Worker Inefficiency (%)

Unions facilitate worker inefficiency	Canada		United States	
	Members	Nonmembers	Members	Nonmembers
Strongly agree	23	32	14	21
Moderately agree	35	37	26	33
Moderately disagree	20	19	26	25
Strongly disagree	22	11	33	17
Don't know	1	3	1	3

Source: Lipset-Meltz survey.
Note: Percentages may not add to 100 because of rounding.

TABLE 5.3
Differences between Union Members in Canada and the United States (%)

Item	Canada	United States
Pride in work	78	92
Children's opportunity to succeed better than yours	22	35
Government should reduce the income gap	49	31
Should be a maximum limit on income	32	23
Workers should take early retirement	50	19
Confidence in unions	27	43
Union leaders are more honest than corporate ones	50	58
Vote for dues increase for organizing campaign	40	61
Unions don't have enough power	22	47
Attend union meetings twice a year or more	44	55
Read union newspaper	34	45

Source: Lipset-Meltz survey.

to agree with social democratic values, while Americans are more likely to exhibit greater levels of pride in work, to believe in their children's opportunity to succeed, and to feel that workers should not take early retirement. But as noted, the same Canadian members are less prone than Americans to say they would vote to retain their union in a decertification election, are less willing to pay increased dues to support an organizing drive, and are less involved in their union, that is, attend fewer meetings and pay less attention to the union newspaper. Do these results make sense?

One way of understanding the discrepancy between more favorable union attitudes in the United States and outcomes that are more favorable to unions in Canada is to look at the most commonly accepted reasons in

TABLE 5.4
Estimates of the Degree of Employer Opposition to Unionization (%)

| How | Canada | | United States | |
Widespread?	Nonmembers	Members	Nonmembers	Members
Very	26	19	25	30
Somewhat	54	55	54	51
Not very	14	19	15	14
Not at all	3	1	2	2
Don't know	4	5	4	3

Source: Lipset-Meltz survey.
Note: Percentages may not add to 100 because of rounding.

the research literature for the greater success of Canada's unions. Success here relates to such things as the supposedly lower intensity of anti-union efforts by Canadian companies and the associated ease of recruiting members and securing collective bargaining rights, as well as the greater union friendliness of the country's labor legislation.

We begin with the view that management is more union friendly in Canada and that this is why unionization is higher north of the border. This view is partially supported by the responses to the query: "How widespread would you say . . . employer resistance to unionization is in Canada/the United States?" U.S. union members are more disposed than Canadian to report opposition, 81 to 74 percent (table 5.4). The differences are most evident in the category "very widespread," 30 to 19 percent. Variations in the same direction occur in the measure of workers' anticipation as to how management in an unorganized company would react to a union organization drive.

The assumption of greater managerial opposition, however, runs counter to data collected on the views of managers themselves. By 44 to 35 percent, more employed Canadians than Americans predict management will go after "workers who try to organize" or "threaten . . . [them with adverse] consequences." To probe more deeply into this question of managerial opposition as a cause of the disconnect between the U.S. desire for unionization and lack of union membership relative to Canada, the attitudes of managers are examined next in detail. In this way, we hope to distinguish between a managerial opposition explanation that is due to a greater antipathy toward unions and one caused by a more lenient approach to anti-union practices south of the border. Essentially, we want to see whether the anomaly carries over when we analyze managers separately from the general population. If it does, then we may want to point the finger at legislative differences between the two countries rather than managerial attitudes as an explanation for more effective managerial opposition.

The Managerial Attitudinal Anomaly

Many labor experts as well as trade unionists have emphasized the greater hostility to labor groups of U.S. management in contrast to Canadian management as one of the most important factors adversely affecting union organizations south of the border. As Itzhak Saporta and Bryan Lincoln note, "researchers have emphasized management attitudes and behavior towards union formation as an important determinant of union success or failure in North America" (1985, 551–52). They echo conclusions reached by industrial relations researchers Richard Freeman, Michael Poule, and Sanford Jacoby that greater management hostility to unions in the United States than in Canada is "the major cause of the decline in private sector density" (Saporta and Lincoln 1985, 552). Although this view has yet to be properly challenged, a debate exists regarding the cause of more effective managerial opposition. Specifically, researchers have asked whether U.S. managers display a greater antipathy toward unions or whether managers are essentially the same in both countries but that the real impediment for U.S. workers lies with less friendly labor legislation.

The management-antipathy view has been countered by Canadian scholar Daphne Taras (1997), who, in summarizing the research literature, concludes that there is no evidence that the attitude of business is driving the U.S. union decline. She notes that Canadian managers hold "virtually identical" views. However, in keeping with the theme of this book, she suggests that cultural factors inhibit anti-union Canadian employers from vigorously acting out their sentiments because their country does not have the U.S. "tradition of union avoidance" and, therefore, "an anti-union stance lacks a sustaining structure in the culture" (309).

What is this anti-union stance? In particular, how does it differ in the two countries? If it does differ, in what direction does it do so and can we conclude that attitudes are not as important as legislation in explaining the paradox? Looking at the most often asked union approval question, a larger proportion of U.S. managers, 68 percent in our survey compared with 57 percent of Canadian managers, say they approve of unions; 38 percent of Canadian managers compared with 26 percent of U.S.

TABLE 5.5
Hypothetical Managerial Reactions to Unionization Campaigns (%)

Reaction	Canada	United States
Welcome the union	7	15
Do nothing	30	44
Oppose with information only	50	35
Oppose by threatening consequences	7	3
Oppose by going after weaker organizers	5	4

Source: Lipset-Meltz survey.
Note: Percentages may not add to 100 because of rounding.

managers report disapproval of unions. Social democratic values are more predictive of managerial feelings toward unions than any other variable tested. Union approval indices, or scales, show a similar pattern. More managers in Canada disapprove strongly or moderately of unions than do those in the United States, 39 percent versus 25 percent, using a general approval index. The general approval scale includes items such as whether unions are good or bad, whether they are still necessary, and whether they make the economy fairer for all segments. Three-fifths of Canadian managers (60 percent) compared with 43 percent of U.S. manager express a negative attitude toward unions on an institutional approval index. The latter scale subsumes questions dealing with union power, involvement in politics, corruption, effect on productivity, inefficiency, wage demands, and effect on competition.

The lesser hostility expressed by U.S. managers toward unions compared with Canadian is shown strikingly in their responses to how they would react to union organization drives (table 5.5). A majority of the U.S. managers (59 percent) say they would welcome the union or do nothing to stop it; a minority of the Canadian managers (37 percent) have comparable opinions. More Canadian managers (12 percent) would oppose unions with strong measures than U.S. managers (7 percent).

A regression analysis demonstrates that the more negative attitude of Canadian managers toward unions remains, even after controlling for the effects of other relevant variables (i.e., personal income, management level, social democratic attitudes, ethnic and racial minorities, number of employees working at a location, religion, age, gender, sector of employment, and unionization of their workplace). A Canadian dummy variable has a stronger statistically significant negative effect on union approval (compared with an American one). The average Canadian manager is 0.44 units lower on the general approval scale and 0.39 units lower on the insti-

TABLE 5.6
Managers' Opinions about the Effects of Unionization on Productivity (%)

Effect	Unionized Workplace		Non-unionized Workplace	
	Canada	United States	Canada	United States
Much higher	15	13	2	5
Somewhat higher	10	24	3	7
About the same	61	50	52	61
Somewhat lower	7	8	29	17
Much lower	6	4	14	10
N	124	119	141	192

Source: Lipset-Meltz survey.
Note: Percentages may not add to 100 because of rounding.

tutional approval scale than the average U.S. manager. These union approval scales run from 1 to 5. As noted earlier, social democratic attitudes have strong effects on union approval among managers, much as among workers. Beta, or standardized, coefficients for the social democratic scale are highest in all regressions.

Managers who work at a unionized workplace tend to express higher levels of union approval than those at a nonunionized company. Canadian managers both in unionized and nonunionized situations tend to be more convinced than U.S. managers that unionization decreases the flexibility of management and productivity of workers (table 5.6). U.S. and Canadian managers in organized workplaces do not differ significantly in their assessment of unionization effects on the organization of workers or on wages.

More surprising than the fact that most North American managers express positive feelings toward unions is that when managers are divided into self-ascribed categories (upper, middle, or lower), by the number of employees managed (more than 40, 16–40, 5–15, or less than 5), or by income (more than $50,000, $40,000–50,000, $30,000–40,000, $20,000–30,000, and under $20,000), the higher-level U.S. managers are more disposed than comparably ranked Canadians to be favorable to unions. U.S. executives are more disposed than Canadian to agree that "Unions are good for working people." When asked the question "When hearing about a labor dispute, whom do you tend to side with?" a majority of Canadian managers reply, "the company." Canadian executives as a group are more pro-business (55 percent) than Americans (35 percent) are, and the minority of high-level managers who favor unions in disputes is larger in the U.S. (36 percent) than in Canada (27 percent). The finding that more U.S. managers, regardless of level, say they will back the union contradicts many academic and most union-leadership consensuses that U.S. managers are inherently more anti-union than Canadian managers.

Our findings are not a challenge to the expert judgments about the way business behaves. Indeed, over four-fifths of all Canadians and Americans, when asked, "How widespread would you say that employer resistance to unionism is in Canada/the United States?" reply "very" or "somewhat widespread." Similarly, in response to a question asking "How do you think management would react to an effort by employees to form a union in an unorganized place of work," the same percentages of employed Canadians and Americans (73–74 percent) predict opposition. Only 8 percent in both countries believe companies would welcome a union, although 18–19 percent think they would do nothing to stop it. We therefore prefer to view unions as facing more effective—rather than more vociferous—opposition from business in the United States than in Canada.

Coincident with our finding that there is *more stated* but *less effective* hostility toward unions among Canadian managers is the survey evidence that employed Canadians are more likely to anticipate aggressive resistance by management than are their U.S. counterparts. Thus, 44 percent of Canadians predict employers will strongly oppose union organization (i.e., by "threatening consequences" or "going after the workers trying to organize") compared with 33 percent of Americans. U.S. managers also show friendlier attitudes than Canadians do when asked directly for their reaction to an attempt to form a union. One-seventh of American executives in unorganized workplaces (15 percent) say that they would welcome a union, while 44 percent would do nothing to stop it. Only 7 percent of Canadian managers would welcome a union, and 30 percent would not try to block it. The small minority of managers who would oppose the union by threatening consequences or by going after the workers who seek to organize it is greater in Canada, 12 percent more than the 7 percent in the United States.

In essence, U.S. managers do not need to be as hostile as Canadian managers in order to thwart a unionization drive; we know (from chap. 3) that legal differences between the two countries make it easier for U.S. opposition to translate into effective anti-union outcomes. There may of course be a self-interested or rational-choice logic behind the assumption that U.S. management is more effective in its resistance to union organizing. David Blanchflower and Richard Freeman (1992) argue that U.S. executives have a stronger reason to effectively oppose unionization because the union wage premium is higher in the United States than in

Canada. In our own survey, when asked whether labor organizations improve the wages and benefits of their members, U.S. unionists are more positive than Canadians are. A majority of U.S. members (55 percent) agree strongly that unions increase wages; the comparable percentage among Canadians is 38. Most of the others replied that they "agree moderately."[6]

Union Power versus Union Approval

Why do Canadians, whether managers or workers, seemingly react more negatively to unions than Americans even though they live in a country with higher union density and a greater commitment to social democratic and communitarian values? Part of the answer may lie in varying cross-national reactions to union power. Although majorities of the general populations and of employed people in both countries (and elsewhere in the industrial world) approve of unions generally and believe that they are good for workers, survey data from different societies indicate that most people regard unions as highly self-interested organizations that benefit their members at the expense of society (or the consumer). Unions generally rank toward the bottom among major institutions in public esteem. Many see union leaders as self-serving or corrupt; 64 percent in the United States and 54 percent in Canada agree, that "there is too much corruption in unions here. . . . " More than one-half of the Canadians (56 percent) and over two-thirds of Americans (68 percent) agree that "wage demands of unions don't reflect economic reality"; and 53 percent of Canadians and 64 percent of American agree that "unions enable workers to get away with being inefficient." Hence, it should not be surprising that the public and even many union members do not want unions to be too strong.

Given this background, it follows that if unions become more powerful or display greater militancy they will suffer in public evaluation. Comparative evidence indicates that perceptions of union strength correspond to reality. In Britain during the late 1970s, when unions had grown to 11 million members and the Labour Party dominated national politics, most British (75 percent) told pollsters that unions had too much power. But in the late 1980s, when the foe of unionism, Margaret Thatcher, held office and union membership had dropped by one-third, national sentiment turned upward—less than 40 percent then said unions had too much power (*Market Opinion Research International* 1976).

Various polls have inquired about the perceived power of unions, often whether they have "too much," "the right amount," or "too little." Given variations in question wording it is difficult to be precise about changes over time. However, the broad picture suggests that the proportion of Americans who believe unions have too much power has declined as density has fallen. A set of surveys dealing with the evaluation of union power by the Opinion Research Corporation between 1971 and 1985 found a falloff in the differences between those answering "too powerful" and "not powerful enough," dropping from 41 percent (55 "too powerful" and 14 percent "not enough") to 26 percent in 1985. The decline was steady from 1977 on. In 1996, only 30 percent said unions have "too much power," contrasted to 25 percent for "not enough."

In Canada, where density has increased since the 1950s, the belief that unions have "too much power" also grew from 32 to 50 to 62 percent in 1950, 1958, and 1968, respectively, and from 65 to 68 percent in the early 1980s. Conversely, those replying "not enough" power fell from 47 to 31 to 27 percent in 1950, 1958, and 1968, respectively, and then to around 6 percent in six polls between 1979 and 1984. In 1984, one poll reported 11 percent (Rouillard 1991, 292). Our 1996 survey found 10 percent.

Comparing the feelings Canadians and Americans express about union power points up the factual dimension of beliefs on the subject. In 1944, when U.S. union density was higher than Canadian (29 vs. 24 percent) a larger population of Canadians (65 percent) than of Americans (37 percent) answered "labor unions" when asked by Gallup whom they would prefer to control the government, labor unions or big business. Today Canadians are more disposed than Americans are to fear union power.

The cross-border findings in our survey correspond to current variations in union strength, since 47 percent of Canadians and 30 percent of Americans reply "unions have too much power" in their country. Only one-quarter of Americans think labor organizations have "not enough," an opinion shared by only 10 percent of Canadians (the rest say "about right").

Most Canadian unions explicitly endorse a political party, the NDP in Anglo-Canada. U.S. labor organizations do not, although most favor the Democrats. Canadians, not surprisingly, lead their neighbors in "strongly" agreeing that "unions are too involved in politics" by 40 to 34 percent.

As noted, the decline in U.S. estimates of union power since the 1970s coincides with the actual falloff in union density, while the much stronger feeling in Canada that unions have "too much power" corresponds to greater membership. Interestingly, whereas a good majority of Canadians,

62 percent (23 percent "strongly"), believe the "union movement is getting weaker," in the United States a more overwhelming 73 percent (32 percent "strongly") agree with this statement. The considerable acceptance in Canada of the belief that unions are growing weaker may seem odd given the much greater strength of organized labor north of the border, but as noted earlier Canadian union density hit its highest point in the mid- to late 1980s at 35–37 percent and has since fallen slightly to 30 percent in 2001.[7]

The more negative feelings toward organized labor expressed by Canadian respondents may be linked to the larger impact of unions on the economy, their greater propensity to strike, and their higher involvement in politics. Unions are more powerful, militant, and politicized in Canada, and their effect on the economy and politics tends to be more visible than in the United States. As noted, the percentages of Canadian respondents who say that unions hurt productivity and the ability of companies to compete in international markets or enable workers to get away with being inefficient are higher than among U.S. respondents. Most Canadian union members (52 percent) and nonmembers (73 percent) agree that the wage demands of unions are unrealistic and do not reflect economic realities. In the United States, 38 percent of union members and 57 percent of nonmembers express this view (table 5.7).[8]

These data are congruent with the hypothesis that perceived power is negatively related to union approval (however measured). If unions are considered weak they are more liked than if they are seen as strong and militant. If the latter, they are a source of concern. However, these findings alone do not prove the inverse power relationship. As noted, we also have survey evidence showing that more nonunionists in the United States (31 percent) than in Canada (22 percent) say they "would personally prefer to belong to a labor union." In tandem with these results, a smaller proportion of nonunion employees in Canada (33 percent; 12 percent "definitely") than in the U.S. (48 percent; 16 percent "definitely") say they would vote for unionization in a collective bargaining election. The overwhelming majority of unionists in both countries, 91 percent in the United States and 86 percent in Canada, report they would definitely or probably vote to keep their union in a decertification election.[9]

A Resolution of the Paradox?

The explanation for differences in union density that focuses on managerial opposition is supported by the stronger legal hindrances to

TABLE 5.7
Opinions about Effects of Unions on the Economy (%)

| | Wage Demands of Unions Don't Reflect Economic Realities | | | | Unions Hurt Country's Companies' Ability to Compete in International Markets | | | |
| | Canada | | United States | | Canada | | United States | |
	Nonmembers	Members	Nonmembers	Members	Nonmembers	Members	Nonmembers	Members
Agree strongly	37	17	19	12	22	9	21	9
Agree moderately	36	34	38	26	36	31	26	18
Disagree moderately	18	29	27	30	25	34	33	30
Strongly disagree	6	18	10	29	11	22	15	39
Don't know/not stated	3	1	6	3	6	4	6	4
N	540	384	952	199	540	384	952	199

Source: Lipset-Meltz survey.
Note: Percentages may not add to 100 because of rounding.

TABLE 5.8
Views on the Extent of Government Protection for the Right to Join a Union (%)

How Much Legal Protection of Rights?	Canada			United States		
	All Workers	Union Members	Nonmembers	All Workers	Union Members	Nonmembers
A lot	16	19	14	14	16	14
Some	50	49	51	54	51	55
Very little	15	16	14	18	19	18
No protection	6	6	6	4	7	4
Don't know	13	10	14	9	7	10

Source: Lipset-Meltz survey.
Note: Percentages may not add to 100 because of rounding.

unionization in the United States than in Canada. Craig Riddell (1993, 109–47), Peter Bruce (1989, 115–41), and Noah Meltz (1989b, 142–58) argue that much of the unionization gap between the two countries can be attributed to distinctions in the legal regimes pertaining to unions and collective bargaining. These variations in the law, however, do not appear to be reflected in the way that workers in both countries experience the role of government, that is, their evaluation of the extent to which "government agencies protect the right to join a union. " Almost identical estimates were given in both countries: 68 percent of nonmembers in the United States and 66 percent in Canada believe that the government gives a lot or some protection; the same proportions, 67 percent of union members in the United States and 68 percent in Canada, share this opinion (table 5.8).

These responses, of course, do not have to bear on the actual variations in policy and action by employers and governments. Nevertheless, the poll data indicate that U.S. employees, as compared with Canadian, do not perceive greater opposition by their employers to or lesser government protection for unionization campaigns. There is however, a serious methodological problem in analyzing and interpreting these results. As we know, Canadian union density is considerably higher than U.S. density, but U.S. nonunionists are much more likely than Canadians to prefer membership. Moreover, the proportion of U.S. unionists who would "definitely" vote to retain the union is higher (70 percent) than Canadian unionists (55 percent). The ratio of proportions is similar among employed nonmembers. Close to one-half of all U.S. workers (48 percent; 16 percent "definitely") report they would vote for a union in a representation election, compared with 33 percent of Canadians (12 percent "definitely"). Something must be preventing these workers from actualizing their desires. Trade union membership, therefore, is obviously not a free choice. Whether one belongs is in large part a function of availability, that is, whether there is a union that can be joined in a place of work, and the character of the organizing effort. A large proportion of the employed labor force cannot easily find a union to join. Beyond this, workers may not be exposed to information about the advantages or disadvantages of union representation. Given the great disparity in union density, it is clear that the opportunities for membership are greater in Canada. This conclusion is congruent with the sociocultural hypothesis underlying this book—that the probability of union membership for any given individual is not only, or even primarily, a function of his or her personal outlook, but also reflects the social environment, contractual obligations or pressures, and ultimately the availability of unions.

The analysis to this point has generated several important findings. First, our interpretation of the data challenges the assumption that variation in intensity of employer animosity to union organizing is the most important factor accounting for cross-border variations in union density. We have seen that managerial views are more or less the same on both sides of the border. This implies that the most likely reason for more effective union opposition south of the border resides with differing legal regimes rather than more militant anti-union attitudes. The differences in legal climate are partially accounted for by the differing value systems in the two countries. The results imply that social democratic values (which indirectly affect the real and perceived power of unions) are inversely related to union approval, which explains why Canadian union approval is lower than that in the United Stated. Finally, the evidence surveyed in this chapter demonstrates that potential union membership in the United States is greater than the actual level observed.

To follow up on this last finding, it is necessary to focus on those workers who seem misplaced: union members who do not want to belong and non-members who would prefer to be part of organized labor. The stronger Canadian movement includes a larger percentage of "unhappy" members than the U.S. movement does, whereas the employed labor force among the United States contains proportionately more nonmembers who would like to be in unions. In the next chapter, we go on to examine the sources or characteristics of these four groups in each country: those members and nonmembers who prefer or reject union membership.

6   Frustrated Demand

More Americans Want to Join Unions

Having just explored the outwardly similar (but fundamentally dissimilar) cultural values underlying the patterns of unionization in the United States and Canada, we now examine what people actually think about unions—in particular, whether employees really want to join them. We begin with an examination of our central paradox—namely, Why is it that more than one out of two workers in the United States say that they would vote for a union, a figure that exceeds that for Canadian workers, yet only 16 percent of U.S. employees in our sample actually belong to unions?[1]

This chapter uses the survey that was conducted for the authors by the Angus Reid Group (now known as Ipsos-Reid). The sample sizes were designed to be representative of the working populations of Canada and the United States and of employees who belonged to unions. In total, 1,750 adults were interviewed in the United States and 1,495 in Canada.[2] We measured, in each country, the extent to which nonunion employees wanted to join a union. Included as well were data on individuals who belong to unions unwillingly. The method employed to analyze these data, as developed by Farber and Krueger (1992) and Riddell (1993), compares the extent to which there are differences in the demand for union membership against the relative supply of unionization. That is, we attempt to measure how hard it is for an employee to fulfill his or her desire to be unionized. We follow convention and term the unavailability of union representation *frustrated* or *unsatisfied demand.*

As we show here, there are many employees in both countries who want to join a union but who, for a variety of reasons, are unable to do so. These reasons include lack of adequate union organizing, lack of appropriate approaches by unions to organizing (for example, inability to appeal to professional or white-collar workers), employer opposition to the formation of unions, and inadequate government protection of the right to unionize.

The key to distinguishing the intention to vote from a worker's actual union status is based on the answer to the following question: "If an election were held tomorrow for unionization at your workplace, how would you vote?" The answers were recorded as:

Definitely vote for a union
Probably vote for a union
Probably vote against a union
Definitely vote against a union

People who were not certain of their response or who chose not to answer were recorded as well. The numbers in this last category were very small, less than 1 percent in total. In the analysis of frustrated demand that follows, individuals who did not respond were removed. The analysis also combines the responses "definitely" and "probably" in each group to determine who would vote for or against a union. Although the rationale for the fourfold response was to properly measure the intensity of desired union membership status, in the event of a real organizing drive each respondent would have to choose between joining or not joining a union. Consequently there is no real-life option to sit on the fence, and we wanted our responses to reflect this reality.

Voting Intentions of Members and Nonmembers

The results of our survey for nonunion employees in the United States (84 percent of all employees) and in Canada (64 percent of all employees) are shown in table 6.1. Almost one-half of workers in the United States (48.2 percent) who did not belong to a union at the time of the survey would vote for a union if they had the opportunity. Of the same group in Canada, 33 percent would vote for a union. What this means is that the larger nonunion group in the United States has a greater desire to belong to a union.

To estimate the total demand for unionization in the two countries, we must add to these figures the voting intentions of workers who already

TABLE 6.1
Voting Intentions of Nonunion Employees in the United
States and Canada, 1996 (%)

Survey Question	United States	Canada
Definitely vote for union	16.4	12.0
Probably vote for union	31.8	21.3
Subtotal: Vote for union	48.2	33.0[a]
Probably vote against union	24.4	25.7
Definitely vote against union	27.4	41.0
Subtotal: Vote against union	51.8	66.7
TOTAL (excluding not stated)	100	100

Source: Lipset-Meltz survey.
[a] Percentages do not add to the subtotal due to rounding.

TABLE 6.2
Voting Intentions of Union Employees in the United States
and Canada, 1996 (%)

Survey Question	United States	Canada
Definitely vote to remain in union	69.9	54.9
Probably vote to remain in union	20.6	30.9
Subtotal: Vote to remain in union	90.5	85.8
Probably vote against union	5.1	8.8
Definitely vote against union	4.4	5.5
Subtotal: Vote against union	9.5	14.2[a]
TOTAL (excluding not stated)	100	100

Source: Lipset-Meltz survey.
[a] Percentages do not add to the subtotal due to rounding.

belong to unions. This is done so as to exclude those people who are not
willing members of unions from the total demand-for-unionization
calculation.[3]

The survey we conducted asked those who already belong to a union—
16 percent of workers in the United States and 36 percent in Canada—the
following question: "If an election were held tomorrow to decide whether
to keep the union where you work, do you think you would: definitely
vote for a union; probably vote for a union; probably vote against a union;
definitely vote against a union?" The results are shown in table 6.2.

The vast majority of union members in both countries would vote to
retain their membership in the union. There is, however, a small but

crucial difference. Whereas 91 percent of U.S. union members would vote to stay with the union, only 86 percent in Canada would vote the same way. Put another way, only 9 percent of U.S. union members can be said to be unwilling unionists, compared with 14 percent of Canadian unionized workers.

Total Demand for Unionization

When the responses of union and nonunion workers are combined, 55 and 52 percent of U.S. and Canadian workers, respectively, would vote to join or retain membership in a union. The calculations combine the union and nonunion weights for the respondents to each question.[4] In both countries, therefore, a majority of workers want to be union members, but once again Americans paradoxically appear to be more supportive of unions when questioned specifically on the desirability of belonging to unions and their willingness to belong. They do not, however, join as much as Canadians do. Why?

Using a statistical decomposition technique that divides the Canada-U.S. union density gap into differences arising from the demand for unionization and the supply, or availability, of unionization, Farber and Krueger (1992) and Riddell (1993) found that a significant factor in the unionization gap was supply-side differences. Riddell (1993), in particular, found that two-thirds of the union density difference resided with supply-side factors and only one-third was due to demand-side differences. That is, Canadians had a greater effective demand for unionization than Americans not because they were more desirous of union membership but because they had fewer barriers to realizing that demand. Not surprisingly, Riddell (1993) found that there was much more frustrated demand for unionization in the United States than in Canada.

In both countries, more workers want to join unions than have the opportunity, as shown by the data in table 6.1, but a higher proportion of Canadians seem able to gain union representation and membership than Americans. Using calculations similar to these conducted by Riddell (1993) and Farber and Kruger (1992), but using the results of our own survey question on union preferences, we found that 90 percent of the unionization gap between the two countries was the result of frustrated demand (supply-side barriers) in the United States and only 10 percent was the result of a lower level of demand. In an estimate using the same voting questions in tables 6.1 and 6.2, we obtain results closer to those of Farber

TABLE 6.3
Voting Intentions of Nonunion Employees by Industry, 1996 (%)

Industry/Sector	United States		Canada	
	Vote for Union	Actual Density	Vote for Union	Actual Density
Private sector	45.5	10.4	30.5	22.5
Primary[a]	33.3	13.8	31.9	40.2
Manufacturing	35.2	17.6	23.9	36.7
Construction	37.8	17.7	12.1	59.6
Transportation and communication[b]	40.8	27.3	28.2	54.8
Wholesale and retail trade	44.0	6.1	31.7	11.6
Finance, insurance, and real estate	39.4	2.1	33.3	3.5
Services[c]	47.1	5.7	36.2	35.9
Public administration	57.8	37.8	43.9	80.6
TOTAL	48.2	16.0	33.0	36.0

Source: Lipset-Meltz survey.
[a] Agriculture, mining, fishing and trapping, and forestry.
[b] Public utilities also included.
[c] Community, health, business, and personal services.

and Krueger and Riddell. The various approaches are discussed in more detail in the appendix to this chapter.

In either case, the primary factor for the gap in unionization rates between Canada and the United States seems to be various kinds of supply-side barriers to union membership. We now explore where these barriers are located. We consider whether frustrated demand for unionization is associated with employees in particular industrial sectors, occupations, or regions or across various demographic characteristics. This discussion acts as a complement to the more general discussion in chapter 3 on how barriers have arisen to a greater extent in the United States than in Canada.

Differences in the Demand for Unionization by Selected Characteristics

Table 6.3 highlights the difference between the voting intentions of nonunion members and actual union density across industrial sectors. What is striking about these figures is that the biggest differences between actual and desired unionization are among workers who belong to industries in the private service sector, that is, finance, insurance, and real estate; wholesale and retail trade; and business services. These are the sectors that

TABLE 6.4
Voting Intentions of Nonunion Employees by Occupational Category, 1996 (%)

| Occupation | United States | | Canada | |
	Vote for Union	Actual Density	Vote for Union	Actual Density
Managerial[a]	30.0	13.8	19.1	13.4
Professional[b]	40.2	23.5	27.6	27.0
Technical[c]	39.6	13.5	24.9	26.5
Clerical[d]	54.5	9.9	41.4	30.7
Laborers[e]	64.4	23.0	52.2	40.4
TOTAL	48.2	16.0	33.0	36.0

Source: Lipset-Meltz survey.
[a] Senior management occupations.
[b] Professional occupations in business and finance, health, natural and social sciences, and art and culture.
[c] Highly skilled administrative, technical, and sales and service personnel; industrial supervisors; and paraprofessionals (police, etc.).
[d] Clerical, service support, intermediate sales and service, equipment operation, maintenance, and service personnel.
[e] Sales and service personnel (cashiers, etc.) and laborers.

are the least organized in each country. The implication to be drawn from these results is clear: the greater the extent of unionization, the lower the degree of frustrated or unsatisfied demand for unionization. The table also shows that the higher the union density in a sector, the lower the gap between desired and actual union density levels.

Turning to the occupations of employees, the figures in table 6.4 tell the same story. There is lower unionization in the United States in all occupational groups and a greater willingness to join a union among nonmembers than is the case in Canada—put simply, the greater the extent of unionization, the lower the degree of frustrated demand for unionization. The comparison, therefore, that we see between the two countries also seems to apply to these findings.

We can also consider within-country differences between nonunion workers' willingness to join a union and the extent of actual unionization. These results are shown in table 6.5. States in particular, and provinces to a lesser extent, display a significant discrepancy between the actual union density at the time of the survey and the percentage of nonunion workers in the state or province who would vote for a union. The largest differences between demand and actual density reside in states and provinces that are the least unionized. Those states that have a high union density tend to have a smaller percentage difference between the voting intentions of non-

TABLE 6.5

Voting Intentions of Nonunion Employees by Region, 1996 (%)

Region	Vote for Union	Actual Density
Canada (total)	33.0	36.0
British Columbia	39.8	36.5
Alberta	30.4	22.9
Manitoba and Saskatchewan	39.1	34.0
Ontario	31.2	29.5
Quebec	40.5	37.2
Atlantic[a]	50.2	38.6
United States (total)	48.2	16.0
Northeast	51.9	19.5
Midwest	44.1	16.5
South	44.5	6.8
West	52.7	17.7

Source: Lipset-Meltz survey.
[a] Nova Scotia, New Brunswick, Prince Edward Island, and Newfoundland.

TABLE 6.6

Voting Intentions of Nonunion Employees by Gender and Age, 1996 (%)

	United States		Canada	
	Vote for Union	Actual Density	Vote for Union	Actual Density
Male	45.6	18.8	37.9	34.4
Female	55.7	14.3	45.7	30.0
Youth (15–24)	60.5	6.6	58.5	10.7
Adult (25+)	45.2	19.8	37.0	35.7

Source: Lipset-Meltz survey.

members and actual density. More nonunion workers in the South, for example, lack union density than is the case in western and northeastern states. The same is true for Canada, but to a slightly lesser extent. In chapter 7 we elaborate on these regional differences.

In the case of all three measures—industry, occupation, and state or province—the lower the union density, the greater the degree of frustrated demand for unionization as represented by the difference in the proportion of nonunion workers who would vote for a union and realized membership rates. Because there are fewer unionized workers in the United

States and because there are more Americans than Canadians not belonging to unions who want to join, the inverse relationship between intention to vote for a union and the degree of unionization across selected characteristics is even stronger south of border.

Finally, what about the extent of frustrated demand for unionization by demographic group, such as gender and age? Table 6.6 compares the intentions of male versus female and young (15–24) versus adult (25 and older) nonunion workers in the two countries to vote for a union with the percentages of unionization in each category. In both Canada and the United States, female and young workers are less unionized than their male and adult counterparts. Comparing the intentions to vote for a union with the actual rate of unionization in both countries indicates a higher degree of frustrated demand for unions among youth and women than among men and adult workers.

The Source of Frustrated Demand

The preceding discussion has documented the considerable frustrated demand for unionization that exists even in Canada but particularly in the United States. What is the source of this frustrated demand and why is it greater south of the border? Earlier (in chapters 3 and 4) we have noted that the greatest proximate sources of the differences in unionization were shown to be the greater extent of (post-1964) government support for unionization in Canada. This support is manifested in legislation, the extent and speed of enforcement of the legislation, and the amount of direct government-funded and other publicly funded employment. Other determinants included the amount of union organizing and the size of the private service sector. The contribution of states and provinces to the cross-border unionization gap is discussed in the next chapter.

Appendix

Tables 6.7 and 6.8 use the technique for estimating frustrated demand for unionization employed by Farber and Krueger (1992) and Riddell (1993). The two tables are based on slightly differently worded questions that capture the desire for unionization. Explanations for the estimation methods found in the tables are follow.

TABLE 6.7
Desire for Unionization Based on the 1996 Angus Reid Survey
Question "If an election were held tomorrow, would you vote
for unionization at your workplace?"

	Probabilities	
	Canada	United States
Pr $(U=1)$	0.36	0.16
Pr $(D=1)$	0.52	0.55
Pr $(D=1|U=0)$	0.33	0.48
Pr $(D=1|U=1)$	0.86	0.91
Pr $(U=1|D=1)$	0.69	0.29
Pr $(D=1|U=0)$	0.21	0.40

Note: U = 1, union member; U = 0, nonmember; D = 1, desires to
become or remain union member.

TABLE 6.8
Desire for Unionization Based on the Question "All things
considered, if you had a choice, would you personally prefer to
belong to a labor union or not?"

	Probabilities	
	Canada	United States
Pr $(U=1)$	0.36	0.16
Pr $(D=1)$	0.37	0.39
Pr $(D=1|U=0)$	0.22	0.31
Pr $(D=1|U=1)$	0.65	0.77
Pr $(U=1|D=1)$	0.97	0.44
Pr $(D=1|U=0)$	0.14	0.26

Note: U = 1, union member; U = 0, nonmember; D = 1, desires to
become or remain union member.

Pr(U= 1): The probability that a worker is a union member. The percentages are
drawn from Bureau of Labour Statistics (BLS, http://stats.bls.gov/) and
Labour Force Survey (LFS, Statistics Canada, http://www.statcan.ca/) estimates of union density. $Pr(U=1) = 0.36$ for Canada and $Pr(U=1) = 0.16$ for
the United States.

Pr(U = 1): Total or hypothetical level of union density or the probability that a worker
desires and receives union representation.* This is the sum of the probability that a
worker is a union member and desires to retain union membership plus the
probability that a worker desires union representation but is not employed
on a union job (union membership plus frustrated demand). Formally, this
is $Pr(D=1|U=1) * Pr(U=1) + Pr(D=1, U=0)$.

Pr(D = 1|U = 0): The probability that a nonunion worker demands union representa-tion. Computed from tabulations of the 1996 Angus Reid survey. Individuals who responded yes to unionization (however measured) were coded $D = 1$.

Pr(D = 1|U = 1): The probability that a union worker demands union representation. Computed from tabulations of the 1996 Angus Reid survey. Individuals who responded yes to unionization (however measured) were coded $D = 1$.

Pr(U = 1|D = 1): The probability of being unionized conditional on the desire to be unionized. This represents the ease of obtaining a union job given that a worker desires a union job. Riddell (1993) interprets this as a measure of relative supply.

Pr(D = 1, U = 0): The probability that a worker demands union representation but is not employed on a union job (frustrated demand). Computed as $\Pr(D = 1|U = 0) * \Pr(U = 0)$. $(D = 1|U = 0)$ is obtained from this table, but $\Pr(U = 0)$ is obtained from BLS and LFS estimates of union density. $\Pr(U = 1) = 0.36$ for Canada and $\Pr(U = 1) = 0.16$ for the United States.

TABLE 7.1
State Union Density for Selected Years, 1939–2001 (%)

State	1939	1953	1964	1974	1982	1987	1992	1996	2001
High-Density States									
1. New York	23.0	34.4	38.5	38.0	35.8	29.4	27.7	26.8	26.7
2. Hawaii	n.a.	n.a.	23.6	36.2	31.5	29.7	28.6	23.2	23.4
3. Alaska	n.a.	n.a.	32.1	26.4	30.4	22.2	20.8	22.5	22.0
4. Michigan	20.0	43.3	42.7	38.4	33.7	26.6	25.6	24.0	21.8
5. New Jersey	16.1	35.2	32.3	28.2	19.9	24.0	22.9	21.8	19.5
6. Washington	41.3	53.3	44.0	36.7	32.9	23.5	23.5	19.8	18.6
7. Illinois	25.9	39.7	38.4	34.9	27.5	22.3	20.5	20.0	18.3
8. Minnesota	24.8	38.1	34.0	25.3	24.5	23.1	22.2	20.3	17.8
9. Ohio	24.4	38.0	36.7	33.2	27.4	22.8	20.4	19.5	17.7
10. Pennsylvania	27.6	39.9	38.7	37.5	27.0	22.0	19.6	17.7	17.1
11. Rhode Island	10.2	27.4	28.3	27.3	19.4	21.2	19.9	19.1	16.8
12. Nevada	18.2	30.4	32.8	27.4	22.1	18.3	18.9	20.4	16.7
13. California	23.4	35.7	33.3	28.2	25.4	19.4	18.2	16.5	16.4
14. Wisconsin	29.1	38.3	33.4	28.7	24.5	21.4	19.9	18.8	16.4
15. Oregon	30.1	43.1	34.2	26.5	27.5	19.7	18.6	18.0	15.5
16. Connecticut	11.3	26.5	27.0	25.1	18.9	18.5	17.9	9.7	15.1
17. Massachusetts	15.5	30.1	28.0	24.4	19.7	17.7	17.0	15.4	14.8
Middle-Density States									
18. West Virginia	41.7	44.1	44.7	38.2	28.9	21.6	18.4	15.7	14.6
19. Indiana	21.7	40.0	36.4	33.2	25.1	21.3	19.2	14.9	14.5
20. Maryland	12.0	25.2	22.9	21.6	18.6	15.7	15.6	14.8	13.7
21. Missouri	21.9	39.7	37.9	32.3	26.6	17.7	13.8	15.4	13.5
22. Iowa	17.3	25.0	22.6	21.2	20.5	14.7	13.6	13.0	13.3
23. Montana	36.7	47.0	35.2	25.7	21.7	17.7	18.8	15.6	13.2
24. Maine	7.2	21.4	20.8	16.2	18.5	19.1	14.9	14.5	12.8
25. Delaware	7.8	18.4	24.0	20.1	20.3	16.8	16.5	12.4	12.4
26. Kentucky	22.5	25.0	27.0	25.1	20.4	16.2	12.6	12.7	11.4
27. Vermont	11.4	18.9	18.7	17.7	11.9	11.2	10.6	9.7	10.7
28. Alabama	16.1	24.9	18.7	19.1	18.2	13.9	13.8	11.4	9.9
29. New Hampshire	7.3	24.6	20.1	15.1	12.3	9.9	9.8	11.2	9.6
30. Kansas	13.4	23.9	18.6	14.1	12.0	12.3	11.5	9.6	9.3
31. Colorado	17.6	27.8	22.3	18.9	18.0	11.5	10.1	16.5	9.2
32. Wyoming	26.7	28.6	19.4	18.2	15.6	13.7	12.0	9.7	9.0
33. Oklahoma	10.4	16.1	15.1	15.0	12.9	10.7	9.4	10.4	8.4
Low-Density States									
34. Nebraska	12.5	19.7	19.2	15.1	16.3	11.2	10.7	8.6	8.0
35. New Mexico	11.2	14.2	14.5	14.1	12.8	8.6	8.8	8.4	8.0
36. Louisiana	9.6	19.5	18.7	16.3	13.8	8.4	7.8	8.1	7.8
37. Tennessee	15.3	22.6	19.2	18.7	17.3	12.1	10.4	9.6	7.8
38. Idaho	13.7	21.5	19.0	15.5	16.1	13.2	9.1	8.7	7.5
39. Georgia	7.0	15.0	14.0	14.5	12.7	9.5	7.3	7.7	7.2
40. North Dakota	10.9	15.6	14.8	15.1	14.2	12.3	9.4	9.1	7.2
41. Utah	19.3	26.3	18.0	14.9	16.8	10.1	9.6	8.4	6.9
42. Florida	11.3	16.2	14.0	12.5	9.6	7.5	8.1	7.5	6.6
43. Arkansas	12.7	21.5	17.0	16.8	13.2	11.0	8.6	7.1	6.3
44. Arizona	16.6	27.7	18.5	16.0	12.8	6.2	7.2	5.9	5.9
45. South Dakota	7.1	14.4	10.0	11.0	10.3	7.9	8.9	7.4	5.8
46. Texas	10.3	16.7	14.1	13.0	12.5	6.5	6.9	6.6	5.7
47. Mississippi	6.5	14.7	13.5	12.0	9.3	8.9	9.1	5.8	5.5
48. Virginia	12.8	17.4	15.8	13.8	10.9	9.0	9.3	6.8	5.3
49. South Carolina	4.0	9.3	7.4	8.0	5.8	5.0	4.9	3.7	4.9
50. North Carolina	4.2	8.3	7.4	6.9	8.9	5.6	4.8	4.1	3.7

Source: Troy and Sheflin (1985); Hirsch and Macpherson (1998, 2002).
Note: Listed by 2001 union density ranking. N.a., not available.

7   The Contribution of States and Provinces to the Cross-Border Unionization Gap

Any cross-border examination of union density differences would be incomplete without an examination of the contribution of the states and provinces to the overall unionization gap between the two countries. Three approaches are used in this chapter to quantify the impact of the within-country differences on the cross-border unionization gap. First, we look at which states or provinces have high, medium, and low union representation and how this has changed over time. The question here is whether states that have relatively high union membership such as New York, Michigan, and Hawaii have always had relatively high density rates and whether states with low union density such as South Carolina, North Carolina, and Mississippi have always been low. We then ask whether this is also true of high-density provinces such as Newfoundland, Quebec, and British Columbia and of the low-union-density provinces, Alberta, Ontario, and Prince Edward Island. We ask whether the states or provinces tend to display the same rankings in both private- and public-sector union membership rates or whether there is a difference among the states or provinces in terms of private- and public-sector density.

Our second approach examines whether regional employment patterns have made a difference in the contribution that states or provinces have made to the unionization gap over time. For example, when unionization in the United States was growing faster than in Canada (our data focus on the period 1939–53) was this because employment shares were generally growing in the industrialized cities and states of the United States that were most connected with the war effort? And by implication, was the decline in union density in the United States after 1956 the result of a shift of employment away from the most unionized states toward the least unionized (our data compare 1953 and 2001)?

Finally, if there is considerable consistency in the rankings of the states or provinces by union density, do we also find that there are significant differences in the attitudes and values of people in the various states or provinces toward those factors that are most associated with favoring or not favoring union membership? In order to answer these questions we begin by describing the regional patterns of union representation in both countries.

Patterns of Union Representation by State and Province over Time

Map 1 is a map of Canada and the United States showing union density rates by state and province in 1996 (the time of our survey). The ranking of the states and provinces in 2001 is given in tables 7.1 and 7.2 (last columns). For the United States, the highest percentages of union members are found in the Northeast, the Great Lakes states, and the Northwest (Washington, Oregon, Alaska, and Hawaii). The least unionized states are in the South and Southwest. For Canada, the far west (British Columbia) and the east (Newfoundland and Quebec) are the most organized of the provinces. Two other major observations are immediately apparent. First, of the ten Canadian provinces, eight have higher densities than any state in the United States, and only New York, Michigan, Hawaii, and Alaska have higher densities than the least organized province of Alberta. Second, most of the high-union-density states border Canada.

To explore the consistency in the ranking of the states and provinces by union density over time, we have used available data from Troy and Sheflin (1985) and the Bureau of National Affairs (Hirsch and Macpherson 2002) for selected years from 1939. These years include some of the turning points in union density that are identified in chapter 3 (i.e., 1939, 1953, 1964, 1974, 1982, 1987, 1992, 1996, and 2001). Table 7.1 shows the union density rates for states for these years in descending order, based on the 2001 rankings. In the table, states are divided into three roughly equal groups ranked by the extent of union density: high density, medium density, and low density. Data for Canadian regions are available from 1921, as shown in table 7.2, but data for all ten provinces are available only since 1966; hence we group the Prairie and Atlantic provinces for all time periods.

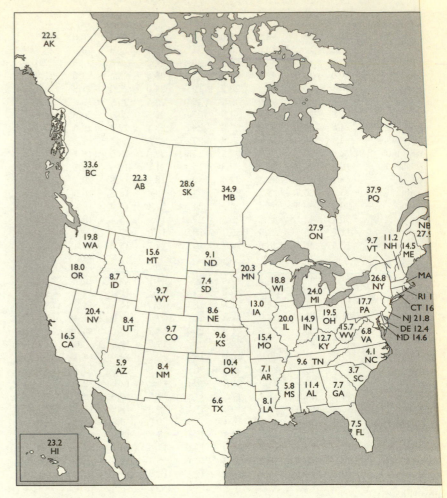

MAP 1

Interstate and interprovincial union density ranking, 1996. (*Source*: U.S. data from Bureau Labor Statistics 1997, http://stats.bls.gov/; Canadian data from Labour Force Survey Statistics Canada, http://www.statcan.ca/.)

The Interstate Pattern

Table 7.1 indicates a high degree of consistency over time in the rank of states by union density. The bottom third is the most consistent. Three quarters of the states that were in the low group in 1996 were in the group virtually throughout the period since 1939. In particular, the sta

TABLE 7.2
Provincial Union Density, 1921–2001 (%)

Province	1921	1939	1946	1956	1966	1976	1992	1996	2001[a]
1. Quebec	8.9	17.0	23.6	24.1	28.1	33.8	40.3	37.8	36.6
2. British Columbia	12.6	20.2	29.9	42.6	36.1	40.5	38.1	34.8	33.1
3. Atlantic[b]	13.3	24.4	21.3	27.2	19.3	33.4	38.8	31.8	30.8
4. Prairies[c]	13.6	17.9	21.6	23.3	19.4	28.8	31.8	30.6	27.3
5. Ontario	10.0	13.1	19.0	29.3	28.3	31.2	31.6	28.3	26.1

Source: Bain and Price (1980); Eaton and Ashagrie (1970); CALURA (1972–1992).
Note: Listed by 2001 union density ranking.
[a] First half.
[b] New Brunswick, Newfoundland, Nova Scotia, and Prince Edward Island.
[c] Saskatchewan, Alberta, and Manitoba.

of South Carolina, North Carolina, Mississippi, Texas, South Dakota, Florida, Georgia, Louisiana, New Mexico, North Dakota, and Tennessee were in the lowest group for each year for which we have data. The states of Virginia and Arkansas were in the bottom one-third for all but one year during more than the six decades that our data cover, and both were just above the bottom group in 1939. Virginia ranked thirtieth and Arkansas thirty-first.

As well, a majority of states that are now highly unionized also had relatively high union density in earlier decades: New York, Michigan, Minnesota, Illinois, Washington, Ohio, Wisconsin, Oregon, and California. Two other states were in the top one-third in all but one year: Alaska and Pennsylvania. For the other states, several moved up during the period: Hawaii, Nevada, Rhode Island, and Connecticut. The top group seems to be slightly more fluid than the bottom group.[1]

The most volatile states are those in the middle. As can be seen in table 7.1, only five of sixteen states in this category remained there throughout the period: Maryland, Iowa, Colorado, Wyoming, and Tennessee. Other states moved into and out of the middle group either from the high end or from the low end. In fact, perhaps there should be a fourth grouping of these borderline or swing states. West Virginia, Missouri, and Indiana were all in the upper group until the mid-1990s, whereas Delaware, New Hampshire, Oklahoma, and Vermont were in the low group until the mid-1990s. As we see later, the biggest source of change for the swing states was the impact of public- versus private-sector unionization. In summary, what changed between the high and low points of unionization was less the ranking than the extent of unionization across all states. The pattern looks something like an accordion, with state unionization growing and then declining but in a generally consistent pattern.

The Interprovincial Pattern

In Canada, as table 7.2 shows, the rankings by region are more volatile. In 1921, Quebec was the least organized region in Canada and the Prairie provinces were the most organized. Eight decades later, Quebec was the most highly organized and the Prairies were close to the bottom. For Quebec, the Quiet Revolution of the 1960s, which transformed the province politically, also did the same for the trade union movement. The two came together in the 1964 legislation that granted public-sector employees the right to organize, bargain, and strike. Although similar legislation had been passed in Saskatchewan in 1944 when the socialist CCF Party was elected, it was the Quebec legislation that was adopted by the federal government and many of the provinces. Union organizing in Canada took a dramatic upward turn in 1964, which was also the beginning of the gap between it and the United States.

Canada versus the United States

The overall unionization gap in 1996 between the United States and Canada was 18 percentage points (32 percent in Canada vs. 14 percent in the United States), but the variation in the percentage of employees who belonged to a union was far greater among the various states and provinces. From table 7.1, we can see that in the United States, the range from the highest, New York at 26.8 percent, to the lowest, South Carolina at 3.7 percent, was 23.1 percentage points. Put another way, workers in the state of New York were more than seven times as likely to belong to a union than workers in South Carolina. In Canada, workers in the most organized province, Newfoundland (39.3 percent), were less than twice as likely to be a member of a union than workers in the least organized province, Alberta (22.3 percent).

The smaller range in union membership among Canadian provinces than among U.S. states may appear surprising in view of the fact that provinces, rather than the federal government, set labor laws for about 90 percent of Canada's workforce. This is far higher than the approximately 10 percent that is the responsibility of state governments in the United States.

TABLE 7.3
State and Provincial Correlations between 1996 and 2001
Union Density and Historical Averages

Canada

	1927–56	1966–92	1939–92	
1996	0.30*	0.67**	0.51**	
2001	0.31*	0.65**	0.52**	

United States

	1939–64	1939–74	1939–92	1982–92
1996	0.77***	0.82***	0.89***	0.96***
2001	0.79***	0.83***	0.91***	0.96***

* $p < 0.10$. ** $p < 0.05$. *** $p < 0.01$.

As discussed in chapter 3, despite much more discretion in labor relations matters than their counterparts to the south, provinces have tended to adopt similar approaches to labor matters. Beginning near the end of World War II, with only the few recent exceptions noted in chapter 3 such as the Conservative government elected in 1995 in Ontario, Canadian legislation has moved toward enshrining support for unions, whereas U.S. federal and state legislation has slowly eroded union protection.

Estimates of the Stability of the Rankings of States and Provinces

We need a more precise measure of the stability of ranking of union density in states and provinces. Table 7.3 contains the correlation coefficients between union density at the time of our survey (1996) and in 2001, and the historical average across states and provinces for several time periods. In the case of the United States, the correlation coefficients are all statistically significant at the 0.01 level of significance, indicating a relation between the period 1929–64 and 1996 that explains 50 percent of the observed difference in union density and between the period 1982–92 and 1996 that explains 90 percent. The level of significance for the correlation coefficients is somewhat lower in Canada in the early period, and overall the degree of explanation is also lower, although it should be noted that the time periods are different. Figure 7.1 is a scatterplot of union density by state, comparing the historical average for 1939–64 with union density in 1996. The upward slope of the plots is clearly visible, indicating the close

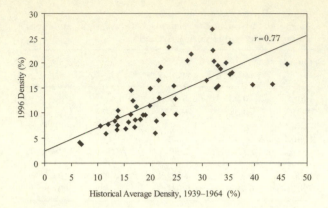

FIGURE 7.1
Scatterplot of union density by state, historical average (1939–1964) versus 1996.

association (correlation) between the historical average and 1996 union densities by state.

The results clearly show that there is a higher degree of persistence in rankings and variations in union density in the states than in the provinces. To put these results another way, the probability of a state remaining in the bottom one-third or the top one-third of union density rankings is greater than that of a province.

Sources of the Unionization Gap
Geographic Shifts in Employment

When union density rates tend to move together, how much of the unionization decline is due to the differing trends in density rates within the states and how much is due to the weighting of these rates by the proportion of employees in the states? In tables 7.4a–c we present three sets of calculations that separate the impact of these two measures (employment shares and density rates), comparing 1939 and 1996, 1953 and 1996, and 1939 and 1953. The technical term for these calculations is shift-share analysis. In each comparison we are asking how much of the change in overall union density is the result of the geographical shift of employment across states and how much is due to the change in union density within all states.

For the period 1939–96, union density declined by 7.2 percentage points. Of this, 1.8 percentage points (or 26 percent of the total decline)

TABLE 7.4a
Decomposition 1: Shift-Share Analysis (1939–1996)

	Percentage Points
Average probability of union membership in 1939[a]	21.22
Average probability of union membership in 1996[b]	14.05
Average probability of union membership in 1996 with 1939 interstate density[c]	19.39
Difference due to interstate density change (R)	5.3 (74)
Difference due to interstate employment share change (C)	1.8 (26)
Total difference due to density and employment share $(R+C)$[d]	7.2 (100)

Note: Numbers in parentheses represent the proportion (in percent) of the total difference in adult-youth preferences. The probabilities (in percent) are calculated and defined in notes a–d, where E is Employment share and U is Union density in state i

a $\bar{P}_{39} = \sum_{i=1}^{51} F[E_{39}U_{39}]_i.$

b $\bar{P}_{96} = \sum_{i=1}^{51} F[E_{96}U_{96}]_i.$

c $\bar{P}_{96}^{39} = \sum_{i=1}^{51} F[E_{96}U_{39}]_i.$

d $\left|\bar{P}_{39} - \bar{P}_{96}\right| = \underbrace{\bar{P}_{96} - \bar{P}_{96}^{39}}_{R} + \underbrace{\bar{P}_{96}^{39} - \bar{P}_{39}}_{C}.$

TABLE 7.4b
Decomposition 2: Shift-Share Analysis (1953–1996)

	Percentage Points
Average probability of union membership in 1953[a]	32.61
Average probability of union membership in 1996[b]	14.05
Average probability of union membership in 1996 with 1953 interstate density[c]	30.06
Difference due to interstate density change (R)	16.0 (86)
Difference due to interstate employment share change (C)	2.6 (14)
Total difference due to density and employment share $(R+C)$[d]	18.6 (100)

Note: Numbers in parentheses represent the proportion (in percent) of the total difference in adult-youth preferences. The probabilities (in percent) are calculated and defined in notes a–d, where E is Employment share and U is Union density in state i.

a $\bar{P}_{53} = \sum_{i=1}^{51} F[E_{53}U_{53}]_i.$

b $\bar{P}_{96} = \sum_{i=1}^{51} F[E_{96}U_{96}]_i.$

c $\bar{P}_{96}^{53} = \sum_{i=1}^{51} F[E_{96}U_{53}]_i.$

d $\left|\bar{P}_{53} - \bar{P}_{96}\right| = \underbrace{\bar{P}_{96} - \bar{P}_{96}^{53}}_{R} + \underbrace{\bar{P}_{96}^{53} - \bar{P}_{53}}_{C}.$

TABLE 7.4c
Decomposition 3: Shift-Share Analysis (1939–1953)

	Percentage Points
Average probability of union membership in 1939[a]	21.22
Average probability of union membership in 1953[b]	32.61
Average probability of union membership in 1953 with 1939 interstate density[c]	21.01
Difference due to interstate density change (*R*)	11.7 (101)
Difference due to interstate employment share change (*C*)	−0.3 (−0.1)
Total difference due to density and employment share (*R* + *C*)[d]	11.4 (100)

Note: The numbers in parentheses represent the proportion (in percent) of the total difference in adult-youth preferences. The probabilities (in percent) are calculated and defined in notes a–d, where *E* is Employment share and *U* is Union density in state *i*.

a $\bar{P}_{39} = \sum_{i=1}^{51} F[E_{39}U_{39}]_i.$

b $\bar{P}_{53} = \sum_{i=1}^{51} F[E_{53}U_{53}]_i.$

c $\bar{P}_{53}^{39} = \sum_{i=1}^{51} F[E_{53}U_{39}]_i.$

d $|\bar{P}_{39} - \bar{P}_{53}| = \underbrace{\bar{P}_{53} - \bar{P}_{53}^{39}}_{R} + \underbrace{\bar{P}_{53}^{39} - \bar{P}_{39}}_{C}.$

was the result of the geographic shift in employment from higher- to lower-union-density states. The larger share, 5.3 percentage points (or 74 percent of the total decline), resulted from a decline of union density within all states.

The period 1953–96 approximates the change from the high point in U.S. union density to the low point. In this case, union density overall plummeted by 18.6 percentage points. Of that total, 16.0 percentage points (or 86 percent of the total decline) resulted from declines in union density within states and only 2.6 percentage points (or 14 percent of the total decline) resulted from a shift in employment to lower-density states.

Strikingly, within-state density changes, as opposed to shifts in employment share, accounted for all the increase in density between 1939 and 1953, when the labor movement in the United States grew the most. Demographic and employment share shifts would have actually reduced union density in the country.

The results of the analysis therefore show that the largest contributor by far to the increase in union density in the United States in any period was the increase, and later the decrease, in union density rates within all states, whether they were high or low to begin with.

Public- and Private-Sector Differences

A second set of calculations relates to the composition of employment in the two countries by sector. We have used the division between private- and public-sector employment because there is such a large difference between the union density rates in these sectors within the two countries. In chapter 3 we note that the unionization gap between Canada and the United States opened up after 1964 and that it had two primary causes. First, there was more growth in public-sector unionization in Canada, which also has a larger public sector. Second, the rate of unionization in the private sector in Canada did not decline as much as in the United States because Canadians were more successful in continuing to organize in the private sector.

Turning now to the state or provincial experience in this regard, we first present public- and private-sector union density rates in 1997 in table 7.5. Canadian provinces rank at the top of both the private- and public-sector lists, with only two exceptions: Alberta and Prince Edward Island in the private sector and Nova Scotia in the public sector. Similarly, when the private- versus public-sector differences are considered, Canadian provinces tend to show the biggest differences, with the exception of the states of Rhode Island, New York, and Connecticut, where a very high rate of public-sector union density was associated with low rates of private-sector density. In the case of the state of New York, private-sector union density in 1997 was well above average, but the reason New York led the nation in union density was because of the very high level of public-sector density, 69.9 percent in 1996.

Differences in Attitudes and Values by State and Province

The preceding analysis indicates that there were deeply embedded state and, to a lesser extent, provincial differences in union density throughout most of the twentieth century. These differences are important contributors to the unionization gap because, as has been shown, the individual U.S. states have maintained their relative union density rankings for more than half a century. The largest source of the increase (and then decrease) in union density in individual states was the change in the extent of unionization within all states as opposed to a shift of employment from the Northeast to the nonunion Sunbelt. The question to be explored now is whether these state or provincial differences in union density are consistent with the measures developed in earlier chapters at the national level

TABLE 7.5
State and Provincial Union Density Rankings, 1997

Rank by Sector				Rank by Difference between Sectors			
Private Sector		Public Sector					
State/Province	%	State/Province	%	State/Province	Public Sector (%)	Private Sector (%)	Difference (%)
1. Quebec	32	1. Quebec	84	1. P.E.I.	77	13	64
2. B.C.	28	2. B.C.	81	2. Rhode Island	69	11	58
3. Newfoundland	26	3. Manitoba	79	3. Saskatchewan	77	22	55
4. Manitoba	25	4. Newfoundland	78	4. Alberta	71	16	55
5. Saskatchewan	22	5. Saskatchewan	77	5. Manitoba	79	25	54
6. Ontario	21	6. P.E.I.	77	6. New York	70	16	54
7. Nova Scotia	19	7. Ontario	75	7. Ontario	75	21	54
8. New Brunswick	18	8. New Brunswick	72	8. B.C.	81	28	54
9. Michigan	18	9. Alberta	71	9. New Brunswick	72	18	53
10. Hawaii	18	10. New York	70	10. Newfoundland	78	26	52
11. Alberta	16	11. Nova Scotia	69	11. Quebec	84	32	51
12. New York	16	12. Rhode Island	69	12. Connecticut	62	11	51
13. Nevada	16	13. New Jersey	62	13. Nova Scotia	69	19	50
14. New Jersey	15	14. Connecticut	62	14. New Jersey	62	15	47
15. Illinois	15	15. Michigan	58	15. Massachusetts	55	9	46

Note: Top fifteen listed in order for each category. B.C., British Columbia; P.E.I., Prince Edward Island.

to distinguish among the attitudes and values in the populations. In particular, we want to know whether interstate differences in preferences for unions, social democratic values, and individualistic versus communitarian attitudes are as consistent across states as they are between Canada and the United States. If union density differences at the state level are associated with other common factors, this provides additional information explaining the unionization gap between Canada and the United States.

The results of our survey suggest that there are fundamental differences among states that appear to predate available measures of attitudes and union density by state or province. For example, a disproportionate number of low-density states are located in the South, where states appear to have always been hostile to unions. These attitudes predate the passing of their union-unfriendly laws—euphemistically known as right-to-work provisions. In addition, many states, mostly in the South and West, prohibited union-shop agreements, provisions that in a Canadian context would be described as the right to free-ride on the benefits gained by a union. Canada took the opposite approach, giving unions the option of requiring the payment of union dues by nonunion employees who are a part of the bargaining unit and, hence, benefit from the gains attained through collective bargaining for all employees.

We explored a number of considerations in attempting to determine whether state differences in attitudes are correlated with differences in union density. Answers to eight questions produced significant differences between union density rates for states and provinces; those findings are summarized here.

Job satisfaction: Comparing employees in high- and low-union-density states, those states with high union densities had employees whose level of job satisfaction was significantly lower than that of employees in low-union-density states.

Fair treatment by employer: Employees in states with a high union density had a significantly lower rating of employers' fair treatment of employees than did employees in low-density states.

Paid fairly last year: Employees in high-union-density states responded that they felt they were paid less fairly than did employees in low-density states.

Loyalty to employer: A surprising finding in view of the foregoing is that employees in high-density states were more loyal to their employers than were employees in low-density states. Perhaps this is explained by the fact that unionized employees tend to stay with an employer longer than do nonunionized employees.

Religious attendance: There appears to be an inverse relationship between the degree of church attendance and union density. In low-union-density states, church attendance was significantly higher than in high-union-density states. Could unions be a substitute for church attendance, and if so, why?

Union side favored in labor dispute: Not surprisingly, people in high-density states and provinces favored the union in labor disputes to a much greater extent than did employees in low-density states.

Union approval: As we would expect, there is a significant difference in union preferences between individual employees in low-union-density states and high-density states. When union members are excluded from the sample, the results are not as dramatic or as significant. It appears that among nonunion members, the approval of unions is quite similar across states with wildly differing union-density levels. This suggests that there is an unmet demand for union representation in low-density states.

Intention to vote for a union: In terms of voting intentions, there is no appreciable difference across high- and low-union-density states. Because the actual rate of unionization differs markedly, this again reinforces the observation that there are unmet union representation needs in low-union-density states.

The Impact of State and Provincial Differences

The analysis of the relation between state or provincial differences and the cross-border unionization gap leads to the following conclusions:

1. There is considerable stability in the ranking of states, and to a lesser extent provinces, in the percentage of union members, even though the rates have risen and then declined over time.

2. States with low union density remain low over a period of more than six decades; states with high union density have a similar pattern. The consistent low union densities in certain states therefore preceded the

introduction of right-to-work laws in the states at the bottom of the density ranking.

3. Provincial rankings are relatively more volatile, although Ontario has been low for most of the period and British Columbia high.

4. Shift-share analyses show that the declines (and increases) in national union density rates in the United States have not been due to a movement of employment to nonunion states. This means that although states have maintained their relative rankings in terms of union density, levels of union density have generally fallen or risen across the whole country.

5. Workers in states with high density display a relatively greater belief in receiving less-fair treatment by employers in general and in less-fair pay in particular, as well as feeling less satisfied with their jobs, than workers in low-density states.

6. People in states where church attendance is high are less likely to belong to unions and vice versa. That is, union membership and church attendance are inversely related.

In summary, these findings point to the substantial influence of interstate and interprovincial factors in explaining the cross-border differences in unionization highlighted in earlier chapters. It could be said that Canada and the United States are both diverse countries that contain in some cases (more in the U.S. than the Canadian case) as much heterogeneity within as across national borders.

8 Unions among Professionals and Other White-Collar Workers in the United States

It has been forty years since Seymour Lipset (1962/1967) first sought to analyze the attitudes and behavior of professionals and other white-collar workers, such as technical, clerical, and sales workers, toward unions.[1] Noting the weakness of unionism among professionals and other white-collar employees in the United States, the original paper discussed the main obstacles among this nonmanual stratum, focusing on structural factors and attitudes toward labor organizations. Social stratification effects along class and gender lines were associated with the position of organized labor among this group. In general, white-collar workers saw themselves as having higher status than manual workers, even when their wages were lower. The professional associations seemingly associated with status served as functional alternatives to unions, explaining in part low rates of union membership among professionals. The available survey evidence on attitudes led to a tentative conclusion that nonmanual unionism drew disproportionate support from people who felt resentful about their jobs, who did not identify with the middle class, and who tended to be liberal politically.

During the next four decades, unions and collective bargaining made headway among a number of professions, especially teachers and nurses. The June 1999 decision by the American Medical Association (AMA) to form a union of physicians and the affiliation of the 17,000-member Boeing engineers' and technical workers' society with the AFL-CIO in winter 2000, put doctors and engineers on the frontier of professional unionism. In this chapter, we reexamine the position of unionism among professionals and nonmanual workers generally in the United States. We seek to compare changes that have occurred in the attitudes and behavior

of nonmanual employees—professionals and other white-collar workers—
toward unions since 1962.

Structural Changes and Union Density

The 1962 study points to two facts that stood out in the writing on white-
collar workers and professionals with respect to their orientations toward
unions. First, inherent in the various changes in the technological and business practices of modern industry had been a rapid increase in nonmanual
work. The study notes that in the United States the occupations called
white-collar had grown from 17.6 percent of the employed labor force in
1900 to 31.1 percent in 1940 to 42.4 percent in 1959 (Lipset 1962/1967,
525). Data from the Bureau of Labor Statistics (BLS) indicate that these
structural changes continue. The proportion of white-collars in the labor
force reached 60 percent by 1998 in the United States. There are now
many more nonmanual employees than manual ones, and the steady trend
has widened the discrepancy. In the Unites States, the number of blue-
collar workers topped at 41.1 percent in 1950, up slightly from 35.8
percent in 1900, but then fell off steadily to 24 percent in 2001 (fig. 8.1).
The primary reason for the reduction in the number of blue-collar workers
was the decline in the proportion employed in manufacturing, from 26.1

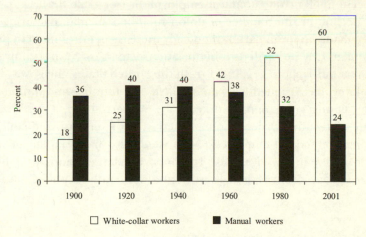

FIGURE 8.1

Employed people by major occupation group, 1900–2001 in the United States (% distribution). Includes self-employed. (*Source: Current Statistics* 1998, 3; Bureau of Labor Statistics
2002, http://stats.bls.gov/.)

percent in 1960 to 16.4 percent in 1995 in the Unites States. This down-ward trend characterizes all major industrialized countries (see table 8.1).

Second, nonmanual employees were less likely to belong to labor unions than manual workers in most countries, not just in the United States. A comparative study of white-collar unionization in industrialized nations in the early 1960s reported that, with the possible exception of Japan, the rates of union density among white-collar workers were lower than among manual workers (Sturmthal 1966, 375–77). Two sets of the 1996 data show anew that white-collar employees have disproportionately lower rates of union membership than blue-collar workers. According to the BLS, as of 1996 the rate of union membership among white-collars in the United States is half (11 percent) that of blue-collar workers (23 percent). Our own 1996 survey (Lipset-Meltz) reports a similar relationship: 14 percent of the nonmanual employees were union members compared with 30 percent of blue-collar workers. Union membership among white-collar workers has not changed significantly since the 1950s, when it numbered around 12 percent (Blum et al. 1971, 7).

Changes in industrial structure explain part of the decline in union density, which dropped in the Unites States from 32.5 percent in 1953 to 13.5 percent in 2001.[2] The declining manufacturing sector has been the traditional stronghold of unionism. But union membership also fell greatly within it. Density was even lower in the other private nonagricultural sectors. As of 2001, it was 14.6 percent in manufacturing, compared with 9.0 percent in all private nonfarm employment (see table 8.2).

The decline in the number of union members in manufacturing jobs has been made up for in part by the steady increase in enrollment in public employment. U.S. union density in the latter sector has grown steadily from 11.6 percent in 1953 to 37.4 in 2001. In the United States, the government as employer has frequently been positive for unions, and unions are stronger among government workers (see Western 1997, 17). President Kennedy's Executive Order 10,988, issued in 1962, encouraged collective bargaining for federal employees. Most states also have similar laws (see Freeman and Ichniowski 1988). Teachers, the largest and most highly unionized group of professionals, work predominantly in public schools.

Differentiation within the Nonmanual Stratum

In analyzing attitudes and behavior within the nonmanual stratum toward unions, it is necessary to differentiate among the various groups. As noted,

TABLE 8.1
Civilian Employment by Economic Sector in Selected Countries (%)

Country	Agriculture[a]			Manufacturing			Mining & Construction			Services[b]		
	1960	1980	1995	1960	1980	1995	1960	1980	1995	1960	1980	1995
United States	8.5	3.6	2.9	26.1	22.1	16.4	7.3	7.2	6.6	58.1	67.1	74.1
Canada	13.3	5.4	4.1	24.7	19.7	15.3	7.3	7.7	6.6	54.7	67.2	74.0
Australia[c]	9.7	6.5	5.0	26.2	19.4	13.6	9.6	9.2	8.3	54.5	64.8	73.1
Japan	29.5	10.1	5.5	21.7	25.0	22.7	6.8	10.1	10.4	41.9	54.8	61.4
France	23.2	8.5	4.7	28.2	25.8	20.4[d]	9.3	9.3	7.4	39.3	56.4	69.8[e]
Germany	13.9	5.2	2.8[f]	34.4	34.0	29.1[g]	11.6	8.9	5.7	40.2	51.9	62.4[h]
Italy[i]	32.5	14.2	7.4	24.0	26.9	24.4	10.2	11.2	8.1	33.4	47.7	60.1
Netherlands	10.3	5.2	3.9	29.0	21.3	16.4	10.0	8.4	6.4	50.8	65.1	73.4
Sweden	15.8	5.6	3.5	31.6	24.3	19.0	8.0	7.2	6.0	44.6	62.9	71.5
United Kingdom	4.7	2.6	2.1	36.0	28.3	19.1	10.1	7.9	7.6	49.2	61.2	71.2

Source: Bureau of Labor Statistics (http://www.bls.gov/fls/flsfore.txt).
[a] Agriculture, forestry, hunting, and fishing.
[b] Transportation, communication, public utilities, trade, finances, public administration, private household services, and miscellaneous servies.
[c] 1965 data are earliest data available.
[d] For 1992.
[e] Preliminary data.
[f] For 1994.
[g] For 1993.
[h] For 1994.
[i] 1995 figures are preliminary.

TABLE 8.2
Union Density by Industry in the United States (%)

Industry	1930	1940	1953	1966	1970	1980	1989	1995	1998	2001
Manufacturing	7.8	30.5	42.4	37.4	38.7	32.3	21.6	17.6	15.8	14.6
Mining	21.3	72.1	64.7	35.7	35.7	32.1	17.5	13.8	12.2	12.3
Construction	64.5	77.0	83.8	41.4	39.2	31.6	21.5	17.7	17.8	18.4
Transportation and public utilities	22.6	47.3	79.9	n.a.	44.9	48.0	31.6	27.3	25.8	23.5
Services, trade, finance, insurance, and real estate	2.3	5.7	9.5	n.a.	7.8	11.6	5.5	5.4	5.0	4.1

Source: Troy (1986, 87); *Statistical Abstract of the United States* (1996, 438; 1991, 425); Bureau of Labor Statistics (1999; 2002).
Note: Excludes self-employed and farm workers. Because of changes in industrial classifications, data are not always strictly comparable. N.a., not available.

the most important structural correlate of union membership has been the position in the stratification structure, with some major exceptions. The more privileged a group is in terms of income or status, the more likely it has been to reject the appeal of trade unions (Lipset 1962/1967, 526).

Our 1996 survey reports the percentages of respondents in the non-manual stratum belonging to unions by occupation as follows: 5 percent in the executive, administrative, and managerial occupations; 10 percent of professionals (excluding teachers and professors); 50 percent of teachers and professors; 8 percent in sales; 14 percent in technical positions; 15 percent in clerical jobs; 14 percent in service occupations; 34 percent of precision production, craft, and repair workers; and 28 percent of operators, fabricators, and laborers.[3] We consider teachers and professors as a separate category because they are very much more likely to belong to unions than any other segment of the stratum (table 8.3).

Expressed preference to join unions shows the same pattern as union membership. The survey found that a desire to join a union is voiced by 26 percent of nonunionists in the executive, administrative, and managerial occupations; 23 percent of professionals (excluding teachers and professors); 27 percent in technical positions; 31 percent in sales; 26 percent in clerical; 43 percent in service jobs; 36 percent of skilled workers; and 37 percent of less-skilled workers. Teachers and professors are close to the top at 38 percent. More nonunionists in all occupational categories said that they would vote for a union if a collective bargaining election were held tomorrow than expressed a desire to be members. The proportions are also inversely related to occupational status (table 8.3).

The unionization rate among professionals in the United States has almost doubled since the 1962 article was first published. According to the 1996 survey, it reached 19 percent for the group as a whole. But, as noted, without teachers and professors it is 10 percent. Membership among teachers has increased enormously, contrasting with the decline or stagnation of unionization among workers in general and among other categories of nonmanual employees in particular. For example, the 1996 survey found a 13 percent unionization rate among clerical and sales workers compared with the 17 percent reported in the 1962 article.

The earlier paper notes a then-little-known fact that "within the ranks of the white-collars the number of people employed in professional, technical, and managerial tasks is now greater than the number in clerical and sales work and the rate of growth of the former remains higher" (Lipset 1962/1967, 527). This structural development has continued. According

TABLE 8.3
Union Density, Preference to Join a Union, and Union Approval by Occupational Group in the United States (%)

	Executive, Administrative and Managerial	Professionals[a]	Teachers and Professors	Technical Occupations	Sales	Clerical Occupations and Secretaries	Service Occupations	Precision Production, Craft, and Repair	Operators, Fabricators, and Laborers
Union members									
Yes	5	10	50	14	8	15	14	34	28
No	95	90	50	86	92	85	86	66	72
N	139	201	62	71	87	154	162	74	184
Prefer to belong to unions[c]									
Yes	26	23	38	27	31	26	43	36	37
No	58	59	62	59	52	58	41	61	54
Don't know/not stated	16	18	0	15	17	16	16	3	9
N	89	122	21	41	54	88	94	33	89
General union approval index[b]									
Disapprove	28	28	19	20	19	17	15	12	16
Neutral	21	21	19	27	20	33	12	24	22
Approve	51	51	62	54	61	50	73	64	62
N	89	122	21	41	54	88	94	33	89

Source: Lipset-Meltz survey.
Note: Percentages may not add to 100 because of rounding.
[a] Excluding teachers and professors.
[b] Nonmembers.

to the BLS, professional, technical, managerial, and administrative workers constituted 22.1 percent of the employed workers in 1960, 24.7 in 1970, and 27.3 in 1980. Clerical and sales workers formed 21.2 percent of the employed workers in 1960, 23.6 in 1970, and 24.9 percent in 1980 (*Statistical Abstract of the United States* 1996, 401).

Any further trend analysis is complicated by the fact that the occupation classification system used by the BLS has changed since 1980 (*Statistical Abstract of the United States* 1981, 391) so that the criteria used in the 1990s by the BLS differ from earlier years. Technicians and related support workers are now a separate subcategory and are included in the category of technical, sales, and administrative support workers. However, when we employ the old classification for purposes of comparison, managerial, administrative, executive, professional, and technical workers add up to 32.8 percent of employees in 1998 compared with 26.1 percent of sales and administrative support workers.

Stratification and Gender Roles

It has been difficult to relate the stratification position of nonmanual workers to union behavior and attitudes without dealing with the interrelation of stratification and gender within the stratum. The earlier paper documented the privileged position of males. Men held 84 percent of managerial and 64 percent of professional and technical positions in 1950. Women were much more likely to be found in lesser-status and lower-paid occupations; for example, women occupied 62 percent of clerical positions in 1950 (Lipset 1962/1967, 528).

Gender-related differences in the occupational structure have diminished significantly since the 1950s. Women's labor force participation rate has increased from 34 percent in 1950, to 38 percent in 1960, to 52 percent in 1980, to 59 percent in 1994 (Spain and Bianchi 1996, 81). According to the BLS, the proportion of women in executive, administrative, and managerial positions reached 43 percent in 1995, up from 16 percent in 1960. As well, women held the majority of professional jobs at 53 percent in 1995 (*Statistical Abstract of the United States* 1996, 405). Women constituted a majority of teachers (75 percent), registered nurses (93 percent), dietitians (93 percent), librarians (84 percent), and social workers (68 percent). They had increased their numbers but were still a minority among natural scientists (27 percent in 1995 compared with 11 percent in 1960), engineers (8 vs. 1 percent), physicians (24 vs. 7 percent), and lawyers (26 vs. 4 percent) (*Statistical Abstract of the United States* 1996, 405; 1963, 232).[4] However, women still formed a large majority of the lower-level support staff, including clerical positions (80 percent).

A comparison of survey data cited in the 1962 paper with information obtained from a 1997 *Washington Post*–Kaiser Family Foundation–Harvard University national poll reveals dramatic changes in the attitudes of female workers toward their role in the economy. The older research reported that absolute majorities of white-collar workers, 85 percent of men and 65 percent of women, preferred a male supervisor (Lipset 1962/1967, 529). But when questioned in the 1997 survey about whether they personally preferred to deal with a male or female supervisor at work, a much smaller, but similar proportion across gender lines, 39 percent of men and 37 percent of women, chose a man. Almost half, 46 percent of men and close to one-third of women (30 percent) responded that the gender of a supervisor did not matter. One-third of women (33 percent) and almost one-seventh of men (15 percent) prefer female supervisors.

When asked in the 1950s "Is it your ambition to hold the same position as your supervisor in your company or isn't that important to you?" one-half of men (48 percent) compared to 27 percent of the women answered that they desired a supervisory position (Lipset 1962/1967, 529). But when queried in the 1997 *Washington Post* study "Would you like to have a top executive or professional position where you work, or isn't that something you'd be interested in doing?" almost the same proportion, 38 percent of male respondents and 34 percent of female respondents answered "yes" (*Washington Post* 1998 database, http://www.washingtonpost.com/wp-srv/politics/polls/vault/stories/98gender_data_a.htm).

Unlike the situation in the 1950s, the Lipset-Meltz 1996 survey indicates that there are no longer any significant gender differences in union density in most groups of white-collar workers. Similar proportions, 4 percent of the female respondents and 6 percent of the male respondents in the executive, administrative, and managerial category, and 13 percent of female and 15 percent of male respondents in the technical, sales, and clerical group were union members as of the late 1990s. Gender, however, differentiates among the professionals and managers. Female teachers and professors are more likely than males to be union members, 53 versus 42 percent, and to prefer to belong to unions, 62 versus 49 percent. Non-teaching professionals show the same pattern. Among managers, the preference to join a union is significantly higher among women than men, 36 to 14 percent (table 8.4).[5] However, these gender differences may result from the fact that much higher proportions of women than men work at the lower levels of management.

Obstacles to White-Collar Unionism

As noted earlier, social stratification factors have influenced union membership rates. The 1962 paper indicated that white-collar workers viewed themselves as having higher status than blue-collar workers. This sense of greater prestige appeared to have presented an obstacle to union growth among the nonmanual workers (Lipset 1962/1967, 531).

The 1996 survey data indicate that the pattern continues. White-collar employees still consider their social status to be higher than manual workers. Three-quarters of the executive, administrative and managerial respondents (74 percent); 70 percent of the nonteaching professionals; 72 percent of the teachers and professors; 59 percent of the technical workers; 55 percent of the sales workers; and 54 percent of the clerical workers and secretaries identify themselves as members of the middle or upper class, compared with 45 percent of the service workers; 58 percent of the precision production, craft, and repair workers; and 42 percent of the operators, fabricators, and laborers.

As noted, unionization is much stronger in government employment than in the private sector. The 1996 survey finds that union density in the public sector is almost three times higher than in the private sector, 38 and 13 percent, respectively. The BLS figures are similar. Rates of unionization are significantly higher in the public sector across every major occupational category. Among public-sector employees, one-third of professionals (34 percent), and 39 percent of technical, sales, and clerical workers belonged to unions, compared with 8 percent of both groups in the private sector. Three-fifths of teachers and professors (59 percent) employed by government reported themselves to be union members, compared with 26 percent employed by private schools. The discrepancy between these figures gathered in a national survey by the BLS and the membership reports from the unions may result from around 1 million NEA members' not reporting themselves as union members.

Teachers and professors had the highest proportion employed in the public sector among professional groups—73 percent of teachers and professors compared with 24 percent of other professionals. Three-fifths of nonteaching professional (59 percent) were employed in the private sector, while only 9 percent of the teachers and professors were.

TABLE 8.4
Union Membership and Preferences by Occupational Group and Gender in the United States (%)

	Executive, Administrative, and Managerial		Professionals[a]		Teachers and Professors		Technical Occupations	
	F	M	F	M	F	M	F	M
Union members								
Yes	4	6	11	8	53	42	13	15
No	96	94	89	92	47	55	87	85
N	67	40	108	92	35	26	36	35
Prefer to belong to unions								
Yes	36	14	31	22	62	49	32	36
No	47	75	46	68	38	49	45	63
Don't know/not stated	17	11	23	10	0	2	24	1
N	67	40	108	115	35	26	36	35

Source: Lipset-Meltz survey.
Note: Percentages may not add up to 100 because of rounding.
[a] Excluding teachers and professors.
[b] The number of observations in this category is very small.

The 1962 paper discussed some of the ways that the work milieu affects union numbers and prospects. The greater strength of unions in big companies, then and in 1996, seems to relate to the facts that the larger the size of the job environment the more impersonal the relationship between the supervisors or owners and workers, and that unions are better able to reach workers in large plants; the engineers at Boeing are probably in a situation closer to this than professionals elsewhere. It is also a supply-side phenomenon in that it pays for unions to direct more organizing efforts toward large establishments. The cost of organizing small companies is often prohibitive, especially in the face of managerial opposition.

White-collar workers expressed more positive attitudes than manual workers about their relations with management. Significantly more nonmanual employees, at all levels, than blue-collar workers believed that interests of employers and employees are the same. Smaller proportions of the executive, administrative, and managerial respondents (17 percent); teachers and professors (13 percent); sales workers (14 percent); and clericals and secretaries (19 percent) said that they received poor or very poor treatment by employers, as compared with technical workers (29 percent); operators, fabricators, and laborers (28 percent); and service workers (26 percent) (table 8.5).

Sales		Clerical Occupations and Secretaries		Service Occupations		Precision Production, Craft, and Repair		Operators, Fabricators, and Laborers	
F	M	F	M	F	M	F[b]	M	F	M
9	6	14	20	8	22	—	34	28	28
91	94	86	80	92	78	—	66	72	72
42	45	109	41	92	68	—	95	57	164
41	29	31	42	49	43	—	53	52	49
31	67	55	42	39	39	—	43	38	44
28	3	14	15	12	17	—	4	11	7
42	45	109	41	89	60	—	95	57	164

Nonmanual workers tended to give their management higher evaluations than blue-collar workers for appreciating what they (the workers) did. White-collar employees were also more likely than blue-collar and service workers to side with the company when they heard about a labor dispute. Clericals and secretaries, although relatively low in status and pay, perform work duties that put many of them in close contact with management. They showed higher degrees of loyalty toward employers than did blue-collar workers. They were more likely to back the company in a labor dispute, to believe that employees and employers interests are the same, and to report better treatment and appreciation from management than blue-collar workers do (see table 8.6).

Not surprisingly, professionals and managerial personnel were less likely to approve of labor unions and exhibit less confidence in organized labor and labor leaders than blue-collar workers (Brint 1985, 394–95). As expected, all groups of nonmanual workers, except teachers and professors, exhibited lower levels of general union approval than the blue-collars in the 1996 survey. It is noteworthy that union approval among clerical workers and secretaries, low-paid occupations, was significantly lower than union approval among higher-wage blue-collar workers (table 8.3).

TABLE 8.5
Attitudes toward Management by Major Occupational Group in the United States (%)

	Executive, Administrative, and Managerial	Professionals[a]	Teachers and Professors	Technical Occupations	Sales	Clerical Occupations and Secretaries	Service Occupations	Precision Production, Craft, and Repair	Operators, Fabricators, and Laborers
Employees' and employers' interests									
Opposite	33	35	31	39	36	41	40	55	46
Same	67	65	69	61	64	59	60	45	54
N	135	198	61	69	87	153	161	74	178
Treatment of employees by management									
Very good	37	32	35	26	36	32	30	30	26
Good	47	46	53	44	50	48	45	46	46
Poor	12	19	12	25	10	13	19	19	18
Very poor	5	3	1	4	4	6	7	4	10
N	137	200	61	70	89	154	161	74	183
Management's appreciation of what you do									
Very good	41	34	39	31	37	35	36	28	26
Good	40	46	46	43	47	45	40	44	44
Poor	14	15	14	16	11	13	15	18	14
Very poor	6	5	1	10	5	7	9	9	16
N	137	198	60	71	87	154	161	74	183
Hearing labor disputes sides with[b]									
Union	42	59	78	58	55	58	72	80	70
Company	58	41	22	42	45	42	28	20	30
N	105	154	47	50	65	128	124	53	142

Source: Lipset-Meltz survey.

Note: Percentages may not add to 100 because of rounding.

[a] Excluding teachers and professors.

[b] Excludes Don't know/not stated.

Where Is Nonmanual Unionism Found?

The earlier research reported that "among low-level white-collar workers, strong unionism is generally found in situations where the work conditions are similar to those of the manual workers, often also involving the employment of a significant number of males" (Lipset 1962/1967, 534). Reflecting the significant changes in the employment patterns of women over the last generation, gender in the 1990s had a much smaller effect on unionization than in the 1950s.

Clerical employees in the railroad industry and white-collar workers in postal, telegraph, and telephone occupations were all well organized in the 1950s. Unionization rates among them were higher than for many manual positions. Labor unions in such nonmanual occupations were predominantly male with few exceptions. Since then, the proportion of women workers has increased significantly in these categories, but they remain strongholds of unionism. An overwhelming majority, 81 percent of post office mail carriers, 74 percent of postal clerks, and 23 percent of telephone operators compared to 13 percent of all clerical and kindred workers belonged to unions in 1998. Technological changes resulted in a disappearance of telegraph operators and ticket, station, and express agents as separate occupation categories in the 1998 Current Population Survey (data provided by Barry Hirsch; see Hirsch and MacPherson 1993). In 1980, 62 percent of telegraph operators and 34 percent of ticket, station, and express agents, compared with 16 percent of all clerical and kindred workers, belonged to unions (Kokkelenberg and Sockell 1985). Closer links to manual workers in the industries in which they worked may explain the higher union density.

The analysis of the Lipset-Meltz survey indicates that, compared to nonunionists, union members in the United States are more welfare-state-oriented and more likely to identify with and vote for the Democratic Party. Almost one-half of union members (45 percent) in precision production, craft, and repair, compared to 28 percent of nonmembers, identified with the Democratic Party. The percentages among operators, fabricators, and laborers are 39 and 26 percent. Professionals and clericals showed the same pattern of party sentiment. However, some groups, such as service occupations, were exceptions (table 8.6).

Leftism among unionized teachers and professors was expressed not in being more supporting of the Democrats but in rejecting both major parties. Unionists among the teachers and professors scored higher on a social democratic attitudes scale than nonunion people. Other data indi-

TABLE 8.6
Relation of Union Membership to Political Identification by Occupation in the United States (%)

	Executive, Administrative, and Managerial		Professionals[a]		Teachers and Professors		Technical Occupations	
	Member	Nonmember	Member	Nonmember	Member	Nonmember	Member	Nonmember
Party identification								
Republican	46	32	19	29	25	29	30	32
Democratic	31	31	45	36	37	43	45	44
Independent[b]	22	37	37	35	38	29	25	24
N	17	88	52	121	78	21	23	41
Social democratic scale								
Libertarian	58	44	47	48	38	67	43	37
Neutral	42	49	44	44	58	33	41	49
Social democratic	0	7	9	7	4	0	16	15
N	18	89	52	122	79	21	25	41

Source: Lipset-Meltz survey.
Note: Percentages may not add to 100 because of rounding.
[a] Excluding teachers and professors.
[b] Includes Other and Nothing.

cate that National Education Association (NEA) members are much less social democratic than American Federation of Teachers (AFT) members. And a significant proportion, almost one-half of the former, do not consider the NEA to be a union.

Professionals and Trade Unions

One of the major distinctions between professionals and other occupations is that professionals are assumed to be concerned with the fulfillment of certain intrinsic values, such as disinterested service and universalistic standards based on science or intellect, which are different from and even opposed to the money-making emphasis of business (Lipset 1962/1967, 537–38; Lipset and Schwartz 1966, 307; Parsons 1949). A prime characteristic of professionals is a desire for a high degree of independence and for control and evaluation by their own group, not by employers (Ladd and Lipset 1975, 244).

With the possible exception of large business owners and managers, professionals as a group are the most privileged and satisfied stratum in the society. They are accorded more prestige by the general public and receive

Sales Occupations		Clerical Occupations and Secretaries		Service Occupations		Precision Production, Craft, and Repair		Operators, Fabricators, and Laborers	
Member	Nonmember	Member	Nonmember	Member	Nonmember	Member	Nonmember	Member	Nonmember
32	33	26	21	36	23	22	38	15	25
12	31	54	29	33	42	45	28	39	26
56	36	20	50	31	35	33	34	46	49
16	52	57	87	57	93	60	32	130	88
23	33	27	38	39	21	24	33	23	39
54	61	63	58	50	65	68	58	64	45
23	6	10	5	11	14	8	9	14	16
17	54	61	88	57	94	65	33	132	89

higher pay than other occupational categories.[6] Therefore, it is not surprising that professionals are more likely to perceive themselves to be in the middle and upper classes. Those in professional positions have been found to exhibit a high degree of job satisfaction, perhaps because these positions provide more autonomy, freedom for personal decision, and individual creativity than other occupations (Lipset and Schwartz 1966, 300). These characteristics help explain the greater aversion of U.S. professionals to labor unions compared to manual workers because they undermine the desire to organize and act collectively to achieve some greater measure of standing and voice vis-à-vis a dominant outside party, such as business management. The more recent turn toward unionization among physicians is a direct consequence of their loss of autonomy to HMOs.

Social status is closely associated with occupational autonomy. Members of occupations characterized by a high degree of self-control have a greater sense of individual standing and importance, one that they guard jealously. The more collectivist and egalitarian norms of unionism have been more readily acceptable by those with lesser personal status and freedom of action (Ladd and Lipset 1975, 244–45).

Thorstein Veblen (1933), Talcott Parsons (1949, 186), and Bertrand de Jouvenal (1954, 118–20) suggested that the professions face a conflict between professional norms and the demands of the market. Modern society relies mainly on the market to distribute rewards, but many professionals believe practitioners rather than the market should determine quality in their fields. It may be inferred that they tend to view the market and employers with disdain (Lipset 1960/1981, 341–42; Lipset and Schwartz 1966; Lipset and Dobson 1972; Ladd and Lipset 1973, 1975). The conflict between professional norms and the demands of the market may be one of the main factors explaining the spread of unionism and leftist policies among the more artistic and intellectual professionals (Bendel 1991, 26–27). The 1962 paper reports that actors, musicians, journalists, airline pilots and flight engineers, ship captains, marine engineers, teachers, nurses, and social service employees had their own unions or professional associations involved in collective bargaining. The professions that in 1998 showed the highest propensity for unionization were quite similar—teachers and nurses have gained the most (see table 8.7).

Teachers

Teacher unions have grown considerably since the 1950s. The AFT, the "pure" teacher union that is affiliated to the AFL-CIO, has almost 1 million members, compared to 50 thousand in 1959 (Kassalow 1966, 340). The larger independent union, the NEA, reports a membership of almost 2.5 million as of 1998. The NEA was a professional association, not a union, in the 1950s. Its leadership, reacting to the growth of the AFT, gradually transformed the organization into one that engaged in collective bargaining, union representation elections, and strikes (Lieberman 1997).

Several explanations have been put forward to explain the strength of teacher unionism. Saltzman (1985) argues that the enactment of mandatory bargaining laws was the main factor in their growth in the public sector (see also Saltzman 1988). Organizational rivalry also helps explain the rapid increase in unionism among teachers. Competition between the AFT and the NEA for new members has been intense. The American Association of University Professors (AAUP) also takes part in the competition, although only in higher education (Garbarino 1986; Ladd and Lipset 1975, 248–50).

The history of the NEA provides an explanation for the numerical spread of unionism. The NEA originally served as a professional association of teachers. In 1956, it reported a membership equaling 53 percent of all elementary and secondary schoolteachers (Lipset 1962/1967, 546). At that time, it opposed collective bargaining as alien to the goals of teaching professionals. Faced with competition for members from the growing AFT, however, the NEA became involved in collective bargaining, union representation elections and strikes, and by the end of the 1960s the NEA had become a full-fledged teachers' union, in fact if not in name (Ladd and Lipset 1975, 247–50). Its leaders and publications describe the organization as a union (Murphy 1990; Lieberman, Haar, and Troy 1994; Lieberman 1997).

Surveys appear to underestimate union density among teachers. The Current Population Survey data indicate that about 2,200,000 teachers are union members (data from Barry Hirsch; see Hirsch and MacPherson 1993), but the combined reported membership in the NEA and the AFT is more than 3,300,000 (tables 8.7 and 8.8). One reason for the discrepancy is that many teachers who are NEA members give a negative response when asked in surveys whether they are union members, presumably reflecting their preference for a professional association and seemingly still thinking of the NEA as a professional organization, not a union. Surveys of the membership of both organizations indicate that NEA members are more conservative politically than AFT adherents and that many of the former dislike the AFL-CIO. The perception of the NEA as a professional association by a significant number of its members undoubtedly contributed to the failure of a proposal for a merger with the AFT that had been accepted by the leaders of both groups.

The hypothesis that social status and union membership among professionals are inversely related is supported by the fact that union density among professors (16 percent) is much lower than union density among teachers in schools (44 percent) (table 8.7). Within higher education, the less prestigious institutions demonstrate a much higher propensity to unionize (Garbarino 1986, 271–72; Ladd and Lipset 1973, 25–33).

Other Professions

Similar factors apply to the increase in unionization among nurses and other professionals or semiprofessionals with relatively low status and income. Fifteen percent of the 2 million registered nurses reported belonging to unions in 1998. The American Nurses Association (ANA), like the NEA, originated as a professional association. The ANA took over collective bargaining functions after the end of the World War II and takes part in union representation elections (see Kassalow 1966, 351–52). It has 210,000 members. Like NEA members, many belonging to the ANA

TABLE 8.7
Ranking of Union Affiliation of Professionals in the United States, 1998

	Employed Wage and Salary (thousands)	Union Density (%)
Professionals, total	17,628.6	19.5
Professionals, excluding teachers and professors	11,697.0	9.1
Teachers	5,005.7	44.3
Speech therapists	93.3	44.1
Urban planners	13.9	30.9
Forestry and conservation scientists	24.0	26.6
Librarians, archivists, and curators	227.7	25.9
Social workers	742.7	24.0
Psychologists	160.9	22.7
Professors	925.9	16.3
Respiratory therapists	104.3	15.1
Other physical scientists	40.5	14.9
Registered nurses	1,999.1	14.7
Metallurgical and materials engineers	37.3	12.0
Therapists	101.5	12.0
Musicians and composers	100.9	12.0
Other artists, performers, and related workers	96.8	11.6
Occupational therapists	60.8	10.5
Civil engineers	271.7	10.4
Actors and directors	103.1	9.6
Physicians' assistants	63.7	9.5
Statisticians	32.8	9.1
Dietitians	79.8	9.1
Authors and technical writers	109.4	8.7
Agricultural and food scientists	32.1	8.4
Athletes	82.8	8.1
Aerospace engineers	77.6	7.7
Sociologists and social scientists	34.4	7.6
Other engineers	310.3	7.5
Editors and reporters	248.8	7.1
Operations and systems researchers and analysts	212.9	6.6
Photographers	67.4	6.3
Announcers	52.7	6.3
Physicians	505.7	6.1
Pharmacists	166.9	6.1
Biological and life scientists	101.7	5.5
Designers	496.7	5.1
Painters, sculptors, craft-artists, and artist printmakers	109.1	5.0
Chemists, except biochemists	131.6	4.6
Physical therapists	121.4	4.6
Public relations specialists	148.9	4.6
Architects	105.9	4.5
Mechanical engineers	325.2	4.5
Electrical and electronic engineers	616.3	4.4
Recreation workers	137.8	4.4

TABLE 8.7—cont.

	Employed Wage and Salary (thousands)	Union Density (%)
Lawyers and judges	611.7	4.4
Other health-diagnosing practitioners	91.8	4.3
Industrial engineers	254.1	3.9
Geologists and geodesists	50.5	3.6
Computer systems analysts and scientists	1,349.3	3.1
Surveyors and mapping scientists	11.6	3.0
Medical scientists	88.2	1.9
Chemical engineers	68.3	1.6
Economists	108.2	1.3
Actuaries and mathematical scientists	29.7	0.9
Physicists and astronomers	35.3	0.8
Clergy	312.3	0.7
Petroleum engineers	21.1	0.0
Religious workers	114.0	0.0

Source: Data provided by Barry Hirsch (see Hirsch and MacPherson 1993; 1999).

identify themselves only as professional association members when asked whether they belong to labor unions and professional associations (see also Aronson 1985, 355).

Although librarians, speech therapists and psychologists do not have strong unions, their membership rates are higher than those among all professionals. One-quarter of librarians (26 percent), 44 percent of speech therapists, and 23 percent of psychologists were union members in 1998 (table 8.7).[7] Many of these professionals work in the highly unionized public schools and state colleges and universities.

According to the Current Population Survey, union membership rates appear to have declined significantly in the recent decades among actors (53 percent in 1974, 46 percent in 1980, and 10 percent in 1998), musicians and composers (32, 34, and 12 percent), and authors (13, 15, and 10 percent).[8] The data, as reported in 1998 by the actors and musicians unions, however, do not sustain this conclusion.[9] Membership in the Screen Actors Guild (90,000), the Actors' Equity Association (39,000), and the American Federation of Television and Radio Artists (75,000), which belong along with other actors' unions to the Associated Actors and Artists union, compares with the 58,000 members in the entire Associated Actors and Artists union in 1961. Membership in the American Federation of

TABLE 8.8
Largest Professional Unions and Professional Associations in the United States

Professional Unions	Membership (thousands)	Professional Associations	Membership (thousands)
National Education Association (NEA)	2,376	American Bar Association	375
American Federation of Teachers (AFT)	950	American Medical Association	297
American Nurses Association	210	Institute of Electrical and Electronics Engineers	274
American Federation of Musicians of the United States and Canada	165	American College of Cardiology	241
		National Council of Teachers of Mathematics	215
Screen Actors Guild	90	National Association of Social Workers	155
American Federation of Television and Radio Artists	75	American Chemical Society	151
		American Psychological Association	151
Federation of Nurses and Health Professionals	54	American Dental Association	142
American Association of University Professors (AAUP)[a]	45	American Society of Mechanical Engineers	121
		American Society of Civil Engineers	120
Actors' Equity Association	39		
The Newspaper Guild	32	American Physical Therapy Association	72
International Federation of Professional and Technical Engineers	27	American Computer Scientists Association	60
Committee of Interns and Residents	11	American Occupational Therapy Association	59
Directors Guild of America	10	American Library Association	57
Union of American Physicians and Dentists	10	American Institute of Architects	56
Writers Guild of America, West	9	Society of Professional Journalists	14
National Writers Union	7		
Writers Guild of America, East	4		

Source: Associations Unlimited (1998).
[a] The AAUP consists of a bargaining part and a non-bargaining one. The Collective Bargaining Congress is the bargaining part of the AAUP (see Garbarino 1986, 279–80).

Musicians now stands at 165,000, in contrast to 247,000 in 1961 (*Associations Unlimited* 1998; Kassalow 1966, 340). To complicate the matter, memberships reported by these unions considerably exceed the numbers of those employed as actors and musicians. There are about 100,000 wage and salary employees in each category. The difference is too large to be explained by sampling errors, variations in classification, or the inclusion of self-employed, student, and Canadian members. It seems plausible, however, as some have suggested, that many who joined entertainment unions as young people while working in a band or an off-Broadway play and who subsequently turned to other pursuits continue to hold union cards for prestige or other ego-gratifying reasons.

Journalists, like the creative professionals, often face conflicts between their professional norms and the demands of the market. Reflecting market demands, the great majority of the mass media are superficial in their coverage of serious issues. Journalists, as a group, are much more likely to be liberal Democrats or more left than the rest of the population (Hess 1992; Lichter and Rothman 1981; Lipset 1962/1967, 542; Lipset and Schwartz 1966, 307–8). According to a 1992 survey of journalists, almost one-half (47 percent) described their political leanings as left (Weaver and Wilhoit 1996, 15). But the 1992 Gallup Poll reported that only 18 percent of adult Americans consider themselves to be on the left (reported in Weaver and Wilhoit 1996, 15).

The Newspaper Guild, the main journalist union, had a membership of 32,000 in 1998 compared to 24,000 in 1959 (Kassalow 1966, 340). The guild voted in 1995 to merge with the Communications Workers of America. As with teachers and nurses, however, there may be a problem of underreporting in the surveys. A 1992 survey of journalists reported that only 17 percent belonged to a labor organization but more than one-third of those queried in 1992 (36 percent) reported membership in professional associations (Weaver and Wilhoit 1996, 128–30).

The relatively high rate of union membership among social workers (24 percent in 1998) suggests that clientele may be another factor determining unionism rates among professional workers. Social workers are in daily contact with less fortunate people. Seemingly, social workers develop an affinity for their clients' problems and have liberal attitudes on economic issues, or possibly these are the kinds of people who decide to be social workers in the first place (Lipset 1962/1967, 543; Lipset and Schwartz 1966, 304; *Professional Workers and Unions* 1988).

The 1962 article notes that the jobs of airline pilots are similar in some aspects to manual occupations, although airline pilots form the elite of the transportation industry. Their working conditions create a strong vocational community and promote occupational solidarity. In addition, they have especially strong bargaining power because of the potential effects of their industrial actions on the economy. All these factors seemingly promote unionism among airline pilots and related occupations. Almost two-thirds of airline pilots (64 percent) and 60 percent of air-traffic controllers were union members in 1998.

Until recently, U.S. engineers were unlikely to belong to unions, although some analyses of these professionals, such as Thorstein Veblen's (1933) classic discussion, lead to an expectation that they should. Veblen argued that a basic cleavage exists between the pecuniary norms of modern capitalism and the standards of engineering excellence. He felt that this cleavage in values should lead to discontent with the market among engineers, for much the same reason as in the creative professions previously discussed. There has been little evidence that Veblen was right. The union membership rate among engineers was 6 percent in 1998, and most vote Republican. Other factors seem to have counterbalanced the presumed discontent with free market norms. Engineers have been a major source of recruitment to the top management of corporations (Lipset 1962/1967, 539–40). Nearly 30 percent of the profession occupied management positions in 1978. Many engineers work in small offices where they are closely involved with top executives. Business-oriented norms and values also contribute to engineers' hostility toward unions (see Latta 1981, 37–38).

The successful forty-day-long strike of 17,000 engineers and technical workers in winter 2000 against the country's largest airplane manufacture, Boeing, has upset many of these generalizations about engineers and other professionals, however, and Veblen's predictions may be on the verge of realization. The Society of Professional Engineering Employees in Aerospace (SPEEA) called the strike. This organization began in the early 1950s as a professional association and developed unionlike characteristics in the 1990s, conducting a one-day strike in 1993 and affiliating to the AFL-CIO in October 1998.

Recent changes may be triggering this Veblenian reaction. Boeing engineers are in the situation similar to industrial workers in that they are a mass working for one employer. David Groves of the Washington Labor Council (AFL-CIO), in trying to account for the strike, noted that "there aren't many companies that have thousands of engineers working side by side" (in Fryer 2000, A26). Like factory workers, but unlike most professionals, Boeing engineers are in easy communication with one another. One of their principal demands, as reported in the press and by their leaders, was "respect," a demand acknowledged as legitimate by the company. In the 1990s, they witnessed the emergence of a higher-paid and higher-status subgroup in the high-technology communications firms, many of whom benefited greatly from stock options. *The Economist* comments that in the Seattle area "the explosive growth of Microsoft, Amazon.com and other 'new economy' firms has left the engineers looking old and poor," relatively if not absolutely deprived. "Seattle man has given way to Redmond [Microsoft] man in the local hierarchy" ("United States" 2000, 19).

Of course, traditional economic and stratification factors operated. Technical workers, who constitute over 40 percent of the society's membership, joined the union earlier and in proportionally larger numbers than engineers. The former "voted to strike by a 62 percent margin," while a slight majority of the latter, 51 percent, favored a strike ("17k Technical Workers" 2000, 178). They were undoubtedly influenced by the fact that the company's unionized blue-collar employees had been able to obtain generous settlements prior to the engineers' walkout by threatening to strike. Five years earlier (in 1995) the International Association of Machinists had conducted a very successful sixty-nine-day strike.

Professional Associations

The 1962 article argues that professional associations serve as an alternative to unions among professionals. Many of these organizations undertake economic and status representation functions (Lipset 1962/1967, 545–46). These associations are major representative bodies and serve, in part, as a functional alternative to union representation. According to the National Opinion Research Center's 1993 General Social Survey, 62 percent of U.S. professionals belonged to such organizations (http://www.norc.uchicago.edu/issues/ecopop2.asp). Conversely, relatively few low-level nonmanual workers—21 percent of sales employees, 12 percent of administrative support personnel, and 8 percent of secretaries—reported membership in nonunion occupation-linked associations.

Professional occupations associated with numerically large associations tend to have relatively small professional unions and vice versa (table 8.8). This relationship applies to the previously nonunionized professionals, such as engineers, dentists, lawyers, teachers, musicians, and actors, who had large professional unions, although some of these unions, such as the NEA, appear to play both roles.

Physicians had strong professional associations and weak unions until the AMA voted in 1999 to create a branch that would promote the unionization of doctors employed by HMOs and hospitals. The most common arguments against the organization of medical doctors have been that unions are unprofessional and that strikes by doctors are unethical (Budrys

1997; Lowes 1998; Serafini 1999). These objections were raised anew during the 1999 meeting of the AMA but were ignored, and it voted to create a union affiliate. The AMA, however, does not support the use of strikes by the doctors' union (Greenhouse 1999). Membership in the AMA is almost 300,000, whereas the Union of American Physicians and Dentists represents fewer than 10,000 doctors.[10]

The rise of HMOs has made the physicians who work for them feel like employees. This represents a radical shift from a traditional view of doctors as self-employed professionals. Many physicians view the regulations imposed by HMOs and insurance companies as encroachment on their professional autonomy in treating patients. Frustrated by the loss of their professional independence, a growing minority of doctors seemingly has become attracted to unionism (Carlson 1999; Lowes 1998; Serafini 1999).

Many professionals appear to view their associations as an alternative to unions, and these associations seem to satisfy their needs more adequately than unions. In 1997, the Department of Professional Employees of the AFL-CIO conducted a survey of professional and technical workers at seven enterprises that had been involved in union-organizing campaigns. The study found that about one-third of the respondents (36 percent) would support a union, while 30 percent preferred a professional association. Twelve percent said they would support an employee involvement committee, and 9 percent backed a nonunion workplace association. The remaining 12 percent did not endorse any of these organizations. The respondents who preferred a professional association were significantly less likely than the respondents who supported a union to have sided with the union during the organizing campaign, 29 versus 71 percent (*Organizing Challenge* n.d., 5–6). The interviewees in this small study had been exposed to organizing campaigns and, therefore, are not representative of all professionals; they are more likely to include a larger proportion of pro-unionists.

Not surprisingly, research on the determinants of support for unionism has found that a strong professional identification is negatively related to union support in collective bargaining elections (Hemmasi and Graf 1993). Levitan and Gallo (1989, 24–33) conclude that the issue of professionalism remains "a stubborn impediment to collective bargaining by associations whose memberships are concentrated in the private sector" (1989, 27). Beyond this barrier, David Groves of the Washington Labor Council concludes pessimistically, "professionals are marbled throughout the economy, making a mass labor movement . . . [among them] almost impossible" (in Fryer 2000, A26).

Implications for the Future

In 1962, Lipset wrote that unions of nonmanual workers were unlikely to become a powerful element on the U.S. scene because white-collar employees appeared reluctant to associate themselves with unions. As we have seen, this situation has changed significantly. While membership has dropped considerably among manual workers, it has increased among some important groups of professionals.

In the 1950s, the fact that the lower levels of white-collar occupations were predominantly female contributed to the weakness of unions among them. At the time, women were not expected to identify strongly with their work. Family was primary and many preferred spending more time at home. These gender-related factors are now weaker and the gender variable no longer significantly affects preferences for unions.

Finally, it must be reiterated that opportunities for unionization are more affected by private- or public-sector employment than any other variable. Union density in the public sector has increased significantly and is considerably higher than in private-sector employment across all major occupational categories, including professionals. The most highly unionized occupation, teachers, is overwhelmingly employed by the government.

Variation in the rate of adherence to unions continues to be inversely related to membership in professional associations. Some, such as the NEA and the ANA, have taken over collective bargaining functions and have become de facto, if not explicitly, unions, even though a large proportion of their members are not union friendly. Most of the other associations also seek to improve earning capacity and working conditions and hence constitute functional, if less militant, alternatives to trade unions.

The AMA's decision to create a union affiliate and the successful forty-day strike of engineers at Boeing highlight the conflicting factors affecting professionals. Many physicians and engineers have objected to unionization because they view unions as unprofessional. However, the large proportion of physicians who work for HMOs and the thousands of engineers employed by Boeing in Seattle feel that they have lost their professional independence and favor collective bargaining. The potential for unionism among professionals is a function of the extent to which those in other fields face comparable degrading experiences and will seek to convert their associations into collective bargaining institutions, whether called unions or not. To grow among professionals in private employment, unions must find ways of linking to professional, as distinct from economic and occupational, interests.

The overall U.S. union movement must decide whether it will seek to organize de facto unions (i.e., associations) among groups that disdain the union label. Surveys that have asked nonunionist professionals whether they would vote for a union and separately whether they would endorse an employee association (described as one that "would represent the interests of the employees, meeting regularly with management to discuss important workplace issues") found that 78–79 percent said they would vote for an association (39 percent definitely), compared to 43 percent who would back a union (17 percent definitely). The Boeing engineers first formed a professional association fifty-four years ago, but did not affiliate with the AFL-CIO until October 1999. This association's history, like that of the NEA and the ANA, suggests a path to be followed by the union movement. Even in Sweden, with its 90 percent union density, professional and white-collar employees are in separate federations from blue-collar workers.

9 Unions among Professionals and Other White-Collar Employees in Canada

In chapter 8, we saw that the difference in the rate of unionization between the United States and Canada also applies for specific occupational groups within the U.S. population as a whole. In this chapter we examine the attitudes of professionals and other white-collar workers toward unionization in Canada, as well as comparing these attitudes to those found among the same group of workers in the United States.

The Shift toward White-Collar and Professional Work

As in the United States, in Canada the twentieth century witnessed a transformation in occupation structure, with a fourfold increase in the share of white-collar workers[1] in the work force, from 15.2 percent in 1901 to 59.0 percent in 1998. For Canada, the proportion of blue-collar workers peaked at 37.7 percent in 1951, having grown somewhat from 32.2 percent in 1901. As in the United States the proportion fell after 1951, to 22.6 percent in 1998. In both countries the primary source of the reduction in blue-collar workers was the decline in the proportion employed in manufacturing in the four decades after 1951, from 24.7 to 15.3 percent in Canada.

At the beginning of the twentieth century, union membership consisted almost entirely of skilled workers in manufacturing and mining occupations. From the 1930s to the early 1960s, semiskilled and unskilled workers joined industrial unions in substantial numbers. As noted in the previous chapter, as of the early 1960s the rates of union density among white-collar workers were lower than among manual workers in almost all industrialized nations, with the possible exception of Japan.

This difference continued to the end of the century. As in the United States, manual workers in Canada also had a higher rate of union membership, but the manual-nonmanual gap was much smaller than in the United States. It was 25 percent in Canada (36.8 vs. 28.1 percent), compared with 50 percent in the United States (see Akyeampong 1998, 37; table 8.2). Greater union density in Canada showed up not only in a higher rate for manual workers than in the United States, but also in a much higher rate for white-collar and other nonmanual workers.

As discussed in chapter 2, with only a few exceptions, such as Canada and the Scandinavian countries, union density has dropped significantly in most countries in recent decades. As we have seen, the pattern in Canada has differed sharply from the United States, beginning in the mid-1960s. Whereas the U.S. union movement peaked in the mid-1950s at 32.5 percent, the Canadian peak was in the mid-1980s at 38.8 percent (see chap. 3). Although the share of manufacturing employment in Canada fell as much as in the United States, union density within manufacturing maintained a high level for a decade and a half longer than in the United States, and the decline has been much less precipitous. Union density in manufacturing in Canada in 1970 was 6 percentage points above that in the United States, and by 1997 the gap had widened to 18 percent (see table 9.1). In the 1980s, U.S. union density declined in each of the nineteen subsectors. In Canada, during the same decade, union density rose in one-third of the manufacturing subsectors (Meltz 1994). In the first half of 2001, union density in manufacturing in Canada was 30.3 percent, more than twice the 14.6 percent in the United States. Although there are many potential sources for this gap, the largest single cause for the huge difference is the much greater degree of union organizing in Canada (Meltz and Verma 1996).

Outside of manufacturing, union density grew the most in the public sector in both countries, but again the increase was far more pronounced north of the border. Public-sector union density in 2001 was 71.0 percent in Canada, versus 37.4 percent in the United States. In addition, there was much broader support for unions among nonmanual workers. In the private service sector there were major union gains among a number of the subsectors, including financial services, one of the most difficult sectors to organize (Meltz 1993). As is discussed in more detail later in this chapter, these cross-border differences in unionization among nonmanual white-collar workers are particularly important in understanding the

TABLE 9.1
Union Density by Industry in Canada, 1930–1997

Industry	1930	1940	1950	1960	1970	1980	1990	1997
Primary	n.a.	n.a.	57.5	54.8	51.5	33.0	33.4	29.2
Forestry	n.a.	n.a.	50.1	46.2	56.1	38.6	58.8	n.a.
Mining	38.5	34	58.2	63.7	49.9	32.5	28.4	n.a.
Manufacturing	n.a.	n.a.	32.6	43.2	45.0	41.6	34.9	33.3
Construction	23.8	32.1	29.8	60.2	67.6	57.6	59.6	27.3
Transportation & communication[a]	68.7	n.a.	62.2	71.1	57.2	53.2	54.8	44.4
Public utilities	n.a.	26.0	20.9	47.1	51.2	n.a.	51.9	62.2
Trade	n.a.	n.a.	3.8	5.4	8.4	8.9	11.6	12.0
Services[b]	6.1	6.8	15.4	15.0	13.6	24.2	35.9	37.5
Finance, insurance, & real estate	n.a.	n.a.	n.a.	n.a.	0.8	2.5	3.5	9.2
Public administration	n.a.	n.a.	n.a.	22.9	74.3	67.8	80.6	72.7

Source: 1930–60 data from Bain and Price (1980); 1970–90 data from CALURA (1970, 1980, 1990); 1997 data based on Labour Force Survey (see Akyeampong 1998).
Note: n.a., not available.
[a] Includes utilities in 1980 and 1990.
[b] Includes business services, education, health and social services, accommodation, and other services.

significant differences that arose between the labor movements in the two countries.

Differentiation within the Nonmanual Stratum

Table 9.2 reports the 1996 survey results for union membership by occupation in Canada. For the main white-collar occupations, the union percentages are 20 percent in the executive, administrative, and managerial occupations (United States, 5 percent); 51 percent of the nonteaching professionals (United States 10 percent); 20 percent in sales (8 percent); 57 percent in technical positions (14 percent); 28 percent in clerical jobs (15 percent); and 41 percent of the respondents in service occupations (14 percent). Similarly, for manual occupations the union percentage in Canada is substantially above the U.S. rate: 45 percent of the precision production, craft, and repair workers (United States, 34 percent) and 50 percent of the operators, fabricators, and laborers belong to unions (United States, 28 percent). Whereas teachers and professors are the most unionized professionals in the United States, 50 percent according to the

TABLE 9.2
Union Membership, Preferences to Join Union, and Union Approval by Occupational Group in Canada (%)

	Executive, Administrative and Managerial	Professionals[a]	Teachers and Professors	Technical Occupations	Sales	Clerical Occupations and Secretaries	Service Occupations	Precision Production, Craft, and Repair	Operators, Fabricators, and Laborers
Union members									
Yes	20	51	87	57	20	28	41	45	50
No	80	49	13	43	80	72	59	55	50
N	142	129	57	56	82	119	131	62	133
Prefer to belong to unions[b]									
Yes	14	16	33	21	17	32	30	26	23
No	70	66	67	53	63	51	62	63	58
Don't know/ not stated	16	18	0	26	19	16	8	11	19
N	90	50	6	19	52	68	61	27	52
General union approval index									
Disapprove	36	26	17	37	38	24	25	30	27
Neutral	30	34	33	21	23	25	20	19	23
Approve	34	40	50	42	38	51	56	52	50
N	90	50	6	19	52	68	61	27	52

Source: Lipset-Meltz survey.

Note: Percentages may not add up to 100 because of rounding.

[a] Excluding teachers and professors.

[b] Nonmembers.

Lipset-Meltz survey in 1996, the Canadian equivalent is 87 percent. With the exception of clerical occupations and secretaries, nonunionized Canadians express a weaker desire to belong to unions than do their U.S. counterparts. Cross-border differences in general union approval among nonmembers in different occupational groups follow a similar pattern (tables 9.2 and 8.3).

The patterns of occupational change in Canada have been very similar to those in the United States, as have the factors underlying the changes. Meltz (1965) pointed out the emergence of white-collar workers as the dominant occupation group by the end of the 1950s, and this trend has continued. The pattern that emerged was the growth of clerical occupations, followed by the expansion of professional and technical workers and then managers (Meltz 1965; 1999). Data from the 1996 survey show how close the distributions are for the two countries. Executive, professional specialty, and technical workers were 41 percent in both the United States and Canada, while sales and administrative support workers totaled 21 percent in the United States and 22 percent in Canada. There were, however, more U.S. professional specialists and fewer executive, administrative, and managerial workers than in Canada. The Canadian figures may be attributed to the higher percentage of public-sector employees in Canada.

Stratification and Gender

The figures on gender differences in employment for Canada in 1951 were roughly similar to those for the United States, allowing for possible differences in occupational classification. Men held 91 percent of managerial jobs in Canada (United States, 84 percent) and 64 percent of professional and technical positions (United States, 56 percent in 1950). In the same years women had a majority of clerical jobs, 57 percent in Canada (United States, 62 percent) (Lipset 1962/1967, 528; Meltz 1969).

Similar patterns are evident in the growth of women in the total workforce and within managerial and professional occupations in Canada. To cite only a few statistics, 40 percent of managers (United States, 43 percent), 55 percent of professionals (United States, 53 percent), and 69 percent of teachers (United States, 75 percent) were women (Akyeampong 1999).

The Lipset-Meltz 1996 survey shows that both females and males have much higher union densities in all occupation groups in Canada than in

TABLE 9.3
Union Membership and Preferences by Occupational Group and Gender in Canada (%)

	Executive, Administrative, and Managerial		Professionals[a]		Teachers and Professors		Technical Occupations	
	F	M	F	M	F	M	F	M
Union members								
Yes	22	18	66	37	88	84	53	61
No	78	82	34	63	12	16	47	39
N	74	68	63	67	32	24	27	29
Prefer to belong to unions								
Yes	26	18	53	29	66	59	40	42
No	62	66	38	55	29	22	42	44
Don't know/ not stated	13	16	9	16	6	20	18	15
N	74	68	63	67	32	24	27	29

Source: Lipset-Meltz survey.
Note: Percentages may not add to 100 because of rounding.
[a] Excluding teachers and professors.
[b] The number of observations in this category is very small.

the United States (tables 9.3 and 8.4). The most significant differences between the two countries are that female executive, administrative, and managerial employees have a higher union density than males in Canada, 22 versus 18 percent, but not in the United States, where the respective figures are 4 versus 6 percent.

Canada also leads the United States for both males and females in answering yes to the question "Do you want to belong to a union?" The only exceptions are female executive, administrative, and managerial workers; in the United States 36 percent want to belong to a union compared with 26 percent in Canada. As well, both female sales workers in the United States (41 vs. 20 percent) and female service workers (49 vs. 45 percent) are more interested in belonging to a union than their Canadian counterparts.

Obstacles to White-Collar Unionism

From the discussion in chapter 6, it is clear that there is a lot of unsatisfied demand for unionization in the United States and very little in Canada. In

Sales		Clerical Occupations and Secretaries		Service Occupations		Precision Production, Craft, and Repair		Operators, Fabricators, and Laborers	
F	M	F	M	F	M	F[b]	M	F	M
18	22	25	42	35	48	—	47	47	51
82	78	75	58	65	52	—	53	53	49
41	41	97	22	67	63	—	60	29	105
20	39	39	49	45	44	—	43	59	43
50	56	47	40	43	50	—	51	24	45
30	5	14	11	12	6	—	6	18	12
41	41	97	22	67	63	—	60	29	105

fact there is a significant minority of Canadians who are unwilling union members, especially among professionals and technical employees.

The statistics for Canada show a higher sense of social status among white-collar workers: 79 percent of executives in Canada classify themselves as middle or upper class compared with 74 percent in the United States. The same is true for nonteaching professionals (81 vs. 70 percent in the United States), teachers and professors (82 vs. 72 percent in the United States), and technical workers 69 vs. 59 percent). The figures for sales and service are identical, and they are almost the same for both clerical and secretarial occupations (58 vs. 54 in the United States).

At the same time, manual workers in Canada have a much higher sense of social status than their U.S. counterparts. For example, a majority of Canadian operators, fabricators, and laborers think of themselves as middle class (54 percent), whereas only 40 percent of U.S. operators place themselves in the middle class. A larger group of U.S. operators say they are members of the working class (46 percent), whereas only one-third of Canadians (33 percent) place themselves in the working class. These results are consistent with a stronger union identification among male blue-collar workers in the United States than in Canada.

The concentration of professional and other white-collar workers in the public sector is much greater in Canada than in the United States. For example, 84 percent of teachers and professors and 55 percent of other professionals are employed in the public sector, far greater than the respective figures (73 and 24 percent) for the United States. The difference is due to the larger nonprofit and private sectors in the United States. The Canadian public sector also has a far larger share of all executive, administrative, and managerial personnel (26 percent), two and a half times larger than in the United States (11 percent). As in the United States (which has 39 percent public sector and 6 percent private sector), the unionization rate in Canada is much higher in the public sector (74 percent) than in the private sector (15 percent) among white-collar workers.

With just a few exceptions, there are only small (4 percentage points or less) differences between how Canadians and Americans view employee versus employer interests. Where the differences are large, they are all in the direction of U.S. employees believing that employees' interests are opposed rather than the same as employer interests. For technical workers, 39 percent of U.S. employees said this, versus 30 percent in Canada. For manual workers, there was much more belief in the opposition of employee-employer interests than was the case in Canada—for operators the figures are 46 percent in the United States and 33 in Canada; for precision production workers the figures are 55 percent in the United States and 34 percent in Canada (tables 9.4 and 8.5). The greater U.S. belief in employee-employer opposition is consistent with the almost across-the-board unsatisfied demand for unionization in the United States.

In both Canada and the United States nonmanual workers, more than blue-collar workers, tended to say that their management appreciated what they did. Canadians in technical and clerical occupations felt they were treated even better than their U.S. counterparts did (see tables 9.4 and 8.5).

Where Is Nonmanual Unionism Found?

In general, the greater union strength in Canada extends to the private service sector as well, an area that is the least organized in both the United States and Canada (Meltz 1993). Although the gains are small, Canadian unions have been making headway in finance, insurance and real estate, trade, management, and administrative support, and even in professional, scientific, and technical services (Akyeampong 1999).

TABLE 9.4
Attitudes toward Management by Major Occupational Group in Canada (%)

	Executive, Administrative, and Managerial	Professionals[a]	Teachers and Professors	Technical Occupations	Sales Occupations	Clerical Occupations and Secretaries	Service Occupations	Precision Production, Craft, and Repair	Operators, Fabricators, and Laborers
Employees' and employers' interests									
Opposite	33	39	27	30	39	44	41	34	33
Same	67	61	73	70	61	56	59	66	67
N	139	124	56	56	81	115	127	59	131
Treatment of employees by management									
Very good	37	34	26	35	39	42	34	36	33
Good	54	49	60	45	43	34	50	54	41
Poor	5	15	13	16	11	17	13	5	18
Very poor	4	2	1	4	6	7	3	5	8
N	142	129	57	56	82	118	131	62	133
Management's appreciation of what you do									
Very good	43	43	31	27	43	39	33	32	31
Good	42	40	53	54	43	42	46	56	42
Poor	6	12	11	13	13	14	18	6	16
Very poor	9	5	6	6	1	6	4	6	11
N	142	129	57	56	82	118	131	62	133
Hearing labor disputes sides with[b]									
Union	38	53	74	52	44	56	58	54	61
Company	62	47	26	47	56	44	42	46	39
N	105	97	37	38	67	91	98	45	107

Source: Lipset-Meltz survey.
Note: Percentages may not add to 100 because of rounding.
[a] Excluding teachers and professors.
[b] Excludes Don't know/not stated.

In terms of a social democratic scale of attitudes, Canadian nonmanual workers are more social democratic and less libertarian (free market) than Americans. For example, 26 percent of Canadian unionized professionals, excluding teachers and professors, are social democratic and 16 percent libertarian, versus 9 and 47 percent of Americans. For nonunion professionals, the figures are 10 and 28 percent for Canadians versus 7 and 48 percent for Americans. Among unionized precision, production, craft, and repair workers in Canada 17 percent are social democratic and 19 percent libertarian, versus 8 and 24 percent of Americans. The nonunion figures are 7 and 11 percent in Canada compared with 9 and 33 percent in the United States (tables 9.5 and 8.6).

Americans are much more neutral or noncommitted with respect to the major political parties than are Canadians. For example, 37 percent of unionized nonteaching professionals consider themselves independents in the United States (i.e., neither Republicans nor Democrats), compared with 17 percent in Canada who have no party affiliation or are not affiliated with the one of the five major parties. Among nonunion nonteaching professionals, 35 percent of Americans are independents versus 15 percent of Canadians (see tables 9.5 and 8.6).

The five Canadian political parties range from the right (Reform and Progressive Conservative parties) to the centrist Liberal Party to the left-of-center NDP and Bloc Quebecois. Recall that the NDP was founded in 1961 by the former socialist party, the CCF, and the major federation of the trade union movement, the CLC, and that all Canadian political parties tend to be to the left of their U.S. counterparts.[2] The Conservative Party, which was in power in the province of Ontario from 1943 to 1985, was known as the Red Tory Party. And, as noted earlier, even the former Reform Party (Canada's most libertarian political force) did not identify with the views of Newt Gingrich's Contract with America.

Canadians also tend to be more left of center in their support for political parties. Only 15 percent of unionized executives supported the Conservative and Reform parties (parties of the right), whereas 46 percent of unionized executives in the United States supported the Republican Party. Of nonunion executives, 27 percent supported the Conservative and Reform parties, compared with 32 percent of U.S. nonunion executives who supported the Republican Party. The Liberals were the most popular Canadian party among executives, nonteaching professionals, and unionized teachers. In the United States the two latter groups supported the Democrats. When we combine the NDP and the Bloc Quebecois as left-of-center parties, they lead only among unionized sales, clerical, and service workers and in the two manual occupations, operators and precision, production, craft, and repair. The only white-collar group in which the two left parties are ahead is the nonunion teachers and professors. Fifty percent of this group supported the NDP (however, the number of observations in this category is very small). In the United States nonunion teachers and professors also gave strong support to the Democrats (43 percent).

As noted, given more choice of major political parties within the parliamentary system, Canadians identify to a greater extent with political parties than do Americans. One other curiosity of Canadian politics is worth noting. In the largest province, Ontario, the same political party has not been in power in both the provincial legislature and the federal parliament since the early 1940s.

Professionals and Trade Unions

In chapter 8 it was noted that professionals, U.S. or otherwise, are concerned with the fulfillment of certain intrinsic values, such as disinterested service and universalistic standards based on science or intellect. This creates conflict with the money-making emphasis of business. At the same time, professionals as a group form one of the most privileged and satisfied strata. This factor inhibits the development of unionism among professionals.

Canada being a more communitarian society than the United States exhibits less of an aversion to trade unions among professionals. The rate of unionization of professionals excluding teachers in the United States is 10 percent, compared with 51 percent in Canada. Fifty percent of teachers and professors are organized in the United States, compared with 87 percent in Canada (tables 9.2 and 8.3).

Teachers

In Canada there appears to be less reluctance on the part of teachers to identify themselves as union members than in the United States. According to the Canadian Labour Force Survey, the unionization rate for all teachers in 1998 was 76.4 percent, of which 87.2 percent of secondary and elementary school teachers identified themselves as union members,

TABLE 9.5
Relation of Union Membership to Political Identification by Occupation in Canada (%)

	Executive, Administrative, and Managerial		Professionals[a]		Teachers and Professors		Technical Occupations	
	Member	Nonmember	Member	Nonmember	Member	Nonmember	Member	Nonmember
Party identification								
Progressive Conservative	13	20	7	23	9	0	14	17
Liberal	36	47	36	46	50	17	33	39
New Democrat	7	6	20	10	18	50	14	22
Bloc Quebecois	18	8	13	2	9	17	14	6
Reform	2	7	7	4	2	0	0	6
None or other	24	12	17	15	11	17	26	11
N	35	85	82	48	57	6	39	18
Social democratic scale								
Libertarian	25	37	16	28	22	17	26	42
Neutral	50	53	58	62	63	67	60	42
Social democratic	25	10	26	10	15	17	15	16
N	37	90	86	50	64	6	42	19

Source: Lipset-Meltz survey.
Note: Percentages may not add to 100 because of rounding.
[a] Excluding teachers and professors.

compared with 48.8 percent of professors and other teachers (Akyeampong 1999, 52). Data obtained from the unions themselves showed a figure for education and related services of 70.0 percent for 1995 ("Unionization" 1999).

The growth of teacher unions was part of the wave of worker militancy that transformed professional and public-sector workers from passive employees and civil servants into active unionists. The beginnings were in Quebec in the early 1960s, where the Quiet Revolution transformed the labor relations scene, culminating in 1964 when the Quebec government gave public-sector workers the right to bargain and strike. In 1965 Canadian postal workers carried out a series of illegal strikes (Laidlaw and Curtis 1986) that in 1967 led to the federal government granting its employees the right to bargain and strike under the Public Service Staff Relations Act (PSSRA) (Morton 1990). Nurses were also engaging in militant action across the country and they too received the right to bargain and in some provinces the right to strike. Teachers in provinces other than

Sales Occupations		Clerical Occupations and Secretaries		Service Occupations		Precision Production, Craft, and Repair		Operators, Fabricators, and Laborers	
Member	Nonmember	Member	Nonmember	Member	Nonmember	Member	Nonmember	Member	Nonmember
24	20	8	6	13	14	12	7	15	14
24	30	44	26	35	27	31	27	44	29
20	4	16	22	16	23	12	13	8	25
15	16	11	19	9	11	8	19	12	14
0	4	3	6	7	12	19	8	2	4
17	26	19	21	20	13	19	26	19	15
19	50	64	38	55	60	26	36	48	85
6	33	19	13	16	12	11	19	17	10
58	50	65	61	67	60	81	63	56	60
37	17	16	26	16	28	7	17	27	30
21	52	68	43	61	69	27	36	52	87

Quebec also received the right to bargain and strike in the late 1960s and early 1970s. In some provinces, such as Ontario, the requirement by legislation that teachers be members of one of the professional teachers associations clearly increased the extent of teacher unionization. At the same time, however, it also gave rise to a number of unwilling union members, as has been noted earlier.

Other Professions

A much higher percentage of nurses belong to unions in Canada than in the United States. The union membership rate among Canadian nurses is 79.1 percent (Akyeampong 1999, 52). Collective agreement coverage of Canadian nurses in hospitals is 93.8 percent. Coverage of community health nurses is 88.5 percent. In comparison, U.S. registered nurses have a unionization rate of 14.7 percent (see Bendel 1991, 30–31; table 8.7).

TABLE 9.6
Union Membership by Occupation in Canada, 1994 (%)

Occupation	Union density
Managers and administrators	17
Management and administration related	38
Life sciences, math, and computers	29
Architects, engineers, and related	36
Social science and religion	49
Teaching related	79
Medicine and health	72
Artistic, literary, and recording	35
Stenographic and typing	38
Bookkeeping and account-recording	11
EDP operators and material recording	39
Reception, information, mail, and message	45
Library, file, and other clerical	49
Sales and commodities	7
Sales and services	9
Protective services	40
Food, beverage, accommodation services	16
Personal, apparel, furnishing services	11
Other service occupations	37
Farm occupations	9
Primary occupations	29
Food and beverage processing, etc.	26
Processing occupations (except food)	50
Machine and related occupations	31
Electrical and electronic related	47
Textiles, fur, and leather	19
Wood products, rubber, and plastics	42
Repairmen (except electrical)	37
Excavating, paving, and wire communication	65
Other construction trades	54
Transport operating occupations	33
Material handling	39
Other crafts and equipment	53
Don't know/not stated	54
Total	37

Source: General Social Survey (1995).
Note: Excludes self-employed workers. $N = 1,742$.

There has been a long tradition of Canadian engineers' belonging to unions. A survey in 1994 showed that 36 percent of architects, engineers, and related professionals were union members, up from the 11.6 percent reported collective agreement coverage of engineers in 1989 (see table 9.6; Bendel 1991, 30–31). Associations of engineers have been organized in the Canadian aircraft and aerospace industry, in such large private organizations as De Havilland and Spar Aeorospace. In addition, associations of engineers at public-sector utilities such as Ontario Hydro were transformed into unions in the 1990s (White 1993).

Professional Associations

Under the national health-care system in Canada, the fee schedules of doctors are negotiated between provincial medical associations and provincial governments. On several occasions there have been doctors' strikes, for example, in the province of Ontario in 1986. Although provincial medical associations are not considered to be unions (with the exception of the one-hundred-member Manitoba Medical Association), in many respects they behave like any traditional union would. Indeed, although most medical doctors are treated as independent practitioners and not employees, most aspects of their terms and conditions of practice are established through negotiations with provincial authorities.

A survey of nonunion private service-sector employees in Montreal and Toronto has found that 40 percent were interested in joining a union, whereas 60 percent were interested in joining a professional association. For 20 percent of the employees, a professional association was a substitute for a union (Bergeron 1993).

Not surprisingly, as noted in the preceding chapter, research on the determinants of support for unionism has found that a strong professional identification is negatively related to union support in collective bargaining elections. The findings of our survey show that professionalism is less of an impediment to unionization in Canada than in the United States.

Conclusion

The most highly unionized occupations in Canada are teachers and nurses, along with social workers and health-related professionals working in hospitals. Teachers and nurses also consider themselves to be union members to a greater extent than in the United States. The *Directory of Labour Organizations* in Canada (http://labour.hrdc-drhc.gc.ca/millieudetravail_workplace/ot_lo/index.cfm/doc/english) includes all teachers' federations and associations and the nurses associations and unions. These groups are largely public-sector employees.

In the Canadian context, where the extent of unionization is much greater than in the United States, the move to unionize professionals has gone beyond the push factor of dissatisfaction and unhappy employment experiences and toward the pull of positive benefits that other professionals have received. In Canada, when one professional sector unionized others followed. This was particularly the case in the late 1960s and early 1970s when teacher, nurse, and public-sector worker unionization spread across Canada. In one year, 1974–75, negotiations and strikes by unionized nurses in Canadian hospitals produced wage increases of 50 percent (Meltz 1985).

The idea of establishing separate federations for U.S. professional associations as a means of increasing union membership roles has its merits, and it has been proposed in a Canadian context as well (Meltz 1993). The fact is, however, that even without such federations, Canadian professionals and other white-collar workers are much more highly unionized than their counterparts in the United States. In the case of Canadian professionals, as with other occupations, the more favorable labor legislation and its enforcement have certainly contributed to the differences in union organizing. However, legislation only facilitates union membership where employees want to join a union. With only a few exceptions (such as teachers in Ontario), employees are not required to join a union, although in Canada if there is a union representing a workplace then employees, for the most part, are required to pay union dues (see the Rand Formula; Morton 1990, 186).

In this chapter we also have explored the attitudes of professionals and other white-collar workers toward belonging to unions, social class, political parties and social democratic values, along with gender differences, with some unexpected results. Although Canadians have greater social democratic leanings than Americans, U.S. professionals and other white-collar workers identify with the working class to a greater extent than do Canadians, and more nonunion professionals in the United States want to belong to unions than do nonunion Canadians. In other words, there is greater unsatisfied demand for unionization in the United States.

Professionals and other white-collar workers in the two countries are roughly evenly split among occupation groups over whether the interests of employees and employers are more opposed or similar. More nonteaching professionals, sales, and clerical occupations in Canada believe that employee-employer interests are opposed. Americans also feel less well-treated by management than do Canadians, except for teachers and professors. U.S. teachers and professors and technical workers see their interests as more opposed than do their Canadian counterparts. All these factors suggest that U.S. professionals and white-collar workers should want to belong to unions at least as much as Canadians do. The prediction, therefore, is that if labor legislation were equivalent in both jurisdictions we would see a convergence upward in unionization rates toward the Canadian average.

10 Estimates of Nonunion Employee Representation

How Different Are the Two Countries?

As discussed in chapter 2, there is a general awareness that, with the exception of the Scandinavian countries and a few others, the percentage of employees who belong to unions has been declining worldwide. The International Labour Organization (ILO), for example, in its *World Labour Report 1997–98*, estimates that worldwide trade union membership dropped sharply during the late 1980s and 1990s. Membership declined in seventy-two of the ninety-two countries surveyed. In forty-eight of them, union density dropped below the 20 percent level between 1985 and 1995.

What has not been examined in any systematic way, however, is the extent and direction of change in nonunion employee representation as a possible alternative. As seen in chapter 3, in the 1920s in the United States and Canada, nonunion employee representation plans, known in the United States as the American Plan, were introduced by large corporations as substitutes or replacements for unions. Following the passage of the Wagner Act in the United States in 1935, these plans became fertile organizing grounds for unions on both sides of the border.

In this chapter we present results from our survey on the extent of nonunion representation in Canada and the United States.[1] We also examine some possible hypotheses concerning where this representation is located and who belongs to these organizations. We end by raising some questions concerning the possible effect of these developments on labor relations in the two countries.

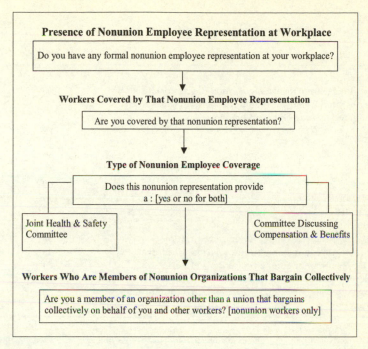

FIGURE 10.1
Measures of nonunion employee representation.

The Survey Questions

The major focus of the 1996 binational telephone survey was the attitudes of Americans and Canadians toward work and unions, but we also included questions on employee representation in general. In one subsection in particular we included several questions concerning nonunion representation.[2] Figure 10.1 sets out the survey questions on which the estimates of nonunion representation are based. The results are drawn from the same sample of interviews, with randomly generated samples of 1,750 adults in the United States and 1,495 in Canada.

The General Results

Table 10.1 indicates the extent of union representation in the two countries at the time of the survey and the proportion of individuals indicating that their workplaces had employees involved in decision making.

TABLE 10.1
Union Density and Employee Involvement, 1996 (%)

	United States	Canada
Union density	16	35
Presence of employee involvement among total workforce	50	51
Presence of employee involvement among total workforce by establishment size (number of employees)		
1–5	29	30
6–10	31	33
11–50	37	41
51–100	51	56
101–500	60	65
501–1,000	70	69
1,001–5,000	73	70
>5,000	90	71
Employee involvement among unionized workforce	58	60
Employee involvement among nonunionized workforce	49	44
Employee involvement among nonunionized but employee-represented workforce[a]	64	71
Employee involvement among nonunionized and nonrepresented workforce	43	36

Source: Lipset-Meltz survey.
Note: Employee involvement includes self-directed work teams, total quality management, quality circles, or other employee-involvement programs.
[a] Nonunion employee representation is measured by the number of respondents answering yes to the presence of nonunion representation at their workplace.

Employee involvement included the presence of self-directed work teams, total quality management, quality circles, and other employee-involvement programs. These were self-reported measures by the employees themselves.

In 1996, 35 percent of Canadians in our survey belonged to unions, compared with 16 percent in the United States. These results are very close to the aggregate figures available from other sources in the two countries.

When employees were asked whether their employers had introduced decision making in new ways to get employees involved (an admittedly crude measure for "the high-performance workplace") one-half of the workers in each country said that they were involved in new forms of decision making (50 percent in the United States and 51 percent in Canada). Perhaps not surprisingly, the extent of employee involvement among workers increased with establishment size, reaching a maximum in both countries within firms employing 5,000 workers or more (90 percent in the United States and 71 percent in Canada).

Of interest is that in both countries a higher percentage of unionized workplaces involved their employees in decision making than did

TABLE 10.2
Nonunion Forms of Employee Representation

	United States	Canada
Presence of formal nonunion employee representation among nonunion workforce	20	20
Nonunionized workforce covered by that formal nonunion employee representation	15	14
Type of nonunion employee representation among nonunion workforce		
Formal nonunion employee representation that discusses compensation and benefits among nonunion workforce	11	10
Formal nonunion employee representation that discusses joint health & safety among nonunion workforce	10	10
Nonunionized workforce who are members of an organization that bargains collectively on their behalf	5	6

Source: Lipset-Meltz survey.

nonunionized workplaces (58 percent vs. 49 percent in the United States and 60 percent vs. 44 percent in Canada). Within the nonunionized sector, workplaces that had formal nonunion employee representation also had a higher percentage of workers involved in some form of employee involvement than did the nonrepresented sector (64 percent vs. 43 percent in the United States and 71 percent vs. 36 percent in Canada).

Next, we move to nonunion forms of employee representation. And here, despite the huge differences between the countries in the extent of unionization, the incidence of nonunion representation is very similar, as is shown in table 10.2. One-fifth of nonunion employees in each country have formal employee representation other than unions present at their workplaces. In terms of coverage (that is, how many workers are not members of these nonunion organizations but are represented by them), the proportion of nonunion employees who are represented by some form of formal nonunion representation is 15 percent in the United States and 14 percent in Canada.

An alternative measure of nonunion representation (and one that may function better in terms of a substitute for unions) is the extent to which these nonunion employer-run organizations discuss compensation and benefits with their nonunion workforce—11 percent in the United States and 10 percent in Canada.

Finally, if we look only at those who belong to (or who state that they are members of) nonunion organizations that bargain over (rather than discuss) compensation and benefits, we find that roughly the same proportion of employees in each country is represented by such organizations (5 percent in the United States and 6 percent in Canada).

Ultimately, no matter which set of figures is used, the results seem clear that the extent of nonunion representation is similar in Canada and the United States. The range of estimates for nonunion representation is 5 percent for employees who say they are members of nonunion organizations (6 percent in Canada), 15 percent for those who claim to be covered (14 percent in Canada) by nonunion organizations, and 20 percent for employees who work in establishments where there is some form of nonunion representation present.

Nonunion Representation by Industry

Tables 10.3 and 10.4 show the estimated union density by industry for the United States and Canada, together with estimates for union density from our survey. For the most part, our survey results are similar to the government estimates. Tables 10.3 and 10.4 also contain three estimates of nonunion representation by industry. The estimates correspond to the first three rows of table 10.2, which include the following measures: (1) the presence of employee representation among nonunion workers, (2) nonunion workers covered by any form of nonunion employee representation, and (3) the percentage of nonunion workers covered by formal nonunion employee representation that discusses compensation and benefits.

There is a large and significant positive correlation between union density and our first measure of nonunion employee representation (the presence of formal nonunion representation across industrial classifications). When the figures for the United States and Canada are pooled, the correlation of union density with nonunion representation (column 3 in tables 10.3 and 10.4) is 0.59. For the United States separately the figure is 0.67 and for Canada it is 0.57.

One possible avenue for analysis is to ask why industries with high union density also tend to have high nonunion representation density. Presumably this is related to underlying factors (such as larger plant size and a manufacturing or blue-collar environment) that make some form of voice and dispute resolution more beneficial for workers and employers.

Examining the data in more detail, however, reveals different patterns in the United States and Canada. In the United States, most of the low-union-density private service sectors and agriculture have nonunion repre-

TABLE 10.3
U.S. Estimates of Union and Nonunion Forms of Employee Representation by Industry, 1996

	BLS Estimate of Union Membership (% of total employment)	Survey Estimate of Union Membership (% of total employment)	Presence of Nonunion Employee Representation (% of nonunion workforce)	Nonunion Workforce Covered by Nonunion Employee Representation (% of nonunion workforce)	Nonunion Employee Representation Discussing Wages and Benefits (% of nonunion workforce)
TOTAL	15	16	20	15	11
1. Agriculture	2	9	11	n.a.	11
2. Construction	19	24	11	11	11
3. Mining	14	n.a.	n.a.	n.a.	n.a.
4. Manufacturing	17	17	17	10	12
5. Wholesale and retail trade	6	6	16	12	12
6. Transportation and storage industries	27	30	19	13	13
7. Communication and public utilities	26	33	21	14	14
8. Public administration	38	26	35	28	31
9. Finance insurance and real estate	2	4	7	3	3
10. Other services	6	9	12	9	3

Source: Lipset-Meltz survey; Bureau of Labor Statistics for 1997 (http://states.bls.gov).
Note: BLS, Bureau of Labor Statistics; n.a., not available.

TABLE 10.4

Canadian Estimates of Union and Nonunion Forms of Employee Representation by Industry, 1996

	LFS Estimate of Union Membership (% of total employment)	Survey Estimate of Union Membership (% of total employment)	Presence of Nonunion Employee Representation (% of nonunion workforce)	Nonunion Workforce Covered by Nonunion Employee Representation (% of nonunion workforce)	Nonunion Employee Representation Discussing Wages and Benefits (% of nonunion workforce)
TOTAL	34[a]	36	20	14	10
1. Agriculture	2	3	7	n.a.	n.a.
2. Construction	27	30	18	6	6
3. Mining	29	32	18	9	9
4. Manufacturing	33	36	33	19	20
5. Wholesale and retail trade	12	14	11	6	9
6. Transportation and storage industries, and communication and public utilities	48	52	19	19	11
7. Public administration	66	73	22	17	11
8. Finance insurance and real estate	9	12	15	7	5
9. Community, business and personal services	35	38	12	8	8

Source: Lipset-Meltz survey; Labour Force Survey 1997; Statistics Canada, http://www.statcan.ca/; Human Resources Development Canada 1997, http://www.hrdc-drhc.gc.ca/.

Note: LFS, Labour Force Survey.

[a] Value from Human Resources Development Canada. Union density of 31.0 percent in 1997 and union membership of 3.6 million in 1997 were reported by the Labour Force Survey.

sentation one and a half times, or more, greater than the union density figures (wholesale and retail trade; finance, insurance, and real estate; and other services). For all of the remaining industry sectors, union density exceeds nonunion representation. In Canada, union density by industry sector exceeds the percentage of nonunion representation in every industry except finance, insurance, and real estate, the sector with the lowest union density (excluding agriculture). The possible meaning of these figures is discussed next.

Interpretation

Several observations can be made concerning the extent and industry location of nonunion representation. If we consider solely nonunion organizational membership, nonunion business organizations have one-third the number of union members in the United States and one-seventh in Canada. If we consider coverage and the presence of nonunion representation at the workplace, the estimates of formal nonunion representation in the United States range from just below to more than union coverage (15 percent and 20 percent, vs. 16 percent). For Canada, nonunion representation is much less than union membership (14 percent and 20 percent vs. 35 percent).

These data underline the importance of knowing more about where the nonunion representation is located (industry, occupation, geographical location, size of organization, etc.), which factors gave rise to it, how close it is to union representation in terms of formally representing employee interests (grievance procedures, profit-sharing plans, etc.), and which direction the numbers are moving.

Is nonunion employee representation simply a substitute for union representation, such that there is an inverse relationship between them? Or, alternatively, is there some complementarity between nonunion and union forms of employee representation, such that firms are more prone to introduce employee representation plans when the extent of unionization in an industry is high rather than when it is low? The survey cannot answer all of the questions, but it can shed light on some of them.

In terms of industry, it appears that the higher the union membership, the greater the nonunion representation. What is most striking, however, is that the differences between union density and nonunion representation are greatest for the low-union-density industries: agriculture; wholesale and retail trade (United States only); finance, insurance, and real estate;

and other services (United States only; community, business, and personal services in Canada). In the case of these industries, it appears that nonunion representation is a substitute for unionization. But for the other industries, the high correlation does not tell us whether greater union representation leads to greater formal nonunion representation or the reverse. Disentangling whether union representation in neighboring firms is the cause rather than the result of nonunion representation requires further exploration.

Concluding Comments

Several tentative conclusions can be drawn from the data presented here. Particularly striking is the similarity in the extent of employee involvement and nonunion representation in the United States and Canada. This is surprising given the huge differences in union density observed between the two countries. The fact that there is a high correlation between union membership by industry and formal nonunion representation suggests once again that differences in union membership across countries are partly the result of differences in the supply of opportunities to join unions rather than in the demand for union services.

Overall, a majority of employees in both countries seem to want some form of voice in the workplace. This is consistent with the late Jack Barbash's (1987) law of equilibrium, which states that there is an equity function to be represented in the workplace and that unions, employers, and governments all compete to represent this function. For U.S. workers, however, our survey results indicate that nonunion representation only partly substitutes in two industry sectors for interest in trade unions. Further analysis must explore in more detail the role of nonunion representation in substituting for or complementing interest in unions.

11 The Legacy of Differing Cultural and Political Histories on Unionization

Most people with even a passing interest in the comparative analysis of employment systems are well aware of the divergence in union membership that exists (and that has existed since the mid-1960s) between Canada and the United States. What continues to make this divergence in union density interesting for social scientists is that the two countries are similar in so many other respects. Canada and the United States are both federal states, they share a common language (with Quebec being the notable exception), their economies are similar and highly integrated, and they appear culturally very much the same. Indeed when viewed from a distance or when compared with other Western democracies, they appear nearly indistinguishable. Perhaps more important, at least in an industrial relations context, the two countries also shared very similar rates of trade union membership until the mid-1960s. Only after that did the patterns of union density observed in both countries begin to diverge dramatically.

The trajectory of trade union membership growth in Canada after the mid-1960s followed the general one observed for Europe as a whole (i.e., a constant or rising level of membership), whereas the pattern in the United States was quite different (i.e., after 1960, a consistent and dramatic free fall). No single explanation has been able to account for this divergence in union density. Not surprisingly, it remains one of the most crucial unsolved problems in the comparative study of Canadian and U.S. labor relations systems.

One traditional answer in the social science literature and described in chapter 3 maintains that the gap is not as large as people commonly assume and that, in any case, the forces of convergence work more slowly in Canada. Given time, the argument goes, Canada will eventually catch up or, in this case, move downward to converge with the U.S. standard. To paraphrase one proponent of this view, Canada is just the United States with a time-lag (Troy 1992).

Another view (ours) is that the two countries actually have quite different social and political cultures; this also has a well-established history in the social science literature. Lipset (1990) has long emphasised that the United States was born of a liberal revolution, whereas Canada provided a refuge for the monarchists and loyalists who fled from that same revolution. In effect, two countries were born out of the American Revolution, not one.

These differing political and social origins make Canada and the United States, despite their outward similarities, fundamentally very different, especially at the twin levels of political culture and deeply rooted social values. The manifestation of these deep-rooted differences is more subtle than is commonly thought, making their detection much more difficult. Therefore, determining the validity of any political culture hypothesis necessitates the use of a wide array of evidence, whereas a test of the convergence hypothesis—with its emphasis on structural and economic efficiency arguments—can make use of widely available economic and labor market data.

Social surveys offer one way to test the political culture hypothesis. A number of such surveys, which sample the opinions and views of citizens in both countries, have in fact been conducted since the 1950s. Some, including our own, have been described in earlier chapters. We discussed the perplexing results that they present in terms of the political culture explanation for the divergence in union density. Chief among these anomalies is that in most cases social surveys, including our own, actually show that unions are more approved of in the United States than in Canada, despite the increased numbers of organized members north of the border (see figs. 1.1 and 1.2 in chap. 1).

Many critics of the political culture hypothesis take these findings as evidence that the theory is too simplistic to account for divergent union density trends. More appealing is the idea that managers have a particular antipathy for unions in the United States that is not shared by similar managers in Canada. Unfortunately, even this view fails to note that, contrary to the opinion of many in the field of industrial relations who attribute lower U.S. union membership to greater managerial hostility, survey data consistently have found similar or lower rates of stated hostility for unions among managers in the United States compared with their Canadian counterparts (Taras 1997).

What critics of the political cultural view and proponents of the managerial hostility school fail to recognize, however, is the crucial distinction between surveys and the measurement of deeply seated values. General social surveys are quite good at measuring attitudes, but attitudes are not the same as values. Attitudes often shift according to changing economic and social conditions, whereas values do not. Unlike opinions about the union movement generally, values—such as a desire to preserve individual freedom above social order—are unlikely to alter in the face of differing material circumstances.

If we are, therefore, interested in the measurement of value differences, we need not only a more sensitive array of survey questions but also an understanding of institutional and cultural history to tease out *how* these value differences affect cross-border outcomes such as divergent union density trends.

In the end, to use a well-worn cliché, the proof of the pudding is in the eating, or in this case the reading. Whether our emphasis on the continued influence of different cross-border organizing principles has helped to explain the distinctive paths of the labor movements in Canada and the United States is for the reader to decide.

General Summary

In this book we have argued that higher union density in Canada, compared with the United States, is rooted in Canada's statist, social democratic traditions, which are in turn attributable to its Tory and decidedly European conservative lineage. The United States has an individualistic, laissez-faire tradition that is generally not supportive of more collectivist approaches. Only in extraordinary circumstances, such as war or prolonged economic downturns, has the United States moved closer to the statist model.

Our own 1996 survey and other data show that Canadians have more social democratic values than do Americans. Americans, irrespective of social class, prefer freedom over equality and, as a result, the state has been much weaker south of the border. Therefore, in order to explain why Canada has historically displayed a higher density rate and diverged so dramatically from the United States after 1960, one does not need to make appeals to the differing tastes or attitudes of managers. One merely has to note that U.S. managers (just as most Americans generally) are less constrained in their day-to-day activities by the state, whereas Canadians face slightly more intervention and have less scope for individual action.

One of the chief implications of the political culture view is that it inverts the causal ordering of much cross-border labor relations research. Rather than asking why union density has fallen so dramatically in the United States since the early 1960s and viewing this as the problem in need of an explanation, our view asserts that the surge in union membership relative to labor-force growth in the United States from 1938 to 1958 is the real anomaly, just as was the surge in union membership during World War I. This reorientation should not be construed, however, as an attempt to view the United States as antithetical to unions. Instead, it is an approach that sensitizes readers to the fact that the United States does not possess a traditional left-wing party and that Americans (generally) are antithetical to almost all forms of large institutional structures and laws that impinge on individual civil liberties and freedoms. Compared with Americans, Canadians are more supportive of left-wing parties and are not as averse to equality or institutional power.

This cross-border view is supported when we look beyond North America, toward the international data reviewed in chapter 2. That evidence indicates a continuing link between trade unionism and the strength of left parties and movements, which in turn is related to the degree of class awareness. Cross-national statistical analysis shows that union density in advanced Western countries is positively associated with the power of left parties in government. Given these international findings, it is not so surprising to see the United States scoring so low on union density.

The real problem for unions in the United States, in contrast to many other advanced Western countries, is that they never created their own labor or social democratic party nor did they support one. By way of contrast, we have seen in chapter 3 how Canadian labor activists took part in the formation of the first electorally viable social democratic party in Canada, the CCF, and played a significant role in the organization of the NDP, the CCF's successor. The real divergence to be explained is therefore the absence of a left-wing party in the United States and the presence of a strong one in Canada rather than the manifestation of this divergence in terms of lower union density.

Could it be a historical accident that one country established a strong labor party and the other did not? Perhaps. But we once again point to the embeddedness of differing political cultures. In this case, one culture (Canada) shares more in common with continental counterparts, whereas the other (the United States) was born out of a liberal revolution that distrusted the concept of interventionist politics. As John Conway, retired professor of Canadian Studies at the University of Massachusetts, Amherst, has stated, "This is the most profound difference between Canadian and American political values and political philosophies. Americans cherish individualism and individuality above community. Canadians have exactly the reverse set of political priorities" (Conway 1988, 385).

That frustrated demand for unionization in the United States is higher than in Canada should therefore not surprise us either. The greater extent of government support for unionization in Canada compared with the United States is the chief source of the differences in unmet demand for unionization. This support is manifested in legislation, the extent and speed of enforcement of the legislation, and the amount of direct government and other publicly funded employment. Therefore, when U.S. workers are asked about joining a union, they quite rightly confirm this view. However, it is the U.S. emphasis on individual freedom combined with a congressional rather than the parliamentary system of government in Canada that has not permitted U.S. federal agencies to override the institutional and legal barriers against unions, except in extraordinary circumstances such as wars and depressions.

This conflict between attitudes and values has an important implication for the future of unionism in the United States and Canada. Holding other factors constant, individualistic and libertarian U.S. values will continue to impede unionism because culture changes slowly. Conversely, social democratic and statist values in Canada will remain a major factor promoting unionism.

The higher *perceived* approval of unions in the United States compared with Canada, discussed in chapter 5, is in fact linked to the *actual* weakness of U.S. unions. In Canada, the greater perceived (and real) power of unions results in lower public approval. Because unions are more powerful, militant, and politicized in Canada, their effect on the economy and politics tends to be more visible than it is south of the border. This is also why, contrary to many expert opinions that attribute lower union membership in the United States to greater managerial hostility, survey data actually show that there is more support for (or less hostility toward) unions among U.S. managers than among their Canadian counterparts. This does not mean that managers are any less effective in their opposition to unions south of the border. In fact, we argue that the exact opposite is implied by these survey responses. U.S. managerial sentiment is less overtly hostile than Canadian sentiment precisely because managers are less constrained in opposing union organizing. Canadian managers face a more militant union movement and more stringent laws that protect unions. It is for this reason that they are more vocal in their stated opposition to unions than Americans.

Another piece of evidence supporting the cultural hypothesis is that, despite considerable variation in the levels of union density among states and provinces as seen in chapter 7, the ranking of states and, to a lesser extent, provinces, has remained relatively stable since the 1930s. The low union densities in most states even preceded the introduction of right-to-work laws.

Another interesting interstate finding is that union membership and church attendance are inversely related; that is, people in states where church attendance is high do not tend to belong to unions, and vice versa. This may, for example, explain the persistence of anti-union enclaves in the Bible belt.

In chapters 8 and 9, we observed that a larger proportion of Canadian than U.S. professionals and other white-collar workers either belongs or wants to belong to unions and approves of unions. The findings imply that the U.S. union movement as a whole must decide whether it should seek to organize de facto unions (i.e., associations) among groups of professionals that disdain the union label. The history of professional associations that have assumed union functions, such as the NEA and the ANA, suggests a path to be followed by the union movement in the United States. Even without these separate associations, however, Canadian professionals and other white-collar workers are much more highly unionized than their counterparts in the United States.

Finally, in chapter 10 we demonstrated that in spite of large differences in union density, there is a similarity in the extent of nonunion representation in the United States and Canada. Overall, a majority of employees in both countries want some form of voice in the workplace. A high correlation between union membership by industry and formal nonunion representation also suggests a complementarity between the two forms of voice.

To end as we have begun, the American Revolution produced two nations, not one. Two centuries after the revolution that gave birth to Canada and the United States, we have compared the two countries along a dimension that differentiates them markedly, namely unionism. Specifically, the book is concerned with the source(s) of the differences in unionization rates between the two countries. Accepting, as we do, that the two

countries differ in their basic organizing principles and that these historical legacies still exert their effect on both countries, we suggest that
perhaps one way in which we can understand the differing trajectory of
U.S. and Canadian unionism over the last thirty years would be through the
prism of value and cultural differences. This perspective does indeed help
us answer one of the most perplexing cross-border questions surrounding
unionism: why there is greater approval of unions in the United States than
in Canada but a lower union membership rate. Other questions still remain
unanswered. It is to this end, and to the research to follow, that this book
is dedicated.

APPENDIX A

UNION MEMBERSHIP AND UNION DENSITY ESTIMATES:
METHODOLOGY AND COMPARABILITY

Preparation of Estimates of Union Membership and Union Density in the United States and Canada in the Early Period: 1901–1936

Some estimates indicate slightly higher union densities in Canada than in the United States prior to the mid-1930s (Bain and Price 1980), but new calculations by the authors show a consistently higher union density in Canada, particularly from World War 1 to 1936. The early union density data series for Canada was constructed using revised estimates of both the size of the Canadian labor force and union membership.

1901–1910

The data for the period 1901–10 are based on estimates derived from the limited available statistics. The only data available for Canadian union membership in this period are from two sources. First, we have two conflicting *Labor Gazette* estimates, one that claims that there were 15,000 members in 1900 and another that recorded an estimate of union members for 1911 as approximately 100,000. Second, Leo Troy estimates the number of Canadian members in U.S. international unions as close to 40,000 in 1901 (Troy and Sheflin 1985).

The first year for which we have reliable estimates of Canadian membership data is 1911. In that year, 70 percent of Canadian members were also members of international unions. We use this percentage to back-cast the Canadian membership data from Troy's estimates of Canadian members in U.S. international unions in 1901. The labor force data needed to construct a union density measure are described next.

1911–1936

For the period 1911–21, we have membership data but no accurate estimate of the size of the labor force. The size of the nonagricultural paid workforce is constructed by inference from census figures for 1901 and 1911. However, there was a change in the calculation of the nonagricultural paid workforce in 1931 in order to take into account the presence of the self-employed in the labor force. Therefore, adjustments are required because previous labor force figures did not include estimates of the self-employed. This omission gives a downward bias to the previous estimates of union density from 1901 onward.

We used the average percentage of self-employment in the 1931 and 1941 census calculations (17.7 percent) to recalculate the size of the nonagricultural paid workforce from 1901 to 1930. This calculation revealed a fifteen-year period from 1921 to 1936 (as opposed to the five-year period using earlier estimates) in which Canadian union density was 7–8 percentage points higher than U.S. union density.

Comparability of Union Density Estimates in the United States and Canada

Estimates of union density in the United States are obtained from BLS. These estimates are derived from the Current Population Survey (CPS) of a national sample of about 60,000 households. The union membership data are confined to wage and salary workers. Self-employed workers are excluded.

Canadian union membership rates for 1963–96 are obtained from the data collected under the Corporations and Labor Unions Returns Act (CALURA) of 1962. The data for 1997–2001 are obtained from the Labor Force Survey. Unionization rates are limited to paid workers. Because of cross-national differences and changes in methodology, union membership rates are not always strictly comparable with U.S. estimates and estimates for earlier years.

APPENDIX B

TRANSCRIPT OF SURVEY ON ATTITUDES TOWARD WORK

Summary of the Survey Methodology

A survey investigating comparative public attitudes in Canada and the United States with respect to work, labor unions, and general public issues was undertaken on behalf of Professors Seymour Martin Lipset of George Mason University and Noah Meltz of the University of Toronto and was conducted by the Angus Reid Group (now Ipsos-Reid Group). The survey involved 3,245 telephone interviews commencing in June 1996. It included samples of 1,750 adults in the United States and 1,495 in Canada.

The survey questionnaire was developed by Lipset and Meltz in conjunction with their research assistants and with researchers from the Angus Reid Group. The questionnaire construction process was partly guided by the academics' and assistants' detailed review of the questioning used in other surveys on work, labor unions, and related issues. In addition, the research specifications provided for the Angus Reid Group to conduct a series of eight focus groups in November 1995 in four selected cities (Windsor, Detroit, Calgary, and Houston). These sessions broadly explored the issues under consideration and qualitatively tested the concepts addressed in the draft survey questionnaire.

The draft questionnaire (similar to the final version, but considerably longer) was subjected to a full pretest survey conducted among a total sample of 231 (116 in the United States, 115 in Canada). The pretest data were tabulated and fully analyzed (including such procedures as factor and regression analysis) in order to assist the process of paring back the survey instrument for the full survey.

The total survey sample of 3,245 was collected in phases as follows:

	Canada	*United States*
General population surveys	1,003	1,000
Special state booster samples	0	117
Workforce boosters (employed 10+ hours/week)	212	206
Union members booster samples	280	358
Spanish-speaking booster sample	0	69

The survey samples for both countries were geographically stratified by province and then to the Current Metropolitan Area/Census Division–level in Canada and to the state level in the United States. Within this stratification, individual households were selected using a modified random-digit dialing procedure. The Canadian sample was generated using the Angus Reid Group's in-house telephone sample database. The U.S. sample was generated from a database provided by Genesys Sampling Systems.

The general population surveys were executed in two proportionate halves. Gender quotas were imposed for the second half of data collection such that the complete general population samples would include a 50-50 gender split at the regional level. The workforce and union member boosters were executed following the general population surveys. Their regional stratification was devised based on the incidences encountered in the initial phase, such that the resulting complete workforce and union member samples would be regionally reflective of their respective populations.

Data collection was conducted by the Angus Reid Group using the firm's network of central location Computer Assisted Telephone Interviewing (CATI) facilities. The one exception was the Spanish-language interviews, which were conducted by MDI Interviewing Services of Chula Vista, California. Interviewing for the general population surveys and the special state boosters was conducted between June 18 and July 3, 1996. The workforce boosters were conducted between July 10 and 15, 1996, and the union member boosters between July 16 and 27, 1996. The Spanish-speaking interviews were conducted between September 9 and 11. All interviews were conducted from central-location facilities. All interviewers had received the Angus Reid Group's basic interviewing procedures training and a specialized briefing for this project.

The response rate was 58.7 percent. A rigorous callback regimen was employed throughout data collection. Numbers were recontacted throughout fielding— including in the daytime and as work moved to new phases. For example, numbers unsuccessfully attempted in the general population samples were reattempted for the workforce and union member booster surveys. Refusals were recontacted (those encountered early enough in the field process) by a different interviewer with a view to enlisting their participation—over 150 initial refusals were success-fully converted.

Weighting

For the purposes of analysis, the survey data have been grouped into six separate samples, three main types for both Canada and the United States:

General population samples. These do not include respondents contacted for the workforce or union member boosters, but the U.S. general population sample does include the special state and Spanish language boosters. (The 1,000+ cases in both countries provide for an overall margin of error of ±3.1 percentage points at the 95 percent confidence level, larger within subgroups.)

Workforce samples. The workforce samples include respondents working full- or part-time 10+ hours/week drawn from both the general population and workforce booster surveys, but not the union member booster surveys. (The 800+ samples afford a standard margin of error of ±3.5 percent.)

Union members samples. The samples of 500+ union members in each country include union members encountered in both the general population and the work-force samples as well as the union member booster samples (standard margin of error ±4.5 percentage points).

These six survey samples were examined against the various sociodemographic and workforce characteristics of the respective populations. The samples are con-sidered to be satisfactorily representative across the range of descriptors examined, with the one exception of reported formal educational attainment, which is higher than the actuals for all six samples. No statistical weighting has been applied to adjust for this skew, primarily because there is no certainty that the less-educated strata captured in the sample are a representative surrogate for the specific segment(s) absent from the sample. Further, trial weighting was applied to investi-gate this issue, and adjusting for the education skew in that way did not have a major impact on the overall pattern of the binational results. One other sample issue worth noting concerns the apparent undersampling of Blacks, or African Americans, which has also not been adjusted for by statistical weighting.

Some statistical weighting has been applied to these data sets to enhance repre-sentativeness. For both the general population and workforce data, weights were applied to adjust for the state and Spanish language boosters in the United States and a modest underrepresentation of Canadian union members in these samples; both samples in both countries were also weighted by respondents' age and sex to more precisely reflect census distributions. The Canadian and U.S. union members samples were weighted by age to reflect available union member-ship profile data.

Questionnaire

Introduction

Hello, this is _____ calling from the Angus Reid Group, a professional public opinion research company. We are doing a survey of people's attitudes toward "work" and some related issues, as part of an important academic study being conducted by a team of Canadian and American researchers.

Your household's telephone number has been selected at random from a computer database—and your participation in this telephone survey would help us to ensure that we include a representative sample of (Canadians/Americans). Let me assure you we're not trying to sell you anything—this is strictly a survey of public opinion, and all responses are entirely confidential. We would really appreciate it if you could spare roughly 20 minutes of your time to talk about different issues related to work. (If now is not a good time, I'd be happy to call you back later this evening or tomorrow to do the survey—*arrange callback.*)

Are you 18 years of age or older? (*If not, ask to speak to someone who is—repeat intro or arrange callback.*)

Record regional data from sample: province/state; city/census division

Record respondent's sex—watch quotas: male; female

1.0 Introductory Questions—Genpop Sample

We'd like to begin the survey with some questions about your current employment status, for our own classification purposes.

1.1 Are you currently employed in a paying job, on either a full-time or part-time basis?

Yes, full-time

Yes, part-time

Yes, both

No, not employed

(*all yes, employed skip to Q. 1.3*)

(*Programming note: all respondents not employed at Q. 1.1 to be asked only Q. 1.2, section 2, section 5.1, Q. 5.2.4, section 7.2.*)

(*Not employed:*)

1.2 How would you describe yourself? Are you (*read list*)? (*Interviewer note: if respondent volunteers they are "laid off," record as "Unemployed."*)

A student

Retired

A homemaker not working outside the home
Unemployed and looking for work
Other

(If employed:)

1.3 In total, how many hours a week do you normally work at your paying job (or jobs)? (*Probe for best estimate. Record figure, not a range.*)

Number of hours: _____

(*Programming note: if work less than 10 hours at Q.1.3, proceed as "not employed" as outlined above—i.e. ask only: section 2, section 5.1, Q.5.2.4 and section 7.2.*)

(*Interviewer note: if "yes, both" at Q.1.1 or if respondent volunteers they have 2+ jobs, ask them to focus on their main job only for all other questions about work.*)

1.4a Are you self-employed—that is, do you work for yourself or own your own company?

(If self-employed at Q.1.4a:)

1.4b How many employees, other than yourself, do you have working for you or your company on a regular basis? (*Record exact number, not a range.*)

Number of employees: _____

(*Programming note: self-employed with 0 or 1 employee to be asked only rest of section 1, section 2, section 5.1, Q.5.2.4, and section 7.2.*)

(If not self-employed at Q.1.4a:)

1.5a Do you work on a personal contract with your main employer, or are you an actual employee of that organization?

1.5b And are you a temporary employee, or are you considered permanent?

(All employed 10+ hours:)

1.6 In at least two words, please state your current occupation. (*Probe thoroughly for full description of job—i.e., if "Salesperson," ask: "What do you sell?"*)

1.7a Would you describe yourself as a "manager"—that is, as someone who participates in establishing policies at your company or organization?

(*Programmer note: Q.1.7a is "filter" for question series in sections 4, 5, and 6. If yes, manager at Q.1.7a, ask Q.1.7b. Others skip to Q.1.8.*)

1.7b And would you say that you are in an upper-, middle-, or lower-management position?

(*All employed 10+ hours:*)

1.8 As an official part of your job, do you supervise the work of other employees or tell other employees what to do?

1.9 Are any of the people working for your employer members of a union?
(*Programmer note: Q.1.9 is "filter" for question series in sections 4, 5, and 6.*)

2.0 General Values and Canadian-U.S. Differences

(*Programming note: section 2.0 to be asked of all respondents.*)
We'd like to begin the main part of our survey by asking people their attitudes about some general issues concerning our society.

2.1 Economic Situation/Public Priorities

2.1.1 To begin with, thinking of the issues presently confronting (Canada/the United States), which one do you feel should receive the greatest attention from (Canada's/America's) leaders? (*do not read list*) What other issues do you think are important for (Canada/the United States) right now? (*do not read list*) (*record up to three others*)

Deficit/debt/spending

Economy—general

Education

Health care/medicare

Jobs/unemployment

National unity/Quebec's future/constitution

Taxes

Other (*specify*)

2.1.2 There is a lot of talk these days about what the aims of this country should be for the next ten years. I'm going to read a list of goals which different people would give top priority. Would you please say which one of these you, yourself, consider the most important? (*read items in random order*) (*one only for first mention*) And which would be the next most important? (*repeat remaining items if necessary*) (*one answer only for next most*)

Maintaining a high level of economic growth

Seeing that people have more to say about how things are done at their jobs and in their communities

A stable economy

Progress toward a less impersonal and more humane society

2.1.3 Do you strongly agree, moderately agree, moderately disagree, or strongly disagree that: (*read items*)

    a. The way things are in (Canada/the United States), people like me have a good chance of improving their standard of living in the next few years.

    b. My present economic situation is not good.

    c. The gap between rich and poor (Canadians/Americans) is too wide.

    d. Businesses put profit too far ahead of the welfare of their employees.

    e. (Canada/The United States) should do more to protect our own industries against foreign imports.

    f. Most people can be trusted.

2.2 Class and Mobility

2.2.1 Imagine two workers of the same age, with the same years of service with their employer, doing nearly the same job. One earns (in Canada: 70 dollars; in the United States: 50 dollars) a week more than the other. The better-paid worker, however, is quicker, more efficient, and more reliable at their job. In your opinion, how fair or unfair is it that one of these workers is paid more than the other: very fair, somewhat fair, somewhat unfair, or very unfair?

2.2.2a If you were asked to use one of four names for your social class, which would you belong in (*read list*): lower, working, middle, or upper?
(*If "middle" at Q.2.2.2a, ask Q.2.2.2b. Others skip to Q.2.2.3.*)

2.2.2b And would that be lower-middle class, upper-middle class, or right in the middle?

2.2.3 How do you think your children's opportunities to succeed will compare to your own—would you say your children will have better opportunities than you, about the same, or not as good opportunities as you? (*Interviewer note: if respondent volunteers they don't have children, ask them to imagine they did.*)

2.3 Individualism versus Group Orientation/Role of Government

2.3.1 Which do you think is more important—(*rotate options*)
Freedom, so that everyone can live and develop without hindrance
or
Equality, so that nobody is underprivileged and social class differences are not so strong

2.3.2 Do you agree strongly, agree moderately, disagree moderately, or disagree strongly with each of the following statements? (*read items—randomize*)

a. It is the responsibility of the government to reduce the differences in income between people with high incomes and those with low incomes.

b. It is the government's responsibility to provide a job for those who cannot find one in the private sector.

c. The government is responsible for the well-being of all its citizens and it has an obligation to help people when they are in trouble.

d. When jobs are scarce, people should be required to retire early.

e. An important government responsibility is to preserve (Canadian/American) society's morality in areas such as gambling, pornography and alcohol.

f. There should be a maximum limit on how much income people can make in salary and bonus.

g. We (Canadians/Americans) have a particular obligation to ensure that no child has to grow up in poverty.

h. Governments should place higher priority on reducing the deficit than on creating jobs.

2.4 Confidence in Institutions

2.4.1 Now I am going to read you a list of institutions in (Canadian/American) society.

Please tell me how much confidence you, yourself, have in each one: a great deal of confidence, quite a lot, some, or very little confidence? (*randomize items*)

a. Labor unions

b. Parliament/Congress

c. Large corporations

d. The news media

e. The (Canadian/U.S.) government

f. The legal system

g. The police

h. Environmental groups

2.4.2 If you had to generalize, who would you say is more honest—(*read items in random order*)?

Union leaders

Corporate leaders

(Both equally)

(Neither)

2.5 Consensual versus Adversarial/Attitudes toward Business

2.5.1 Generally speaking, would you say that employers' interests and employees' interests are, by their very nature, opposed, or are their interests basically the same?

2.5.2 If you had to estimate, what proportion of (Canadian/American) employers would you say do not treat their employees as fairly as they should? Would you say this is true of (*read list*)

Hardly any employers at all
Only a fairly small number
Quite a few
or
Most employers

2.5.3 All other things being equal, should a company that has to lay off people do this on the basis of seniority or merit?

Seniority
Merit
(Both)
(Neither)

3.0 Attitudes toward Work

(*Programming note: sections 3.0 and 4.0 for all those employed 10+ hours. Not employed, working less than 10 hours, and self-employed <2 employees—skip to section 5.0.*)

3.1 General Attitudes toward Work

Now, we want to ask a series of questions about people's attitudes toward their jobs and their workplace.

3.1.1 In general, are you very satisfied, somewhat satisfied, somewhat dissatisfied, or very dissatisfied with your current job?

3.2 Specific Attitudes toward Current Job

3.2.1 Please tell me whether you strongly agree, moderately agree, moderately disagree, or strongly disagree with the following statements. (*randomize*)

a. When it really comes down to it, job security is more important to me than opportunities for advancing my career.

b. I would always do the best I could at any job, regardless of what the pay is like.

c. Employees where I work are afraid to challenge managers when they disagree with a decision that affects them.

d. People at my workplace don't express their real views for fear of losing their jobs or hurting their careers.

3.2.2 Please tell me whether you rate your job as: very good, good, poor, or very poor on each of the following attributes. (*randomize*)

a. Fair treatment of employees by management

b. Opportunity for advancement

c. Management who appreciates what you do

3.2.3 From your most objective viewpoint, have you been compensated fairly for your main employment this past year?

3.2.4a How much pride, if any, do you take in the work that you do: a great deal, some, little, or none?

3.2.4b How loyal would you say you feel toward your employer? Do you feel very loyal, fairly loyal, not very loyal, or not loyal at all?

3.2.5a Over the past three years or so, has your employer experienced: significant downsizing or layoffs, significant expansion or hiring, or has there been no real change in the number of people working for your employer over the past three years or so?

(*If downsized/layoffs or expanded/hiring:*)

3.2.5b And roughly how big was the employee (downsizing/expansion)—that is, roughly what proportion of all employees have been (let go/hired on) in the past three years or so? (*prompt if necessary*)

Less than 10 percent

10 to 20 percent

21 to 30 percent

31 to 40 percent

41 to 50 percent

More than 50 percent

3.2.6a Looking ahead to the near future, would you say you expect your employer will be expanding its number of employees, reducing its number of employees, or not making any changes to the number of people it employs?

3.2.6b How worried are you that your company will be laying off or cutting jobs in the near future? Are you not worried at all, not very worried, somewhat worried, or very worried?

4.0 Attitudes toward Collective Action at Work

4.1 General Attitudes—Decision Making at Work

4.1.1 Overall, how would you rate your company's system for resolving the problems individual employees have at work: excellent, good, only fair, or poor?

4.1.2 At the place where you work, is there a formal grievance procedure—that is, a formal process that employees can use to raise complaints about something the company or management has done?

4.1.3 Some companies are organizing workplace decision making in new ways to get employees more involved—using things like self-directed work teams, total quality management, quality circles, or other employee-involvement programs. Is anything like this now being done by your employer?

4.1.4 Overall, how would you rate the involvement or influence you have in workplace decisions that affect your job or work life: excellent, good, only fair, or poor?

(*Programmer note: if "manager" at Q. 1.7a, skip to section 4.2*) (*Nonmanagers continue.*)

4.1.5a Still thinking about your influence on company decisions that concern you, how much more influence do you think you would have if there was a group of employees who met regularly with management to discuss workplace issues? Do you think a group like this would give you (*read list*)

A lot more influence
Somewhat more influence
Only a little more influence
No more influence at all
(Already have a group)

4.1.5b How would you prefer to solve a workplace problem of your own? Would you feel more comfortable dealing directly with management yourself, or would you feel more comfortable having a group of your fellow employees help you deal with management?

4.1.5c How willing would you be to volunteer two or three hours a month to participate in an employee organization to discuss workplace issues with your employer's management? Would you be (*read list*)?
Definitely willing
Probably willing
Probably not willing
Definitely not willing
(Do not want that organization)

4.1.5d When you, or other employees like you, make suggestions about improving quality or productivity, how often does management take them seriously? Would you say management almost always, sometimes, hardly ever, or never takes them seriously?

4.2 Specific Attitudes on Collective Action

4.2.1 Please tell me how interested you would be in joining an organization that did the following things at your workplace? What about (*read item—randomize*)? Would you: definitely be interested in joining an organization that did that, probably be interested, probably not be interested, or definitely not be interested?
   a. Engage in collective bargaining (or negotiate) on your behalf over wages and benefits
   b. Represent employees who have filed grievances against their supervisors or managers

4.2.2 Do you feel that you are already protected by the law against unfair treatment by your employer?

4.2.3 As far as you're concerned, do you think it should or should not be legal for employers to (*read items—randomize*)? (*separate should/should not response for each*)
   a. Fire an employee for no reason
   b. Hire replacement workers if employees are out on a legal strike
   c. Fire workers who try to start up a union

4.2.4 When you hear about a labor dispute—before you know the specific details—who do you tend to side with (*read items—rotate*)?
The union
The company

5.0 Attitudes toward Unions

(Programming note: section 5.1 and Q5.2.5 to be asked of all respondents.)

This last major part of the survey contains a series of questions about labor unions. Please don't worry if you're not a member of a union—we're simply interested in your personal views and attitudes, based on whatever you may have heard and on your general impressions.

5.1 General Attitudes

5.1.1 All things considered, would you say unions are good for working people, bad for working people, or make no real difference either way?

5.1.2 And what about for (Canada/the United States) as a whole—are unions good, bad, or do they make no real difference?

5.1.3 Do you think that labor unions today have too much power, not enough power, or about the right amount of power?

5.1.4 Please tell me if you strongly agree, moderately agree, moderately disagree, or strongly disagree with the following statements? (*read items—randomize*)
   a. Unions protect workers against unfair action by their employers.
   b. Unions improve their members' job security.
   c. Unions improve the wages and benefits of their members.
   d. Unions improve the working conditions of their members.
   e. Unions give members their money's worth for the dues they pay.
   f. Unions are too involved in political activities and election campaigns.
   g. Unions are not needed nowadays since most employees now get fair treatment from their employers.
   h. There's too much corruption in the organized labor movement in (Canada/the United States).
   i. The union movement in (Canada/the United States) seems to be getting weaker.
   j. Union leadership just isn't representative of the views of ordinary union members.
   k. Unions have a negative impact on productivity.
   l. Workers as a group will do better than an individual on their own.
   m. Most of my family and close friends don't like unions.
   n. Unions make the (Canadian/U.S.) economy more fair.
   o. The wage demands of unions just don't reflect economic realities.

p. Unions enable workers to get away with being too inefficient.

q. Unions hurt (Canadian/American) companies' ability to compete in international markets.

5.1.5 Do you approve or disapprove of labor unions?

5.1.6 To what extent do government agencies protect the right to join a union? Do they give a lot of protection, some protection, very little protection, or no protection?

5.1.7 Please think for a moment about employers' resistance to union efforts to organize new members into unions. How widespread would you say this employer resistance to unionization is in (Canada/the United States)? Is it very widespread, somewhat widespread, not very widespread, or not at all widespread?

(*Programming note: not employed and self-employed with <2 employees now skip to Q.5.2.4.a & b. Managers at Q.1.7a now skip to section 5.2. If nonmanager at Q.1.7a and employer has a union at Q.1.9:*)

5.1.8 If your employer didn't already have a union, and employees tried to form one, can you imagine how management would react? Do you think they would welcome the union, oppose the union with information only, oppose the union by threatening or harassing some union supporters, or do you think they would do nothing?

(*If nonmanager at Q.1.7a and employer has no union at Q.1.9:*)

5.1.9 If a group of employees at your work tried to form a union, how do you think management would react? Do you think they would welcome the union, oppose the union with information only, oppose the union by threatening or harassing some union supporters, or do you think they would do nothing?

5.2 Union Members and Their Views

(*Q.5.2.1a to be asked of all those employed 10+ hours.*)

5.2.1a Are you yourself currently a member of a union?

(*Programming note: Q.5.2.1a identifies "union members" for latter part of section 5.2. If no to Q.5.2.1a, ask:*)

5.2.1b Are you a member of an organization other than a union that bargains collectively on behalf of you and other workers?

(If no to Q.5.2.1b, ask:)

5.2.1c Are you covered by a collective agreement?

5.2.2a Do you have any formal non-union employee representation at your workplace?

(If yes to Q.5.2.2a, continue with 5.2.2 series. Others skip to Q.5.2.3.)

5.2.2b Are you covered by that nonunion employee representation?

5.2.2c Does this nonunion employee representation provide a *(randomize items—yes/no for each)*?

Joint health and safety committee

Committee which discusses compensation and benefits of employment

5.2.2d Are the nonunion employee representatives elected by employees, appointed by management, or chosen in some other way?

(All those employed 10+ hours:)

5.2.3 Does any other member of your family belong to a union—such as your spouse or your parents?

(Q.5.2.4a to be asked of all nonunion at Q.5.2.1a, plus all not employed and self-employed <2 employees)

5.2.4a Have you ever been a member of a union?

(Q.5.2.4b to be asked of all not employed and self-employed <2 employees)

5.2.4b Suppose you were employed outside the home, and an election was held tomorrow to decide whether your workplace would be unionized or not, do you think you would definitely vote for a union, probably vote for a union, probably vote against a union, or definitely vote against a union?

(Programming note: not employed and self-employed <2 employees now proceed to section 7.2. Q.5.2.4 to be asked of all those non-union at Q.5.2.1a.)

5.2.4 If an election were held tomorrow to decide whether your workplace would be unionized or not, do you think you would definitely vote for a union, probably vote for a union, probably vote against a union, or definitely vote against a union?

(Programming note: all nonunion at Q.5.2.1 now skip to section 6.0 if manager, section 7.0 if not. Union members at Q.5.2.1a continue.)

5.2.5 If a new election were held tomorrow to decide whether to keep the union where you work, do you think you would definitely vote for a union, probably vote for a union, probably vote against a union, or definitely vote against a union?

5.2.6 Do you strongly agree, moderately agree, moderately disagree, or strongly disagree with this statement: People like me don't have any say about what the union does?

5.2.7 And how satisfied are you with your union's efforts to influence public policy: very satisfied, somewhat satisfied, not too satisfied, or not at all satisfied?

Some people are more involved in their union than others. Can you give me an idea of how involved you yourself are in the following different union activities?

5.2.8a First, over the past two years, how many regular meetings for the general membership would you say your union has held? (*Probe for best estimate. Get a figure, not a range.*)
Number of meetings: _____

5.2.8b And how many of those regular meetings would you yourself have attended? (*Probe for best estimate. Get a figure, not a range.*)
Number attended: _____

5.2.9a And the last time your union local held elections, did you yourself vote?

5.2.9b Do you recall if your union's last local election was competitive—that is, was it contested by more than one candidate or was there just one candidate?

5.2.10 And the last time your union held national (or unionwide) elections, did you yourself vote?

5.2.11 What about the last time your union ratified a contract—did you yourself vote?

5.2.12 Have you ever held a position within your union? (*If yes*: Was it an elected or appointed position?)

5.2.13 How often do you take a good look at your union newsletter/newspaper: never, rarely, sometimes, most of the time, or always?

5.2.14 How willing would you be to pay a small increase in union dues to support efforts to organize more workers into unions? Would you be very willing, somewhat willing, not very willing, or not at all willing?

5.2.15a Have you ever filed a formal grievance against your employer through your union?

(*If yes at Q.5.2.15a.*)
5.2.15b How satisfied were you with the way the union handled your grievance: very satisfied, fairly satisfied, not very satisfied, or not at all satisfied?

5.2.16 Have you ever been out on strike?

6.0 Managers' Views of Unions

(*Note: section 6 is for "managers" at Q.1.7a. All others skip to 7.0.*)

6.1 Suppose there was an employee organization formed to discuss workplace issues with management. How willing would you be to work with such an organization in solving workplace problems? Would you be (*read list*)?
Definitely willing
Probably willing
Probably not willing
Definitely not willing
(Do not want that organization)

6.2 When employees make suggestions about improving quality or productivity, how often do you find these suggestions useful (*read list*)?
Almost always
Sometimes
Hardly ever
Never
(Don't receive suggestions)

We wanted to ask people working in a management capacity—like yourself—some questions about any experiences you might have had with unions in the workplace.

6.3 In your current management role, are any of the employees you are responsible for represented by a union?
(*If yes to Q.6.3, skip to Q.6.5. If no at Q.6.3, ask Q.6.4, then skip to Q.6.6.*)

6.4 Have you ever managed unionized employees?

(If yes to Q.6.3:)
6.5a Can you give me an estimate of what proportion of all the employees you are responsible for are unionized? (*Probe for best estimate—record a percent figure, not a range.*)

_____%

6.5b   How many different unions would operate in the areas you are directly responsible for? (*record number*)

Number: _____

(*Programming note: Q.6.6 to be asked of all managers at workplaces with unions at Q.1.9. Managers with no union at Q.1.9, ask Q.6.7 & 6.8.*)
We'd like to get an idea of what kind of impact managers believe unions have had at their company or organization.

6.6a What about the wages paid to your employees? Generally speaking, would you say wages at your workplace are higher as a result of unionization, lower, or about the same? (Much or somewhat higher/lower?)

Much higher
Somewhat higher
About the same
Somewhat lower
Much lower

6.6b And what about the productivity at your workplace—generally speaking, would you say productivity is higher, lower, or no different as a result of unionization? (Much or somewhat higher/lower?)

Much higher
Somewhat higher
No different
Somewhat lower
Much lower

6.6c And how has unionization at your workplace affected your overall ability to be flexible and responsive to changing conditions—have unions improved your flexibility, worsened it, or had no impact? (Improved/worsened a lot or a little?)

Improved a lot
Improved a little

No impact
Worsened a little
Worsened a lot

(*Managers at union workplaces now skip to Q.6.9. Ask Q.6.7 & 6.8 of all managers at workplaces with no union at Q.1.9.*)

We'd like to get an idea of what kind of impact managers think a union would have at their company/organization.

6.7a What about the wages paid to employees? Would you say wages at your workplace would be higher with a union, lower, or about the same? (Much or somewhat higher/lower?)
Much higher
Somewhat higher
About the same
Somewhat lower
Much lower

6.7b And what about the productivity at your workplace—would you say productivity would be higher, lower, or no different if there were a union? (Much or somewhat higher/lower?)
Much higher
Somewhat higher
No different
Somewhat lower
Much lower

6.7c And how would a union at your workplace affect your ability to be flexible and responsive to changing conditions—would a union improve your flexibility, worsen it, or have no impact? (Improve/worsen a lot or a little?)
Improve a lot
Improve a little
No impact
Worsen a little
Worsen a lot

6.8a If a group of your employees tried to form a union, how do you think you and other managers would react? Would you welcome the union, oppose the union with information only, oppose the union by threatening or harassing some union supporters, or would you do nothing?

(*If oppose—either with info or threats—at Q.6.8a:*)

6.8b What are the main reasons your organization would oppose a union? (*Do not read list or prompt. Probe for up to three responses.*)

Don't like unions—general

Would hurt productivity

Would be too inflexible

Would push wages up/cost money

Other (*specify*)

(*Q.6.9 is for all managers.*)

6.9 I'm going to read you a short list of actions that organizations might take to try to keep a union out. For each one, please tell me if you think that action is very reasonable, reasonable, unreasonable, or very unreasonable. (*randomize items*)

a. Run an information campaign describing why the organization opposes a union.

b. Quietly threaten to dismiss those trying to organize the union.

c. Introduce a wage increase for all workers.

d. Suggest that if a union comes, some operations will be moved elsewhere.

7.0 Workplace Descriptors and Demographics

(*Note: section 7.1 is for employed 10+ hours only. Others go to 7.2.*)

7.1 Workplace Descriptors

Before I let you go, I've got some questions about your work that will help with the analysis of the survey results.

7.1.1 On your (main) job, do you (*read items, in order*)? (*obtain separate yes/no response for each*)

a. Receive any bonuses

b. Participate in an employee stock ownership or ESOP (EESop) plan

c. Receive fully paid vacations (i.e., a regular pay cheque while on vacation)

7.1.2 From the following list choose which, to the best of your knowledge, most accurately describes how your employer is owned or controlled. (*one only*)

Corporate ownership—stock is traded on an open market

Privately held—including proprietorship, partnership, or family owned business

Government controlled—a local or national agency, ministry, or department, a business wholly or mostly owned by the government, or a public university or college

A nonprofit, charitable or religious organization, or a private university or college

Other

7.1.3 I need to get a good idea of which industry sector your employer is involved in. (*Probe for detailed description—at least two words.*)

7.1.4a How many people across the country work for your employer? (*Record figure, not a range.*)
Number: _____

7.1.4b How many people work at the location you do?
Number: _____

7.1.4c How many people do you work with directly?
Number: _____

7.1.5 What languages are spoken at your place of work?
English only
French only
Spanish only
English & other(s) (*specify*)
French & others(s) (*specify*)
Other(s) only (*specify*)

7.1.6 Have you received any formal training that lasted at least one day or more—but not counting any orientation to a new job—from your employer in the past year or so?

7.1.7a For how many years have you worked for your employer—at any location or job?
Number of years: _____

7.1.7b How many years have you been in the workforce?
Number of years: _____

(*Note: section 7.2. is for all respondents.*)
7.2 Demographics

Now I've just got a final series of questions that will help us with our statistical analysis.

7.2.1 (*Do not ask: rerecord respondent's gender.*)

7.2.2 What was your year of birth?

7.2.3 What is your marital status? Are you (*read list*)
Now married
Living as married
Widowed
Divorced
Separated
Never been married

(*Canada interviews:*)
7.2.4a We are all (Canadians/Americans), but our ancestors come from all over the world. Can you please tell me how you would describe your own ethnic or racial background? (*accept up to two responses*)
    1st response: _____
    2nd response: _____

(*U.S. interviews:*)
7.2.4b Could you please tell me how you would describe your race? Are you (*read list as needed*)?
    White
    Black or African American
    Hispanic
    Asian
    Native American
    Multiracial
    Other (*specify*)

7.2.5 And were you born in (Canada/the United States)?
Yes
No

7.2.6 What is the highest level of formal education that you have completed?
Grade school or some high school
Complete high school
Technical or trade school/community college
Some university
Complete university degree
Postgraduate degree

(*Employed 10+ hours only:*)

7.2.7a Are you paid an annual salary or an hourly wage?

Annual salary

Hourly wage

Other

(*Employed 10+ hours only:*)

7.2.7b Into which of the following broad ranges would you place your personal annual pretax employment income? (*read list*)

Under $10,000

$10,000 to $19,999

$20,000 to $29,999

$30,000 to $39,999

$40,000 to $49,999

$50,000 to $59,999

$60,000 to $69,999

$70,000 to $79,999

$80,000 to $99,999

$100,000 to $124,999

$125,000 and over

(*All respondents:*)

7.2.8 Into which of the following broad ranges does your annual household income fall—that is, the total pretax income of everyone in your household combined. (*read listed categories*)

Under $10,000

$10,000 to $19,999

$20,000 to $29,999

$30,000 to $39,999

$40,000 to $49,999

$50,000 to $59,999

$60,000 to $69,999

$70,000 to $79,999

$80,000 to $99,999

$100,000 to $124,999

$125,000 and over

7.2.9a Do you ever think of yourself as part of a religious tradition, such as Protestant, Catholic, Jewish, other Christian, something else, or nothing in particular?

Protestant

Catholic

Jewish

Other Christian

Something else

Nothing in particular/not religious

(*If "Protestant," "Other Christian," or "Something else" at Q.7.2.9a, ask Q.7.2.9b.*)

7.2.9b What specific denomination is that? (*Do not read list. Record all others carefully.*)

Anglican/Episcopalian

Baptist

Lutheran

Methodist

Nondenominational

Pentecostal

Presbyterian

United Church

Other (*specify*)

(*For United States: if "Baptist" at Q.7.2.9b, ask:*)

7.2.9c And would you describe your congregation as Southern Baptist?

(*Ask everyone:*)

7.2.9d Which of the following statements best describes how often you attend religious services? (*read in order—one only*)

I never, or almost never, attend religious services.

I attend religious services on occasion.

I attend religious services once a month or so.

I attend religious services once a week or so.

7.2.10 Other than religious or church groups or labor or professional associations, are you yourself involved in any other voluntary associations—such as fraternal, charitable, or recreational organizations?

(*United States only:*)

7.2.11 In politics today, do you consider yourself to be a (*randomize two parties only*), or an Independent?

Republican

Democrat

Independent

(Other)

(Nothing)

(*Canada only:*)

7.2.12 In Canadian politics, which party do you traditionally associate most closely with your own political views? (*randomize parties*)

Progressive Conservative

Liberal

New Democrat

Bloc Quebecois (*Quebec only*)

Reform (*non-Quebec only*)

(Other)

(None)

7.2.13 In politics, you hear people talk about the "left" and the "right." How would you describe your own political views? Would you say you lean far to the left, moderately to the left, moderately to the right, or far to the right, or are your views right in the political center?

THANK YOU VERY MUCH FOR TAKING THE TIME TO DO THIS SURVEY—WE REALLY APPRECIATE IT!

NOTES

Chapter 1

1. The Canadian government introduced a form of wage and price control in 1975 for a three-year period, administered by an administrative tribunal established for that purpose, the Anti-Inflation Board. At the time inflation was at historically high levels and, in the view of many in the government and among the public, large union wage settlements were the cause of the inflation.

Chapter 2

1. The limited union membership in France is mostly a result of voluntary decisions. Unions generally include the most militant and politically active employees (see Rojot 2000).

2. The union membership rates among wage and salary workers and the dependent labor force differ somewhat, because the second measure includes the unemployed.

3. Our statistical analyses deal with the eighteen industrialized Organization for Economic Cooperation and Development (OECD) countries, which were democratic after World War II. Iceland, Israel, and Luxembourg are not included because of their small size and a lack of data.

4. Professional (occupational) associations can serve as alternatives to labor unions, especially among professionals in many countries. A measure of such association membership using the 1990 World Values Survey is not significantly related with 1995 union density in advanced Western countries.

5. Cameron (1984, 159–60), Redding and Viterna (1999), Western (1994, 1329), and Wilensky (1981) use somewhat different measures of left party representation. These indexes differ somewhat in time period (1962–82, 1970–90, 1919–1970s, and 1965–77) and in the number of countries they cover, as well as in the components they include. However, all left party representation indexes are highly intercorrelated and are positively correlated with union density in 1995. The left-right measure derived from the 1995 and 1990 World Values surveys for seventeen advanced Western countries is negatively correlated with both the left power indexes and union density.

6. The index was developed by Armingeon (see Wessels 1996, 20–22).

7. The index follows Cameron (1984), as modified by Redding and Viterna (1999).

8. The centralization of the labor market, the organizational unity of labor, and the scope of collective bargaining are significantly related to union density (Visser 1994). Western (1997, 94–95), however, reports a weak effect of the labor-market-centralization variable on union density, although his measure of centralization is somewhat different.

9. The 1950–92 averages of these measures of bargaining correlate positively with union density and other indexes of corporatism obtained from Bruno and Sachs (1985), Cameron (1978), Crouch (1985), Redding and Viterna (1999), and Western (1997). However, the correlation coefficient among these corporatism indexes and between them and union density ranges from 0.21 to 0.95 and from 0.36 to 0.69. Such disparity reflects a focus on different aspects of corporatism and a difference in the time period covered.

10. Western (1997, 135) attributes the occupational gap in the unionization rate to the degree of labor market centralization, or corporatism.

11. The correlation coefficient for twenty-two countries is 0.55.

12. The religious split variable, which measures the representational strength of religious unions, is not associated with union density in our analysis. The same applies to the political split variable, which reflects the combined strength of communist and socialist unions.

13. The economic concentration variable is "the percentage of employment, shipments, and production accounted for by the four largest enterprises" (Stephens 1991, 945). Stephens also estimates concentration data indirectly by looking at the GDP for nine out of twenty countries.

14. The union density figure also was more than cut in half in Portugal. But changes in political system and data quality problems may have affected the density figures there.

15. As we discuss in chapter 3, our reestimated figure is higher than Visser's 6.8 percent.

Chapter 3

1. Even at the turn of the twentieth century, however, there were a number of distinctly Canadian unions including the Canadian Brotherhood of Railway Employees, the Amalgamated Building Workers of Canada, and the broad-based Canadian Federation of Labour.

2. For a discussion of King's role in shaping Canadian labor regulation see Taras (1997, 295–341).

3. In the 1945 election, however, almost half the TLC leaders (45 percent) and almost all the CCL leaders (93 percent) backed the CCF instead of the Liberals (Morton 1990).

4. In the mid-1990s, the estimates were that 23.7 percent of employees in Canada were in the public sector, compared with 16.1 percent in the United States. See discussion by Troy (1990, 1992) on the impact on unionization of the larger public sector in Canada.

5. Interestingly, a decade later, in response to a similar question, 50 percent of Americans said that Reagan had not made the right decision, while 39 percent agreed with him (Lipset and Meltz 1997).

6. However, the new legislation did provide for a vote on certification within five days of a union applying for certification, which reduced the time period during which

employers could mobilize an anti-union drive. The net effect, however, was still reduction in union membership.

7. For an early examination of this issue see Crispo (1967).

Chapter 4

1. The socialist party, the Cooperative Commonwealth Federation (CCF), and the national trade union federation, the Canadian Labour Congress (CLC), founded the NDP in 1961.

2. As discussed in chapter 3 and later in this chapter, the Taft-Hartley Act of 1947 extended the scope of state legislation by permitting states to prohibit the inclusion in collective agreements of a union shop clause (i.e., the requirement that all employees represented by the union be required to join the union). In Canada, a 1946 decision by Supreme Court Justice Ivan Rand in the Ford Motor Company strike permitted the inclusion of a clause requiring all employees covered by a collective agreement to pay union dues, even though they did not have to join the union. This became known as the Rand Formula and is now standard in all Canadian jurisdictions.

3. See also Ostry (1985, 23); Pritchard (1982).

4. See "Canadians' Perceptions" (1997).

5. Part of the comparability results from standards established by the Canada Health Act as a condition for federal funding.

Chapter 5

1. Both aggregate and our survey data indicate that trade union membership is also related to public rather than private employment, work in larger as opposed to smaller work locations, manual rather than nonmanual positions, higher income, and increased age. Minority ethnic/racial status—Black and Hispanic in the United States, French speaking in Canada—is correlated with union membership, but the relationships are not statistically significant, presumably because occupation and income override them. Gender and religion do not show up as major sources of differentiation.

2. The exceptions are the positional ones of manual job, public employment, and size of work unit.

3. Moreover, as we know, the state has been much weaker in the United States. The Republican Party is the only major party that is libertarian in its economic outlook in the democratic world. The Democrats, although much more statist and communitarian than their Republican rivals, are committed to a free market economy and in practice (if not always in word) favor a weaker welfare state than Canada's. No U.S. socialist or social democratic party has ever secured more than 6 percent in a presidential election (this occurred once in 1912). Conversely, all five parties represented in the Canadian Parliament have supported, to a varying degree, the country's extensive welfare state, including its single-payer government-financed medical system. The country's most laissez-faire–oriented party, the Reform (now Alliance) Party, secures less than one-fifth of the national vote and, as noted in chapter 4, is less libertarian than the Republican Party.

4. Recall from chapter 4 that the francophones were turned down because the NDP refused to give consent, which is necessary under the International's rules.

5. The employed U.S. nonunionist population, 84 percent of the total, includes a greater percentage of pro-union workers than is found among the smaller proportion of Canadian nonmembers, 64 percent. This may be a large part of the reason that equal numbers of Canadians and Americans answer that they would prefer to belong to a union.

6. A smaller proportion of U.S. managers in unionized firms are less likely than their Canadian counterparts to believe in a union effect on wages. When queried whether wages are higher or lower as a result of unionization, fewer U.S. managers in unionized workplaces (19 percent) than comparably placed Canadians (24 percent) say that unions produce much higher wages.

7. The 1980 figures are based on the long-term union density series prepared by the Workplace Information Directorate of Human Resources Development Canada, based on surveys of unions. Statistics Canada's Labour Force Survey added a question on union membership in 1997 to the monthly Labour Force Survey, a source more comparable to the source of the U.S. figures.

8. It should be noted that the pattern of greater hostility toward unions by Canadians than Americans does not hold up on all issues. The most noteworthy exception bears on union leader corruption, behavior that the U.S. media are more prone to emphasize and report on than the Canadian media. Union members vary cross-nationally in the same way as the general populations. More U.S. union members (51 percent) and nonmembers (63 percent) than Canadian members (47 percent) and nonmembers (51 percent) believe that there is too much corruption in labor unions.

9. Because only three Canadian provinces provide for representation elections, it is difficult to compare the results of actual contests.

Chapter 6

1. The equivalent Canadian figure is 36 percent. These figures approximate the actual union densities in the two countries in June–July 1996, when the survey was conducted.

2. Because of their relatively small numbers, union members were oversampled. We used weights to account for this oversampling.

3. This possibility exists in Canada and the United States because of agency-shop arrangements. These arrangements oblige all workers covered by a collective agreement to pay union dues. This is true in all ten Canadian provinces and in a majority of United States states.

4. Thus, for the United States 40.5 (48.2*0.84) plus 14.5 (90.5**0.16) = 54.9 percent who would vote for a union. For Canada 21.3 (33.3*0.64) plus 30.9 (85.8*0.36) = 52.2 percent.

Chapter 7

1. If the District of Columbia is included in this division, it ranks fifteenth in 1996 and thirteenth in 2001. The union density in the District of Columbia was 17.2 in 1996 and 16.7 in 2001.

Chapter 8

1. One approach to studies of the occupational structure of the work force is to group workers into white-collar, blue-collar, service, and resource workers. White-collar workers include professional, technical, clerical, and sales workers. Blue-collar workers include skilled, semiskilled, and unskilled factory workers. Service workers are in protective and maintenance work, such as police, firefighters, and janitors and cleaners. The resource worker category covers farm, mine, forest, and fishing workers (Meltz 1969).

2. Koeller (1994) finds that structural factors explain much of the decline in union density among states during the period 1958–1982.

3. We employ the U.S. Bureau of Census occupation typology. This typology roughly reflects the social stratification system (Hall 1969, 7–8).

4. See Spain and Bianchi (1996) for a discussion of changes in the female occupation structure and their causes.

5. The National Labor Relations Act of 1935 (the Wagner Act) and its subsequent amendments, decisions of the National Labor Relations Board, and court decisions do not grant the right to unionize to managers and supervisors (see Bendel 1991). The Supreme Court's Yeshiva University decision in 1980, which held that university professors were managers under certain conditions, limits faculty unionization in private universities (see Rabban 1990 on the legal environment for unionization of professionals).

6. Median earnings of salaried professionals in 1998 were $763 per week, compared to $755 for managers and executives; $477 for technical, sales, and administrative support employees; $327 for service workers; $572 for precision production, craft, and repair workers; and $415 for operators, fabricators, and laborers (Bureau of Labor Statistics 1999).

7. The question of whether the American Library Association should be involved in collective bargaining is being debated by librarians (Hovekamp 1997, 241–42).

8. The 1974 and 1980 data are moving averages calculated by Kokkelenberg and Sockell (1985, 507–8). The 1998 data are provided by Barry Hirsch (see Hirsch and MacPherson 1993).

9. The Current Population Survey probably underestimates union membership rate of performers. Because of the transitory character of their work, many professional performers may have specified other occupations in the survey (*Working* 1981). Jack Golodner, president of the Department of Professional Employees, AFL-CIO, estimates that about 80 percent of performers are union members (personal communication).

10. Physicians are the most highly paid and high-status group of professionals. However, physicians are relatively more liberal than lawyers, engineers, and business professionals (Brint 1985, 403).

Chapter 9

1. As discussed in chapter 8, white-collar workers include professional, technical, clerical, and sales workers. Blue-collar workers include skilled, semiskilled, and unskilled factory workers. Service workers are people in protective and maintenance work, such as police, firefighters, and janitors and cleaners. The resource worker category covers farm, mine, forest, and fishing workers (Meltz 1969).

2. This situation may change with the birth of the Canadian Alliance in spring 2000. The federal party is an amalgam of members from the Reform and the Progressive Conservative parties and is decidedly much more right wing than any party in Canadian

history. It also has the backing of one of Canada's largest national newspapers, the *National Post.*

Chapter 10

1. Bruce Kaufman commented on an earlier version of this chapter, which appeared in Bruce E. Kaufman and Daphne Gottlieb Taras, eds., *Nonunion Employee Representation: History, Contemporary Practice, and Policy* (Armonk, N.Y.: M.E. Sharpe, 2000), 223–30. Copyright © 2000 by M.E. Sharpe, Inc. Reprinted with permission. We appreciate Bruce Kaufman's comments and editorial suggestions.

2. Daphne Taras and Tom Kochan suggested these questions. We appreciate their advice and assistance.

REFERENCES

Adams, Roy J. 1994. "The Administrative Approach and Union Growth in Canada and the United States, 1929–1955." *Proceedings of the 31st Conference of the Canadian Industrial Relations Assess.* Quebec: CIRA.

——. 1995. *Industrial Relations under Liberal Democracy: North America in Comparative Perspective.* Columbia: University of South Carolina Press.

Akyeampong, Ernest B. 1998. "The Rise of Unionization among Women." *Perspectives on Labour and Income* 10 (winter): 30–41.

——. 1999. "Unionization—An Update." *Perspectives on Labour and Income* 11 (autumn): 45–65.

Alston, Jon P., Theresa M. Morris, and Arnold Vedlitz. 1996. "Comparing Canadian and American Values: New Evidence from National Surveys." *American Review of Canadian Studies/Canadian Review of American Studies* 26 (autumn): 301–14.

Aronson, Robert. 1985. "Unionism among Professional Employees in the Private Sector." *Industrial and Labor Relations Review* 38 (April): 353–64.

Associations Unlimited. 1998. Gale Group. Available from http://www.galenet.com (accessed 1999).

Babcock, Robert. H. 1974. *Gompers in Canada: A Study of American Continentalism before the First World War.* Toronto: University of Toronto Press.

Bain, George, and Robert Price. 1980. *Profiles of Union Growth: A Comparative Statistical Portrait of Eight Countries.* Oxford: Blackwell Press.

Bancroft, Gertrude. 1958. *The American Labor Force: Its Growth and Changing Composition.* New York: Wiley & Sons.

Barbash, Jack. 1987. "Like Nature, Industrial Relations Abhors a Vacuum." *Relations Industrielles* 42 (winter): 168–79.

Bendel, Michael. 1991. "Professional and Managerial Staff: Their Place in the Labour Relations System of Canada and the United States." Working paper, International Labor Organization, Geneva.

Bergeron, Jean-Guy. 1993. "Private Service Sector Unionization in Canada." Ph.D diss., Centre for Indsutrial Relations, University of Toronto.

Bergman, Brian. 1993. "The Crusader." *Maclean's,* 25 October, pp. 14–17.

Bertrand, Charles. 1992. "Italy." In *European Labor Unions,* edited by Joan Campbell, pp. 350–69. Westport, Conn.: Greenwood Press.

Bianchi, Giampiero. 1996. "Between Identity and Pragmatism: Italian Trade Unionism on Its Way to Europe." In *The Lost Perspective? Trade Unions between Ideology and Social Action in the New Europe*, edited by Patrick Pasture, Johan Verberckmoes, and Hans de Witte, pp. 52–90. Aldershot: Avebury.

Blanchflower, David, and Richard Freeman. 1992. "Unionism in the United States and Other Advanced OECD Countries." *Industrial Relations* 31 (winter): 56–80.

Blendon, Robert J. 1989. "Three Systems: A Comparative Survey." *Health Management Quarterly* 11 (first quarter): 8–9.

Blum, Albert, Marten Estey, James Kuhn, Wesley Wildman, and Leo Troy. 1971. *White-Collar Workers*. New York: Random House.

Brint, Steven. 1985. "The Political Attitudes of Professionals." *Annual Review of Sociology* 11: 389–414.

Broeck, Gilbert. 1992. "Belgium." In *European Labor Unions*, edited by Joan Campbell, pp. 27–38. Westport, Conn.: Greenwood Press.

Bruce, Peter G. 1989. "Political Parties and Labor Legislation in Canada and the U.S." *Industrial Relations* 28 (spring): 115–41.

Bruno, Michael, and Jeffrey Sachs. 1985. *Economics of Worldwide Stagflation*. Cambridge, Mass.: Harvard University Press.

Budrys, Grace. 1997. *When Doctors Join Unions*. Ithaca: Cornell University Press.

Bureau of Labor Statistics. 1999. Union Members in 1998. Available from http://stats.bls.gov/newsrels.htm.

——. 2000. Union Members in 1999. Available from ftp://146.142.4.23/pub/news.release/union2.txt.

——. 2002. Union Members in 2001. Available from ftp://146.142.4.23/pub/news.release/union2.txt.

CALURA, Part Two: Labour Unions, 71-202. 1962–1992. Ottawa: Statistics Canada.

Cameron, David. 1978. "The Expansion of Public Economy: A Comparative Analysis." *American Political Science Review* 72 (December): 1243–61.

——. 1984. "Social Democracy, Corporatism, Labour Quiescence and the Representation of Economic Interest in Advanced Capitalist Society." In *Order and Conflict in Contemporary Capitalism*, edited by John Goldthorpe, pp. 143–78. Oxford: Clarendon Press.

"Canada Fails Litmus Test." 1989. *Wall Street Journal*, 1 May, p. A14.

"Canadians" Perceptions of the "Health Allowance System." 1997. Available from: http://www.angusreid.com/media/dsp_displaypr_cdn.cfm?id_to_view=877 (accessed 1999).

Carlson, Robert. 1999. "Is There a Physician Union in Your Future?" *Family Practice Management* 6 (January): 21–25.

Chang, Clara, and Constance Sorrentino. 1991. "Union Membership Statistics in 12 Countries." *Monthly Labor Review* 114 (December): 46–53.

Conway, John. 1988. "An 'Adapted Organic Tradition.'" *Daedalus* 117 (fall): 381–96.

Crispo, John. 1967. *International Unionism: A Study in Canadian American Relations*. Toronto: McGraw Hill Canada.

Crouch, Colin. 1985. "Conditions for Trade Union Restraint." In *The Politics of Inflation and Economic Stagflation*, edited by Leon Lindberg and Charles Maier, pp. 105–39. Washington, D.C.: Brookings Institution.

Current Statistics on White Collar Employees: 1998 Edition. 1998. Washington, D.C.: Department of Professional Employees, AFL-CIO.

Davies, Robertson. 1977. "Dark Hamlet with the Features of Horatio: Canada's Myths and Realities." In *Voices of Canada: An Introduction to Canadian Culture*, edited by Judith Webster, pp. 42–47. Burlington, Vt.: Association for Canadian Studies in the United States.

de Jouvenal, Bertrand. 1954. "The Treatment of Capitalism by Continental Historians." In *Capitalism and the Historians*, edited by Friedrich Hayek, pp. 93–123. Chicago: Chicago University Press.

Denton, Frank T., and Sylvia Ostry. 1967. *Historical Estimates of the Canadian Labour Force.* Ottawa: Dominion Bureau of Statistics.

Directory of Labour Organizations in Canada. 1911–1998. Ottawa: Department of Labour.

Eaton, J.K., and Kebebew Ashagrie. 1970. *Union Growth in Canada 1921–1967.* Ottawa: Canada Department of Labour.

Ebbinghaus, Bernhard. 1993. "Labour Unity in Union Diversity: Trade Unions and Social Cleavages in Western Europe, 1890–1989." Ph.D. diss., European University Institute, Florence, Italy.

——. 1996. "From Ideology to Organization: The Transformation of Political Unionism in Western Europe." In *The Lost Perspective? Trade Unions between Ideology and Social Action in the New Europe*, edited by Patrick Pasture, Johan Verberckmoes, and Hans de Witte, pp. 28–59. Aldershot: Avebury.

Ebbinghaus, Bernhard, and Jelle Visser. 1999. "When Institutions Matter: Union Growth and Decline in Western Europe, 1950–1995." *European Sociological Review* 15 (June): 1–24.

——. 2000. *Trade Unions in Western Europe since 1945.* London: Macmillan.

Esenwein, George. 1992. "Spain." In *European Labor Unions*, edited by Joan Campbell, pp. 401–27. Westport, Conn.: Greenwood Press.

Evans, Robert G. 1988. "'We'll Take Care of It for You': Health Care in the Canadian Community." *Daedalus* 117 (fall): 155–89.

Farber, Henry, and Alan Krueger. 1993. "Union Membership in the United States: The Decline Continues." In *Employee Representation: Alternatives and Future Directions*, edited by Bruce Kaufman and M. Kleiner, pp. 70–79. Madison: Industrial Relations Research Association.

Farber, Henry, and Bruce Western. 2002. "Ronald Reagan and the Politics of Declining Union Organization." *British Journal of Industrial Relations* 40 (September): 385–402.

Fiorito, Jack, Lee P. Stepina, and Dennis P. Bozeman. 1996. "Explaining the Unionism Gap: Public-Private Sector Differences in Preferences for Unionization," *Journal of Labor Research* 17 (summer): 463–78.

Freeman, Richard. 1990. "On the Divergence of Unionism among Developed Countries." In *Labour Relations and Economic Performance*, edited by Renato Brunetta and Carlo Dell'Aringa, pp. 304–22. New York: New York University Press.

Freeman, Richard, and Casey Ichniowski, eds. 1988. *When Public Sector Workers Unionize.* Chicago: University of Chicago Press.

Fryer, Alex. 2000. "Strike Heralded as Dawn of New Age." *Seattle Times*, 19 March, p. A26.

Galenson, Walter. 1960. *The CIO Challenge to the AFL: A History of the American Labor Movement, 1935–1941.* Cambridge, Mass.: Harvard University Press.

——. 1998. *The World's Strongest Trade Unions: The Scandinavian Labor Movement.* Westport, Conn.: Quorum.

Garbarino, Joseph. 1986. "Faculty Collective Bargaining: A Status Report." In *Unions in Transition*, edited by Seymour Martin Lipset, pp. 265–86. San Francisco: ICS Press.

General Social Survey. 1995. Cycle 9: Education, Work and Retirement, 1994. Statistics Canada.

Gifford, Court. 1998. *Directory of US Labor Organizations.* Washington, D.C.: Bureau of National Affairs.

Glaser, William. 1984. "Health Politics: Lessons from Abroad." In *Health Politics and Policy*, edited by Theodore J. Litman, pp. 319–32. New York: John Wiley.

Golden, Miriam, and John Londregan. 1998. "Globalization and Industrial Relations." Paper presented at the 1998 Annual Meeting of the American Political Science Association, Boston.

Golden, Miriam, Michael Wallerstein, and Peter Lange. 1999. "Postwar Trade-Union Organization and Industrial Relations in Twelve Countries." In *Continuity and Change in Contemporary Capitalism*, edited by Herbert Kitschelt, Peter Lange, Gary Marks, and John Stephens, pp. 194–230. New York: Cambridge University Press.

Gomez, Rafael, Seymour Martin Lipset, and Noah Meltz. 2001. "Frustrated Demand for Unionization: The Case of the United States and Canada Revisited." *IRRA 53d Annual Proceedings*, pp. 163–72. Champaign, Ill.: Industrial Relations Research Association.

Greenhouse, Steven. 1999. "A.M.A.'s Delegates Decide to Create Union of Doctors." *New York Times*, 24 June, p. A1.

Gruner, Erich. 1992. "Switzerland." In *European Labor Unions*, edited by Joan Campbell, pp. 445–62. Westport, Conn.: Greenwood Press.

Hall, Richard. 1969. *Occupations and the Social Structure*. Englewood Cliffs, N.J.: Prentice Hall.

Handbook of Labor Statistics. 1909–1971. Lanham, Md.: Bernan Press.

Harbridge, Raymond, and Anthony Honeybone. 1996. "External Legitimacy of Unions: Trends in New Zealand." *Journal of Labor Research* 17 (summer): 425–45.

Hattam, Victoria C. 1993. *Labor Visions and State Power: The Origins of Business Unionism in the United States*. Princeton: Princeton University Press.

Hemmasi, Masoud, and Lee Graf. 1993. "Determinants of Faculty Voting Behavior in Union Representation Elections: A Multivariate Model." *Journal of Management* 19 (spring): 13–32.

Hess, Stephen. 1992. "All the President's Reporters: A New Survey of the White House Press Corps." *Presidential Studies Quarterly* 22 (spring): 311–22.

Hirsch, Barry, and David MacPherson. 1993. "Union Membership and Coverage Files from the Current Population Surveys: Note." *Industrial and Labor Relations Review* 46 (April): 574–78.

———. 1998. *Union Membership and Earning Data Book*. Washington, D.C.: Bureau of National Affairs.

———. 2002. *Union Membership and Earning Data Book*. Washington, D.C.: Bureau of National Affairs.

Hofstadter, Richard. 1972. *The Age of Reform: From Bryan to F.D.R.* New York: Alfred A. Knopf.

Horowitz, Gad. 1968. *Canadian Labour in Politics*. Toronto: University of Toronto Press.

Hovekamp, Tina. 1997. "Professional Associations or Unions? A Comparative Look." *Library Trends* 46 (fall): 232–44.

Huber, Evelyne, Charles Ragin, and John D. Stephens. 1997. *Comparative Welfare States Data Set*. Northwestern University and University of North Carolina.

International Labour Organization (ILO). 1997. *World Labour Report, 1997–98*. Geneva: International Labour Office.

Jackson, R. W. 1998. "Diabolical Dictionary of Modern English." *Maclean's*, 29 December–5 January, p. 28.

Kassalow, Everett. 1966. "White-Collar Unionism in the United States." In *White-Collar Trade Unions*, edited by Adolf Sturmthal, pp. 305–64. Urbana: University of Illinois Press.

King, William Lyon Mackenzie. 1918. *Industry and Humanity*. New York: Houghton Mifflin.

Kjartansson, Helgi. 1992. "Iceland." In *European Labor Unions*, edited by Joan Campbell, pp. 231–38. Westport, Conn.: Greenwood Press.

Kochan, Thomas A. 1980. "Toward a Behavioral Model of Management under Collective Bargaining." MIT Sloan School of Management Working Paper 1164–80.

Kochan, Thomas A., and Harry C. Katz. 1989. *Collective Bargaining and Industrial Relations: From Theory to Policy and Practice.* New York: McGraw-Hill.

Kochan, Thomas A., Harry C. Katz, and Robert B. McKersie. 1994. *The Transformation of American Industrial Relations.* Ithaca: ILR Press.

Koeller, Timothy. 1994. "Union Activity and the Decline in American Trade Union Membership." *Journal of Labor Research* 15 (winter): 19–32.

Kokkelenberg, Edward, and Donna Sockell. 1985. "Union Membership in the United States, 1973–1981." *Industrial and Labor Relations Review* 38 (July): 497–543.

Kudrle, Robert T., and Theodore R. Marmor. 1981. "The Development of Welfare States in North America." In *The Development of Welfare States in Europe and America*, edited by Peter Flora and Arnold J. Heidenheimer, pp. 81–121. New Brunswick, N.J.: Transaction Books.

Kumar, Pradeep. 1993. *From Uniformity to Divergence: Industrial Relations in Canada and the United States.* Kingston, Ont.: Industrial Relations Center, Queen's University.

Kumar, Pradeep, and Noah M. Meltz. 1992. "Industrial Relations in the Canadian Automobile Industry." In *Industrial Relations in Canadian Industry*, edited by Richard P. Chaykowski and Anil Verma, pp. 39–86. Toronto: Dryden.

Ladd, Everett Carl, and Seymour Martin Lipset. 1973. *Professors, Unions, and American Higher Education.* Washington, D.C.: American Enterprise Institute for Public Policy Research.

Ladd, Everett Carl, and Seymour Martin Lipset. 1975. *The Divided Academy: Professors and Politics.* New York: McGraw-Hill.

Laidlaw, Blair, and Bruce Curtis. 1986. "Inside Postal Workers: The Labor Process, State Policy and Worker Response." *Labour/LeTravail* 18 (fall): 139–62.

Lange, Peter, Michael Wallerstein, and Miriam Golden. 1995. "The End of Corporatism? Wage Setting in Nordic and Germanic Countries." In *The Workers of Nations*, edited by Sanford Jacoby, pp. 76–100. New York: Oxford University Press.

La Porta, Rafael, Florencio Lopez-de-Silanes, Andrei Shleifer, and Robert Vishny. 1998. "The Quality of Government." NBER Working Paper 6727, National Bureau of Economic Research, Cambridge, Mass.

Latta, Geoffrey. 1981. "Union Organization among Engineers: A Current Assessment." *Industrial and Labor Relations Review* 35 (October): 29–42.

Lester, Richard. 1958. *As Unions Mature: An Analysis of the Evolution of American Unionism.* Princeton: Princeton University Press.

——. 1964. *Economics of Labor.* 2nd ed. New York: Macmillan.

Levitan, Sarand, and Frank Gallo. 1989. "Collective Bargaining and Private Sector Professionals." *Monthly Labor Review* 112 (September): 24–34.

Lichter, Robert, and Stanley Rothman. 1981. "Media and Business Elites." *Public Opinion* (October/November): 42–46.

Lieberman, Myron. 1997. *The Teacher Unions.* New York: Free Press.

Lieberman, Myron, Charlene Haar, and Leo Troy. 1994. *The NEA and AFT: Teacher Unions in Power and Politics.* Rockport, Mass.: ProActive Publications.

Lipset, Seymour Martin. 1950/1968. *Agrarian Socialism: The Cooperative Commonwealth Federation in Saskatchewan.* Berkeley: University of California Press.

——. 1960/1981. *Political Man: The Social Bases of Politics.* Baltimore: John Hopkins University Press.

——. 1962/1967. "White Collar Workers and Professionals—Their Attitudes and Behavior towards Unions." In *Research Development in Personnel Management.* Los Angeles: Institute of Industrial Relations, University of California. Reprinted in

Readings in Industrial Sociology, edited by William Faunce, pp. 525–48. New York: Appleton-Century-Crofts.

——. 1983. "Radicalism or Reformism: The Sources of Working-Class Politics." *American Political Science Review* 77 (March): 1–18.

——. 1986. "North American Labor Movements: A Comparative Perspective." In *Unions in Transition*, edited by Seymour Martin Lipset, pp. 421–52. San Francisco: ICS Press.

——. 1990. *Continental Divide: The Values and Institutions of the United States and Canada*. New York: Routledge.

——. 1996. *American Exceptionalism: A Double-Edged Sword*. New York: W.W. Norton.

——. 1998. "American Union Density in Comparative Perspective." *Contemporary Sociology* 27 (March): 123–25.

Lipset, Seymour Martin, and Richard Dobson. 1972. "The Intellectual as Rebel: With Special Reference to the United States and the Soviet Union." *Daedalus* 101 (summer): 137–97.

Lipset, Seymour Martin, and Ivan Katchanovski. 2001. "The Future of Private-Sector Unions in the U.S." *Journal of Labor Research* 22 (spring): 229–44.

Lipset, Seymour Martin, and Gary Marks. 2000. *It Didn't Happen Here: Why Socialism Failed in the United States*. New York: W.W. Norton.

Lipset, Seymour Martin, and Noah Meltz. 1997. "Canadian and American Attitudes towards Work and Institutions." *Perspectives on Work* 1 (December): 14–19.

——. 2000. "Estimates of Nonunion Employee Representation in the United States and Canada: How Different Are the Two Countries?" In *Nonunion Employee Representation: History, Contemporary Practice, and Policy*, edited by Bruce E. Kaufman and Daphne Gottlieb Taras, pp. 223–30. Armonk, N.Y.: M.E. Sharpe.

Lipset, Seymour Martin, Noah M. Meltz, and Rafael Gomez. 2002. "Religiosity and Unionization: A Cross-Country Comparison." In *Proceedings of the 36th Canadian Industrial Relations Association Conference*, pp. 293–304. Quebec: CIRA.

Lipset, Seymour Martin, and Stein Rokkan. 1967. "Cleavage Structures, Party Systems, and Voter Alignments: An Introduction." In *Party Systems and Voter Alignments: Cross-National Perspectives*, edited by Seymour Martin Lipset and Stein Rokkan, pp. 1–64. New York: Free Press.

Lipset, Seymour Martin, and William Schneider. 1983. *The Confidence Gap: Business, Labor, and Government in the Public Mind*. New York: Free Press.

Lipset, Seymour Martin, and Mildred Schwartz. 1966. "The Politics of Professionals." In *Professionalization*, edited by Howard Vollmer and Donald Mills, pp. 299–310. Englewood Cliffs, N.J.: Prentice Hall.

Lipset, Seymour Martin, Martin Trow, and James Coleman. 1956. *Union Democracy*. Glenco, Ill.: Free Press.

Lowes, Robert. 1998. "Strength in Numbers: Could Doctor Unions Really Be the Answer?" *Medical Economics* 75 (June 29): 114–20.

Lubell, Samuel. 1941. "Post-Mortem: Who Elected Roosevelt?" *Saturday Evening Post*, 25 January.

Macleod, James T. 1976. "The Free Enterprise Dodo Is No Phoenix." *Canadian Forum* 56 (August): 8.

Market Opinion Research International. 1976–2000. October (http://www.mori.com/international).

Marks, Gary. 1989. *Unions in Politics: Britain, Germany, and the United States in the Nineteenth and Early Twentieth Centuries*. Princeton: Princeton University Press.

Meltz, Noah M. 1965. "Changes in the Occupational Composition of the Canadian Labour Force, 1931–1961." Occasional Paper No. 2, Economics and Research Branch, Department of Labour. Ottawa: Queen's Printer.

——. 1969. *Manpower in Canada 1931–1961: Historical Statistics of the Canadian Labour Force.* Ottawa: Queen's Printer.

——. 1985. "Labour Movements in Canada and the United States." In *Challenges and Choices Facing American Labor,* edited by Thomas A. Kochan, pp. 314–34. Cambridge, Mass.: MIT Press.

——. 1989a. "Industrial Relations: Balancing Efficiency and Equity." In *Theories and Concepts in Comparative Industrial Relations,* edited by Jack Barbash and Kate Barbash, pp. 109–13. Columbia: University of South Carolina Press.

——. 1989b. "Interstate vs. Interprovincial Differences in Union Density." *Industrial Relations* 2 (spring): 142–58.

——. 1990. "Unionism in Canada, U.S.: On Parallel Treadmills?" *Forum for Applied Research and Public Policy* 5 (winter): 46–52.

——. 1993. "Unionism in the Private Service Sector: A Canada-U.S. Comparison." In *Canadian and American Labor Respond: Economic Restructuring and Union Strategies,* edited by Jane Jensen and Rianne Mahon, pp. 207–25. Philadelphia: Temple University Press.

——. 1994. "Manufacturing Sector Unionism: Canada-U.S. Comparisons." In *Proceedings of the 30th Annual Meeting of the Canadian Industrial Relations Association,* edited by Esther Deom and Anthony E. Smith, pp. 165–77. Quebec: CIRA.

——. 1999. "The Managerial Workforce in Canada: A Century of Change." Technical paper, Human Resources Development Canada, Hull, Quebec.

Meltz, Noah M., and Anil Verma. 1996. "Beyond Union Density: Assessing Union Strength in Canada and the U.S." Working paper, Centre for Industrial Relations, University of Toronto.

Mercer, John, and Michael Goldberg. 1982. "Value Differences and Their Meaning: Urban Development in the United States." Faculty of Commerce Working Paper 12, UBC Research in Land Economics, University of British Columbia, Vancouver.

Misra, Joya, and Alexander Hicks. 1994. "Catholicism and Unionization in Affluent Postwar Democracies: Catholicism, Culture, Party, and Unionization." *American Sociological Review* 59 (April): 304–26.

Morton, Desmond. 1990. *Working People.* 3rd ed. Toronto: Summerhill Press.

Mouriaux, Rene. 1992. "France." In *European Labor Unions,* edited by Joan Campbell, pp. 119–48. Westport, Conn.: Greenwood Press.

Murphy, Marjorie. 1990. *Blackboard Unions: The AFT and the NEA, 1900–1980.* Ithaca: Cornell University Press.

Neumann, George, Peder Pedersen, and Niels Westergard-Nielsen. 1991. "Long-Run International Trends in Aggregate Unionization." *European Journal of Political Economy* 7 (April): 249–74.

Norrie, Kenneth, and Doug Owram. 1991. *A History of the Canadian Economy.* Toronto: Harcourt, Brace, Jovanovich.

"OECD in Figures." 1997. *OECD Observer* 206 (suppl.).

Organization for Economic Cooperation and Development (OECD). 1997. *OECD Employment Outlook.* Paris: OECD.

"Official Voting Results of the 36th General Election, 1997." 1997. Elections Canada On Line. Available from http://www.elections.ca/election/results.

Organizing Challenge: Professional and Technical Workers Seek a Voice. n.d. Washington, D.C.: Department for Professional Employees, AFL-CIO.

Ostry, Sylvia. 1985. "Government Intervention: Canada and the United States Compared." In *Government and Enterprise in Canada,* edited by Ken J. Rea and Nelson Wiseman, pp. 20–35. Toronto: Methuen.

Parsons, Talcott. 1949. *Essays in Sociological Theory.* Glencoe: Free Press.

Pasture, Patrick. 1996. "The Unattainable Unity in the Nertherlands" In *The Lost Per-spective? Trade Unions between Ideology and Social Action in the New Europe*, edited by Patrick Pasture, Johan Verberckmoes, and Hans de Witte, pp. 136–79. Aldershot: Avebury.

Pennings, Paul, and Noël P. Vergunst. 2000. "The Dynamics of Corporatist Institutions: Measurements and Linkages. The Dutch Miracle in Comparative Perspective." Paper presented at Politicologenetmaal, May 25–26, Veldhoven.

Pritchard, Rubert S. 1982. *Crown Corporations in Canada*. Toronto: Butterworths.

Professional Workers and Unions. 1988. Washington, D.C.: Department of Professional Employees, AFL-CIO.

Rabban, David M. 1990. "Can American Labor Law Accommodate Collective Bargain-ing by Professional Employees?" *Yale Law Journal* 99 (January): 689–758.

Redding, Kent, and Jocelyn Viterna. 1999. "Political Demands, Political Opportunities: Explaining the Differential Success of Left-Libertarian Parties." *Social Forces* 78 (December): 491–510.

Riddell, Craig. 1993. "Unionization in Canada and the United States: A Tale of Two Countries." In *Small Differences That Matter: Labor Markets and Income Maintenance in Canada and the United States*, edited by David Card and Richard Freeman, pp. 109–47. Chicago: University of Chicago Press.

Rojot, Jacques. 2000. "The Future of the Labor Movement in France: The Decline in the Rate of Organization Reasons and Prospects." Paper presented at the 12th World Con-gress of the International Industrial Relations Association, Tokyo.

Rouillard, Jacques. 1991. "Le syndicalisme dans l'opinion publique au Canada." *Rela-tions Industrielles* 46 (spring): 277–305.

Saltzman, Gregory. 1985. "Bargaining Laws as a Cause and Consequence of the Growth of Teacher Unionism." *Industrial and Labor Relations Review* 38 (April): 335–51.

———. 1988. "Public-Sector Bargaining Laws Really Matter: Evidence from Ohio and Illi-nois." In *When Public-Sector Workers Unionize*, edited by Richard B. Freeman and Casey Ichniowski, pp. 41–78. Chicago: University of Chicago Press.

———. 1997. "The Impact of Social Class on Attitudes towards Strikes: A Four-Country Study." *Labor Studies Journal* 22 (fall): 28–48.

Saporta, Ishak, and Bryan Lincoln. 1985. "Managers' and Workers' Attitudes toward Trade Unions in the U.S. and Canada." *Relations Industrielles* 5 (summer): 550–67.

Schonhoven, Klaus. 1992. "Germany to 1945." In *European Labor Unions*, edited by Joan Campbell, pp. 149–66. Westport, Conn.: Greenwood Press.

Serafini, Marilyn. 1999. "Physicians, Unite." *National Journal* 31 (June 5): 1524–28.

"17k Technical Workers Walk Out at Boeing." 2000. *Electronic Engineering Times*, 14 Feb-ruary, p. 178.

Soikkanen, Hannu. 1992. "Finland." In *European Labor Unions*, edited by Joan Campbell, pp. 101–18. Westport, Conn.: Greenwood Press.

Spain, Daphne, and Suzanne Bianchi. 1996. *Balancing Act: Motherhood, Marriage, and Employment among American Women*. New York: Russell Sage Foundation.

Statistical Abstract of the United States. 1950–2001. Washington, D.C.: U.S. Department of Commerce.

Steinfeld, Robert. 1991. *The Invention of Free Labor*. Chapel Hill: University of North Carolina Press.

Stephens, John. 1991. "Industrial Concentration, Country Size, and Trade Union Membership." *American Political Science Review* 85 (September): 941–49.

Sturmthal, Adolf. 1966. "White-Collar Unions—A Comparative Essay." In *White-Collar Trade Unions*, edited by Adolf Sturmthal, pp. 365–98. Urbana: University of Illinois Press.

Taras, Daphne. 1997. "Collective Bargaining Regulation in Canada and the United States: Divergent Cultures, Divergent Outcomes." In *Government Regulation of the Employment Relaionship, IRRA 50th Anniversary Volume*, edited by Bruce E. Kaufman, pp. 295–342. Champaign, Ill.: Industrial Relations Research Association.

Traxler, Franz. 1996. "Collective Bargaining and Industrial Change: A Case of Disorganization? A Comparative Analysis of Eighteen OECD Countries." *European Sociological Review* 12 (September): 271–87.

Troy, Leo. 1986. "The Rise and Fall of American Trade Unions: The Labor Movement from FDR to RR." In *Unions in Transition*, edited by Seymour Martin Lipset, pp. 75–109. San Francisco: ICS Press.

——. 1990. "Is the U.S. Unique in the Decline of Private Sector Unionism?" *Journal of Labor Research* 11 (spring): 111–43.

——. 1992. "Convergence in International Unionism, etc. The Case of Canada and the USA." *British Journal of Industrial Relations* 30 (March): 1–43.

Troy, Leo, and Neil Sheflin. 1985. *U.S. Union Sourcebook: Membership, Finances, Structure, Directory*. West Orange, N.J.: Industrial Relations Data Information Services.

"Unionization in Canada: A Retrospective." 1999. *Supplement to Perspectives on Labour and Income* 11 (summer): 1–35.

"United States: Slow Death of Boeing Man." 2000. *Economist* (March 18): 29–30.

Veblen, Thorstein. 1933. *The Engineers and the Price System*. New York: Viking.

Verberckmoes, Johan. 1996a. "Germany: Inner Trade Union Diversity." In *The Lost Perspective? Trade Unions between Ideology and Social Action in the New Europe*, edited by Patrick Pasture, Johan Verberckmoes, and Hans de Witte, pp. 180–214. Aldershot: Avebury.

——. 1996b. "The Politics of Ideological Diversity in France." In *The Lost Perspective? Trade Unions between Ideology and Social Action in the New Europe*, edited by Patrick Pasture, Johan Verberckmoes, and Hans de Witte, pp. 7–51. Aldershot: Avebury.

Visser, Jelle. 1993. "Union Organisation: Why Countries Differ." *The International Journal of Comparative Labour Law and Industrial Relations* 9 (fall): 206–25.

——. 1994. "Union Organization: Why Countries Differ?" In *The Future of Industrial Relations: Global Change and Challenges*, edited by J. Niland, R. Lansbury, and C. Verevis, pp. 164–84. Thousand Oaks, Calif.: Sage.

Voorden, William. 1992. "The Netherlands." In *European Labor Unions*, edited by Joan Campbell, pp. 305–22. Westport, Conn.: Greenwood Press.

Wallerstein, Michael. 1989. "Union Organization in Advanced Industrial Democracies." *American Political Science Review* 83 (June): 481–502.

Weiler, Paul. 1980. *Reconcilable Differences*. Toronto: Carswell.

Weaver, David, and Cleveland Wilhoit. 1996. *The American Journalist in the 1990s*. Mahwah, N.J.: Lawrence Erlbaum Associates.

Weiler, Paul. 1983. "Promises to Keep: Securing Workers' Rights to Self Organization under the NLRA." *Harvard Law Review* 96 (June): 1796–1827.

Wessels, Bernard. 1996. "Systems of Economic Interest Groups and Socio-Economic Performance." Paper presented at the 1996 Annual Meting of the American Political Science Association, San Francisco.

Western, Bruce. 1994. "Unionization and Labor Market Institutions in Advanced Capitalism, 1950–1985." *American Journal of Sociology* 99 (March): 1314–41.

——. 1997. *Between Class and Market: Postwar Unionization in the Capitalist Democracies*. Princeton: Princeton University Press.

White, Frank. 1993. "Determinants of Professional Unionization in Canada." Ph.D. diss., University of Toronto.

Wilensky, Harold. 1981. "Leftism, Catholicism, and Democratic Corporatism: The Role of Political Parties in Recent Welfare State Development." In *The Development of Welfare*

States in Europe and America, edited by Peter Flora and Arnold Heidenheimer, pp. 345–82. New Brunswick: Transaction Books.

Working and Not Working in the Performing Arts: A Survey of Employment, Underemployment and Unemployment among Performing Artists in 1980. 1981. Washington, D.C.: Ruttenberg, Friedman, Kilgallon, Gutchess & Associates, Inc.

Wright, Gavin. 1996. "The Origins and Economic Significance of Free Labor in America." Unpublished paper, February, Stanford University.

INDEX

Page numbers followed by *f* or *t* refer to figures and tables respectively.